LLEWELLYN'S

2024

Magical Almanac

Featuring

H. Byron Ballard, Elizabeth Barrette, Mireille Blacke,
Danielle Blackwood, Blake Octavian Blair,
Chic and S. Tabatha Cicero, Monica Crosson, Kate Freuler,
Sasha Graham, Olivia Graves, Raechel Henderson,
Emma Kathryn, Lupa, Tisha Morris, Mickie Mueller,
John Opsopaus, Susan Pesznecker, Diana Rajchel,
Suzanne Ress, Melissa Tipton, Tudorbeth, JD Walker,
Brandon Weston, Charlie Rainbow Wolf,
Stephanie Woodfield, and Natalie Zaman

Llewellyn's 2024
Magical Almanac

ISBN 978-0-7387-6896-0. Copyright © 2023 by Llewellyn Publications. All rights reserved. Printed in China. Llewellyn Publications is a registered trademark of Llewellyn Worldwide Ltd.

Editing and layout by Lauryn Heineman
Cover illustration © Tiffany England
Calendar pages design by Llewellyn Art Department
Calendar pages illustrations © Fiona King

Interior illustrations: © Elisabeth Alba: pages 12, 15, 87, 90, 193, 196, 228, and 233; © Kathleen Edwards: pages 32, 57, 61, 179, 219, 222, 252, and 257; © Wen Hsu: pages 1, 45, 64, 67, 81, 99, 175, 182, 187, 215, 260, 263, and 271; © Jessica Krcmarik: pages 17, 20, 39, 42, 209, 212, and 247; © Mickie Mueller: pages 24, 48, 95, 200, 205, 267, and 275; © Amber Zoellner: pages 5, 8, 71, 74, 108, 113, 236, and 241

All other art by Dover Publications and Llewellyn Art Department

Special thanks to Amber Wolfe for the use of daily color and incense correspondences. For more detailed information, please see *Personal Alchemy* by Amber Wolfe.

You can order Llewellyn annuals and books from *New Worlds*, Llewellyn's catalog. To request a free copy of the catalog, call 1-877-NEW-WRLD toll-free or visit www.llewellyn.com.

Astrological data compiled and programmed by Rique Pottenger. Based on the earlier work of Neil F. Michelsen.

Llewellyn Worldwide Ltd.
2143 Wooddale Drive
Woodbury, MN 55125

Printed in China

Contents

Earth Magic

Air Magic

2024 Almanac

Fire Magic

Water Magic

Coloring Magic

Earth Magic

The Magic of Somatics: Turning Small Movements into Big Change

Melissa Tipton

Gym class, middle school. Everyone's lined up in scratchy polyester shorts, flattering on exactly no one, waiting to reach the head of this slowly shuffling line where, in front of the entire class, we have to do a forward bend, arms hanging limply like a rag doll. The point? To determine whether or not we have scoliosis. I looked up this forward-bend test to see if it's still a thing, and seeing pictures of hunched-over examinees, arms dangling, waiting to be diagnosed, brought back long-forgotten childhood memories.

What I recall most of all is how *final* my scoliosis diagnosis felt. I definitely had it, it wasn't going away, and it would only get worse, likely bringing with it pain and mobility issues. There was apparently nothing I could do besides surgery. It was only many years later that I saw a direct link between those early associations of physicality and finality with what was to become my very unbalanced approach to magic.

Fast-forward to my thirties. I'm incredibly disconnected from my body, treating it like a machine to ferry my head around, which is the body part where I spend the majority of my time. I love analyzing things (and over analyzing them), and I am drawn to magic because it feels like a way to make things happen without actually *doing* them. (Oh, how wrong I was.) It is also a time when my back begins to speak to me in the form of burning achiness and occasionally seizing up at the worst possible moments. I've resigned myself to the "fact" that my back will continue to get worse and, at best, maybe I can delay its inevitable decline.

Interestingly, the more stubborn and defeatist my approach to the physical became, the more fantastical and ungrounded my magical outlook grew. On one hand, I was convinced that nothing I did, practically speaking, could change my back, while on the other, I believed magic would somehow deliver me from all my problems, if only I could find the right spell or teacher. When I finally made a connection between this extremely split viewpoint and a long-standing family pattern, things began to click. I realized that when life didn't go as planned, I'd never been taught how to deal with this frustration. The adults around me, who were equally ill-equipped to handle frustration (theirs and mine), would hurriedly do something to make it go away: give me money, start yelling so we'd have a new problem to focus on instead, plop me down in front of a bowl of ice cream, and so on.

I viewed magic through this very same lens. It became just another tool in the "make it go away" box. But what happens when you're dealing with something, like your own body, that you can't get away from? I was back to the push-pull of the hard stubbornness of physical existence and the ever-changing, "anything is possible" realm of the mind. But what I couldn't see was that magic relies on both. It represents expansive possibilities, yes, but it also works through and on the concrete *is*-ness of material reality. And scoliosis, as it turns out, would become my greatest teacher in learning how to weave the material and the magical together.

My chronically cranky back inspired me first to become a massage therapist, then a personal trainer, and, finally, a Structural Integrator. Throughout this journey, I slowly began to descend from the comforts of my cranium to inhabit the rest of my body too. And what I learned is that, wow, there's *nothing* static and unchanging about physical reality! Once I was paying attention, the constant fluctuations and transformations of matter were everywhere I looked. And this began to radically influence my magical practice.

A LITTLE BIT OF MAGIC

Your body is a record of your experiences, but what has been learned can be unlearned, and the solidity of matter is much more malleable than it appears.

One of the most important tools I picked up along the way is a form of somatics developed by Thomas Hanna, known as Hanna somatics. We're going to stick to the broad strokes, because I want to focus on connecting the dots between this physical practice and increasing your magical power and efficacy. What is Hanna somatics? In a nutshell, it's a movement practice that uses slow and intentional movements to repattern how the nervous system relates to the body, with the goal of improving mobility, reducing pain, and releasing chronic tension. Throughout life, our nervous system is learning how to direct our body so we can stand, walk, sit still, and do all the other dynamic and stationary things we do in a given day. It has to learn which muscles to contract or release, how much, and for how long.

Depending on how we use our bodies, which is hugely influenced by watching other people (in my family, we all share a particular way of cocking one hip to the side when we're tired of standing), our nervous system learns certain patterns: this is our muscle memory. These patterns might help us get the job done, but some do so at the expense of, say, the health of our spine or the integrity of our knee joints. Somatics is a tool for retraining the nervous system toward more efficient, functional patterns that don't lead to pain and damage.

There are numerous ways this relates to magical practice, but here are two biggies. The first is the link between how much energy those unconscious patterns gobble up and how much energy we then have left over for magical purposes. To illustrate this, I'll borrow a term from Moshe Feldenkrais, who heavily influenced Hanna's development of somatics. Feldenkrais called the unconscious tensing of muscles that don't need to be engaged for the task at hand "parasitic tension."

This is a useful term, because it captures how pernicious unconscious, chronic tension can be. For example, many of us have high levels of shoulder tension, resulting in wearing our shoulders as earrings. We don't need to have our shoulders held this high to properly function (in fact, this often *prevents* efficient movement while excessively stressing our joints), so this tension isn't energy

well spent. Then, when we require energy to lug groceries out of the car or cast a spell, we have less available because we've already spent part of it keeping our shoulders jacked up 24/7.

Magic requires energy, and while we can outsource at least part of these requirements by drawing on, for instance, elemental or earth and sky energies, our magic is more effective when we're energetically contributing. Why? Well, one of the primary ways magic helps us get what we want is by changing us from the inside out, and if we're not weaving our own energy into the process, that's a bit like preparing for a marathon by asking someone *else* to go on practice runs for us. Not to mention, if our baseline energy requirements are high because a steady stream is being gobbled up by parasitic tension, even when we do rely on external energy sources, we'll have

to draw in more to compensate. Bottom line: parasitic tension is a drain, and it can affect every area of our life, including our magic.

The second link between magic and unconscious physical patterns has to do with our resistance or willingness to change. Remember what I said about muscle memory? We can think of this as a record of what we've done in the past that's repeatedly influencing what we're able to do in the present. If, as a kid, I learned to hold my shoulders up by my ears, this constrains how well I'm able to move my shoulders today. Yet our muscle memory didn't form in a vacuum, influenced solely by physical forces. My shoulder position has also been influenced by stress levels, body image, relationships, and countless other factors.

Bound up in the physical posture of my raised shoulders are emotional, relational, and mental factors as well, and as long as my shoulders are locked in that position, a part of me is energetically stuck in that stew of mental-emotional factors. When this tension exists on an unconscious level, it's nearly impossible for me to fully shift the associated mental-emotional patterns, because my body serves as a constant, unconscious tug back to my familiar baseline.

Let's say one of my mental-emotional patterns is related to stress around money. I routinely heard my parents fighting about cash flow, and this contributed to my shoulders creeping upward. As an adult, I find myself chronically short on funds, so I cast a spell to improve my financial situation, but I'm not aware that my body has recorded part of this pattern in my shoulders. The spell works for a little while, but before long, I'm back to being broke, and I can't seem to shift my money situation once and for all.

If we compare this to my split perspective on scoliosis (i.e., "There's nothing I can do on a physical level and it's hopeless to even try" versus "Magic will save the day!"), the same dynamic is at work. On one hand, I'm doing very little to shift the tangible, practical aspects of my money situation, like facing my budget head-on or taking the time to meal plan in lieu of ordering takeout every night. Instead, I'm putting all my eggs in one magical basket, which effects short-lived change at best. I don't have a good working relationship between more rapid, dramatic change and grad-

ual, stepwise change. Not to mention, I've categorized all magical actions as fast-acting, while physical reality is consigned to sluggish or nonexistent change. Applying somatics to my scoliosis initiated a paradigm shift, allowing me to see the amazing malleability of matter and the power of letting things gradually build in my magical practice.

I'd like to share two somatic exercises with you, and the aim here is threefold. First, these movements bring your awareness fully into your body, linking the mental and the physical, an important ingredient for effective magic. Second, they help retrain your nervous system and release parasitic tension, which frees up energy and dissolves obstructions to its proper flow, which, again, benefits your magical practice. And third, they give you an embodied sense of just how potent small, incremental changes can be, meaning that your body will help reinforce the awareness, both magical and mundane, that progressively built change can snowball into profound transformations.

To speak to the latter more fully, with daily practice of the first exercise below, my scoliotic pain diminished over the course of a month before disappearing *entirely*. This blew me away and helped dissolve my prejudice against "boring," slow change. Instead, I saw (and felt!) that a little bit, day by day, could dramatically change even the most seemingly concrete physical state, like water wearing a riverbed through solid rock, and this, in turn, opened me up to magic that extended beyond the flash-in-the-pan variety.

Somatic Exercises

Do these exercises on a carpeted floor or yoga mat—something that offers firm support but with enough cushion for comfort (don't do them in bed). Start by standing up in bare feet. Close your eyes and do a body scan, starting with how your feet feel on the floor. Don't try to change or adopt "perfect" posture; simply notice. Continue scanning, seeing how your knees and thighs feel, your hips, your lower back, upper back, shoulders, and neck.

Come down to the floor, lying on your back, knees bent and feet planted. Your feet will be hip-width apart and a comfortable

distance from your butt. Let your arms rest down by your sides. Close your eyes, and take some slow, deep breaths into your belly. See how relaxed you can be in this pose, softening any noticeable tension, perhaps in your neck, your hips, the backs of your knees.

Arch and Flatten

Bring your awareness to your lower back and pelvis. On an inhale, slowly tip your pelvis forward, arching your lower back, creating space between your lower back and the floor. Over simply forcing your pelvis to move, really *feel* your lower back muscles contracting to create an arch in your back, which will naturally tilt your pelvis forward. This doesn't need to be a big movement. On the exhale, as slowly as you can (see if you can count to ten), with control, release the arch in your lower back, letting your pelvis gradually come back to neutral. Rest for a moment.

Inhale and on the exhale, do the opposite motion: engage and hollow out your abdominal muscles to flatten your lower back against the floor, bringing your pelvis into a gentle tailbone tuck.

Then, as slowly as you can (count to ten), release your abdominals with control, letting your back and pelvis come to neutral and rest here.

Repeat this sequence a few times, arching and flattening your lower back, always taking a moment to rest in neutral before transitioning to the next movement. The key is to release out of the arch and the flatten as *slowly* as you can, with control. You might find certain parts of the movement feel a little shaky or clumsy at first. That's totally normal. The more you practice, the more your nervous system will regain awareness of how to release and engage this area of your body fluidly, and moving at a slow pace is crucial to this repatterning process.

Shoulder Release

Still lying on your back with knees bent and eyes closed, clasp your hands behind your head, like you're about to do a sit-up. Let your elbows relax out to the sides. You'll focus now on moving your shoulders. Start by sliding your shoulders along the floor, up toward your ears, really feeling the muscles that need to contract for this movement. Then, as slowly as you can, release this contraction, letting your shoulders return to neutral. Rest for a moment, then do the opposite: Slide your shoulders down your back, feeling your back muscles engaging to create this movement. Then, as slowly as you can, release, allowing your shoulders to return to neutral.

Repeat these movements a few times. You can also mix in a variation: Move your right shoulder up toward your ear while sliding your left shoulder down your back. Then, as slowly as you can, release both shoulders back to neutral. Rest, then repeat in the opposite direction, right shoulder moving down, left moving up. I love how much tension this releases in my shoulder and upper back region, especially after a long day at a computer.

Once you've done both exercises, slowly roll onto one side, and use your hands to press yourself up to sitting. Come to standing, close your eyes, and do another body scan, noticing if you feel any differences. This pre- and post-movement scan is important, because it gradually establishes a new baseline. For instance, perhaps

you notice a new sensation in your lower back after the movements, and this scan allows your nervous system to begin adjusting to, "Oh, hey, this is what it feels like to carry less tension in my lower back. Roger that."

By engaging these somatic practices as close to daily as possible, you'll powerfully link your mind and body, both to each other and to the knowing that change is possible; you'll release parasitic tension that can now be used for other things, including magical workings; and you'll forge new energetic pathways that will support you in making steady, incremental changes, magical and mundane, that can lead to downright surprising transformations.

An Astrological Apothecary for Difficult Times

Danielle Blackwood

I'm blessed to live in a cottage on a tiny island on the west coast of Canada, surrounded by ocean, mountains, and forest. Over the seven summers I've called this magical place home, I've nurtured a Witch's herb garden that now spans an acre, and thus, our micro herb farm Folklore Farm was born.

Although I've been an astrologer for over thirty years and the richly layered symbolism of the Moon, planets, and stars was my first love, plant medicine is a natural fit with my practice. My first astrology teacher was both a clinical herbalist and a practicing astrologer, and she imparted her wisdom on me when I first set out on this path. Over the years, I've studied with a couple of wonderful plant medicine teachers, but much of what I've learned is through independent study, growing and getting to know the plants, and making my own tinctures and teas.

Perhaps the most valuable thing I've learned is that plant allies can bring beneficial support when someone is facing a significant transit to their birth chart. Plant medicine can also help us cope with the kinds of themes and feelings that often accompany stressful world transits.

What Is a Transit?

First, let's take a brief look at what a transit is. There are two kinds of transits: personal transits (to your own birth chart) and world transits (in the collective). You'll know when there's a world transit happening because everyone in the astrological and witchy communities will be talking about it on social media. But to pinpoint the dates when you'll be experiencing significant transits to your own birth chart, you can either use a transit app like *Time Passages* or book a consult with a reputable astrologer.

A transit is the interpretation of the movement of the planets within a specific time frame, when a planet or body forms an angular relationship with another planet or point, by sign and degree. A transit describes the archetypal energy that is activated either in our personal lives or in the collective.

Not All Transits Are Created Equal

Transits are happening in the world and in our birth charts and lives all the time. Some are barely a blip on the radar, and others are serious, intense, and potentially life changing. Typically, if the planet making the transit is an *outer* planet (Saturn, Uranus, Neptune, or Pluto), we're going to feel it. When an outer planet transits a planet or important angle (e.g., the ascendant) in our birth chart, it can last for up to two years. With world transits, again, keep your eye on the outer planets to get an idea of the archetypal energy playing out on the world stage.

We also need to look at the relationship between the planets involved in a given transit. These relationships are called *aspects*.

There are soft aspects and hard aspects. Soft aspects include the trine, sextile, and some conjunctions. They tend to be easygoing, supportive, and constructive. On the other hand, hard aspects include the square, opposition, and some conjunctions, and they tend to be challenging and intense or bring an issue to light that needs resolution.

And finally, we need to look at the archetypal nature of each planet activated. Each planet brings its own field of symbolic resonance that blends with the energy of the other planet it encounters. Specific themes tend to show up when certain planets are activated. If we know the thematic tone that is likely to arise in a given time frame, we can source the best plant allies for our apothecary and have them on hand for when we need them. Most of the following herbs are typically taken as a tea or tincture. Some can also be burned or used in the bath as essential oils.

If one of the outer planets is transiting a planet or point in your birth chart or is coming up as part of a world transit, here are some of the themes that can arise, along with some helpful plant allies. The following guidelines usually align with the hard aspects (the square, opposition, and some conjunctions) rather than the soft aspects. And while some transits from the outer planets can also deliver gifts, it's during the difficult times that we often seek support.

Although all the plant allies listed here are readily obtained in most natural foods stores as well as online, check with your healthcare provider to make sure that a particular herb is right for you, and note that this article does not take the place of medical advice from your doctor. Some herbs have contraindications and don't mix well with other medications. If you are depressed or suicidal, please seek help and see your doctor or healthcare provider.

Medicine for Saturn Times

If you have a Saturn transit on your horizon, be prepared for a reality check. The planet known as Lord Karma can bring depression, melancholy, and divine discontent in its wake. During a Saturn transit, it's not uncommon to feel bouts of loneliness, frustration, or overwhelm. You may feel between a rock and a hard place, up against limitations, blocks, or dead ends. You might feel run down or exhausted and be more susceptible to colds. Whatever the scenario, it's not unusual to feel disconnected, rejected, alone, fragile, withdrawn, overworked, or more serious than usual. Saturn's medicine teaches us the cause and effect of living in a body in a physical world. It embodies the way we have consciously or unconsciously structured our life.

Herbal support for Saturn times can include St. John's wort, which has been shown to be helpful with mild depression but does have potential serious side effects when used with other depression medications. See your doctor before taking St. John's wort. Schisandra berries are an adaptogen that can help with the mental fatigue that can accompany a Saturn transit and may also help with increasing vitality. Ginseng, rhodiola, and maca may help boost energy and combat fatigue and brain fog. Lemon balm and damiana can be beneficial allies that act to gently uplift the mood during Saturn transits.

Medicine for Uranus Times

Uranus times are known for bringing the unexpected and can deliver sudden news, upheaval, and unforeseen change. Although the change that often accompanies Uranus transits can also bring breakthroughs and open new doors, it's sometimes associated with shock or crisis. During a hard Uranus transit, it's not unusual to experience stretches of nervous exhaustion, anxiety, restlessness, and insomnia. Uranus's medicine teaches us that change is necessary to keep growing.

Plant allies for Uranus transits include *nervines*, herbs that support the nervous system, promote relaxation, relieve anxiety, calm circular thinking and panic attacks, and take the edge off in acute situations. They can also be beneficial to take before bed if you're having trouble sleeping. Some helpful nervines include milky oats, passionflower, skullcap, and wood betony. Other allies that can help during high-stress Uranus transits are *adaptogens*, herbs and mushrooms that can help balance the body and help you cope with mental, emotional, and physical stress in the long term. They can be taken as a daily tonic in tea and include ashwagandha, holy basil, reishi, lion's mane, and cordyceps, among others. B_{12} and magnesium can also be beneficial for the nervous exhaustion that often goes along with Uranus transits.

Medicine for Neptune Times

During a Neptune transit, things may not be quite what they seem. These transits can bring confusion, disillusion, and projection (we may see someone or something for what we want to see, not necessarily what is). We can feel emotionally flooded and more sensitive than usual. We may yearn to escape the hard edges of reality. During Neptune transits, our perception can be temporarily distorted. We may lose focus, experience ennui or existential angst, or feel lost in a fog. Neptune's medicine teaches us about surrender, to connect with a transcendent sense of the sacred and bring more meaning into our lives. During Neptune transits, we may feel vulnerable and have the urge to retreat, rest, and gather our strength.

If you have a Neptune transit on its way, you can stock your personal apothecary with two different kinds of allies. On one hand there will be times when it feels appropriate to make space to surrender, let go, dream, and soften the edges. At other times, it will be important to focus, face reality, and clear the fog. For dreaming times and smoothing the rough edges, you might wish to explore the calming, sedative qualities of wild lettuce, chamomile, lavender, motherwort, and valerian root. Rose petal tea has a gentle, uplifting quality that can be helpful for soothing sadness. You can also steep rose petals in a bath. For times you need extra focus to cut through the fog, try peppermint, rosemary, guarana, gotu kola, or ginseng.

Medicine for Pluto Times

If you have a significant Pluto transit coming your way, be prepared for a meeting with the Shadow that can bring catharsis and profound transformation in its wake. Hard Pluto transits are sometimes accompanied by endings and grief. Whatever the specifics, Pluto times can be intense and may bring us into contact with extreme people and situations, drama, and power struggles.

Herbal support for grief that can arise during Pluto transits can include sustainably harvested ghost pipe, which may help us detach from overwhelming acute emotions. Motherwort can be a soothing balm that provides comfort, and holy basil can be beneficial for working through trauma and diffusing intensity.

The Witch's Pantry:
Recharge, Restore, and Revitalize
Your Magickal Supplies

Monica Crosson

There are spaces within the Witch's cottage where the mundane should never tread, rooms filled with the scent of magick in the making, where dark shelves are lined with antique apothecary bottles that are labeled to not reveal the secrets of their power—fairy caps and mother die, graveyard dirt and devil's apple, just to name a few of the mysterious ingredients. There are leather-bound grimoires that contain the spells that have been passed down throughout the generations, not to mention strange taxidermied creatures, skulls, and bones marked with occult symbols. A witch's ladder hangs near bunches of herbs tied up with twine, and bundles of beeswax candles and strange stones are tucked wherever there is room. And of course, there is a cauldron. There is always a cauldron that simmers away in the corner.

I wish I could tell you that I was describing my own Witch's pantry, but alas, I am not. In fact, I don't have a separate pantry dedicated to my Craft at all. My home office holds most of my books, crystals, bones, feathers, candles, and other curios I use in spellcrafting organized in drawers and cupboards. And my herbs . . . well, they are neatly tucked behind the pickles and jam on shelves above my chest freezer and across from my washer and dryer in my pantry/utility room. My favorite cauldron, you ask? Well, as of right now, it is in my dining room holding some essential oils I haven't put away yet. Hey, a modern Witch has got to do what they got to do.

In all seriousness, though, most modern practitioners do not have the perfect "witchy" aesthetic you find in so many posts on social media. Nor do we live in homes that fit the fantasy idea of a Witch (say, *Practical Magic* or *The Chilling Adventures of Sabrina*), but what we do have in common is our use of herbs, crystals, and the other paraphernalia associated with our Craft. But how long can one keep herbs hanging from a drying rack in the pantry or kitchen before they go bad? It seems that the ones in the movies are centuries old (even cobweb covered at times). And what about those dust-covered crystals on our shelves or the athame crammed in a drawer along with the charcoal tabs and spell kit candles? Do they lose their energy after being lost in the junk drawer or even sitting along the windowsill?

I'm going to share with you a few tips, tricks, and good old commonsense practices that I have learned as I have journeyed the spiral path to help you keep spellcrafting ingredients viable and your working space energetically in tune with your magick. Let's get cleaning.

How Old Is Too Old?

Did you know that once you have harvested your herbs, the healing and magickal potency begins to wane immediately? The shelf life, under the best conditions, for herbs is one to two years, and spices last approximately two to three years—even less if not preserved properly. And what about the herbs you buy online? Do you know when they were harvested? And more importantly, how were they stored before they were shipped to you?

I suggest you go through your herbal supplies once a year and ask yourself the following questions to figure out the viability of your herbal stockpile:

- Are the herbs still holding their color?
- Is the herb's scent faint to nonexistent?
- Is there evidence that bugs have gotten into your herbs? Are they webby or chewed?

Unfortunately, a lot of herbs purchased online (especially from large online distributors) will sometimes lack both color and scent on arrival. Even homegrown herbs, if not stored properly, can lose their color and scent quickly. Sadly, these herbs have lost their potent energy and should be composted.

For magick, I always suggest using herbs or foraged material that is available to you fresh and drying it using one of several simple ways, including hanging in a warm, dark space in bunches within paper bags, by using a food dehydrator, or by using your oven set on a low temperature. If you buy your herbs, always buy from a reputable small-scale supplier who will give you specifics on harvesting dates.

When you're ready to store your dried herbs, vacuum sealing is going to preserve them best. In fact, they will be fine to use in tinctures and salves for over a year, as long as there is no exposure to air, and up to several years in magick. Canning jars work great too. Just remember to store them in a cupboard, drawer, or darkened pantry. If you don't have a pantry or room in a cupboard, use amber-tinted or painted jars or stainless-steel tins for herbs to avoid exposure to light. Remember to always mark and date your herbs. And last, try not to crumble your herbs when storing, as this breaks down their potency quickly. Crumble just before use.

Recharging and Organizing Crystals and Tools

The following are several media for recharging crystals or magickal tools that haven't been used for some time, are newly purchased, or were recently rediscovered in the back of a junk drawer.

Water: Water-safe (hard) crystals can be cleared of negative residue by washing or soaking in water. Place your stones in

Moon- or Sun-charged water for several hours. You can also rinse them under the tap for approximately thirty seconds each. To make sure that your crystals are water-safe, use the Mohs hardness scale, which is easily accessible online. If your crystal is a six or higher on the scale, it may be cleansed with water.

Rice: Rice has been associated with spellwork for thousands of years and is a common ingredient in protection spells. Rice can absorb negative energy, so placing your crystals or tools in rice for cleansing makes sense. Fill a bowl with dry rice and bury your items within the grains. Leave overnight. Remember to dispose of the rice when done.

Moonlight: Charging or cleansing your stones or tools under moonlight for a couple of hours is simple and effective. Place your items in a single layer where the rays will touch them and let the Moon clear those negative vibes and energetically reset them.

Sound: Using sound is a beautiful way to clear your crystals and tools of negative energy. Use a bell, a singing bowl, finger cymbals, or a tuning fork or even chant or sing for several

minutes, and allow the vibrations of the sound to weave its way around and through your items.

Soil: Stones come from the earth, so why not cleanse them with soil? Fill a bowl with clean, chemical-free garden soil and tuck your stones into the soil. Leave it overnight, and gently wipe your stones with a clean cloth. Return the garden soil to the compost.

Smoke: Using the smoke of garden sage, cedar, bay, or another purifying herb is a simple and gentle way to cleanse your crystals and magickal tools.

Unlike your herbs, crystals can last you a lifetime with proper care. And though they are lovely sitting on open shelves or in a bowl near your altar where the Sun kisses them with its wonderfully charging energy, there are many crystals that can fade, crack, or become brittle in direct sunlight. Safely storing your crystals in felt-lined wood boxes, bead boxes, or individual drawstring bags will not only help keep you organized but also maintain the beauty and viability of your precious stones.

There are many ways to organize your crystals for storage. My favorite way is by magickal intention. You could also store them by color, size, or hardness. Whatever makes sense to you.

Your magickal tools are best tucked away as well. I keep my wands and athame wrapped in cloth and tucked in a drawer until ready for use. All my divination tools are kept together in a basket in a sideboard cupboard in my office and recharged before every use.

Cleansing Your Magickal Space or Pantry

Now that you have a fresh supply of herbs and your crystals and magickal tools are recharged, organized, and neatly stored, it's time to physically and energetically cleanse your magickal working space or pantry. After giving every nook and cranny a good wipe down, go over the surfaces, windows, and floors of your space with a purification cleanser (see page 22). As you do this, keep your intent in mind. Start in the eastern corner of your space and work clockwise. When you are finished, sprinkle the purification sweep mix (see page 22) across your floor. Sweep in a clockwise manner toward the entrance or use a vacuum. Finally, use your favorite purifying incense to give it a final cleansing with smoke and hang your favorite protective elements (such as a witch's ladder, bells, etc.).

Purification Cleanser
2 cups Moon-charged water
2 cups white vinegar
40 drops lemon oil
40 drops sage oil
20 drops lavender oil

Purification Sweep Mix
½ cup baking soda
2 tablespoons dried garden sage
2 tablespoons dried lavender buds
2 tablespoons dried rosemary

It might feel a bit boring to stand in your magickal space with everything vacuum sealed and tucked away. But this really does ensure that your tools, crystals, and herbs are at their peak, and easy to access so you can really focus on your magickal working. As far as aesthetics, I suggest you find items that suit your vibe in thrift or junk stores or even on clearance after Halloween to decorate your witchy pantry. This may include dried bundles of herbs that can be switched out every year, wands, bones, stones, and other ornaments. I do this and I love the way my space feels. The bonus is that if you do choose to photograph them, they look great in social media posts, but they are not the tools, herbs, and stones we hold as sacred.

The movies and social media paint a beautiful fantasy of Witchcraft. But it is just that—a fantasy. It's up to us, as modern practitioners, to keep the magick real and our tools, herbs, and crystals at their working best.

A Magical Cemetery Walk

Kate Freuler

While cemeteries are often the setting for spooky stories and zombie movies, realistically I think most people find them to be peaceful, pleasant places. In my community, it's common for folks to take their daily walk in the graveyard purely for the quiet. But there are some people who visit because they like the feeling of being near those who have passed. There is no way to deny that upon entering a graveyard, there is a change in the energy around you, and your mind tends to meander down a different path than usual. This could be chalked up to several things: the subject of death in general, the presence of spirits, or even just the culmination of lore surrounding these sacred places.

It's interesting to note that while I, and many others, use the words *graveyard* and *cemetery* interchangeably, *graveyard* actually implies a site that is attached to a church or place of worship, whereas a cemetery is independent and considered nondenominational. This difference might impact the feel of the place, as those who are buried in a churchyard are more likely to have believed in a specific religion and its values.

For me, graveyards and cemeteries are magical. When I enter a cemetery, I experience a shift in consciousness. It's like I've walked into a bubble and am separated from the humdrum of mundane life. The breeze carries the voices of spirits. The earth under my feet holds the ongoing cycle of decay and rebirth. The grave markers, shaped by weather and time, each seem to have a personality of their own. I begin to think about bigger things, like life's purpose, the afterlife, and the invisible powers at play. It can put things in perspective.

For many spiritual people, graveyards and magic go hand in hand, since some spells and rituals involve the spirits of the dead.

Items collected from graveyards, such as dirt and pebbles, have special significance in magic. Due to the ethereal energy of the place and the closeness of the spirit realm, these simple materials are actually tools more powerful than the prettiest of purchased items.

It's extremely important, however, to be sure not to disturb any existing plots, decorations, tombstones, flowers, or statues. To do so is illegal in many places and considered vandalism, not to mention disrespectful. Please never take a piece of a tombstone or other monument, even if it is crumbling or damaged, as this is still vandalism.

There are a few reasons why cemeteries are so special. One is that it is a liminal space. "Liminal" refers to a threshold between two states of being, a seemingly empty space that is simultaneously nothing and everything. Liminality occurs between endings and beginnings. Where there is emptiness, there is po-

tential. Physically speaking, consider how those who have been buried are transitioning between forms; their physical remains are turning into fertile earth that will nourish new growth. This is a corporeal display of the constant change that generates life. The grass, trees, and flowers serve as reminders that from death springs birth and from endings grow beginnings. In terms of the spirit, it is the place hovering between this life and the next. As an earthly life concludes, the spirit continues into the unknown. Liminal spaces are a gateway where anything can happen.

Another magical element of graveyards is of course the spirits of the dead, who, depending on your intention, can be communicated with or involved in rituals. Contrary to popular belief, spirit contact in a cemetery is usually a subtle, calm experience. For those who are working on strengthening their skills in spirit communication, it's a good place to begin.

Last, there is a very special atmosphere in the graveyard that can't be found anywhere else. While it's difficult to define this feeling, the fact that it exists makes for powerful magic. Mood, emotion, and atmosphere all contribute to successful rituals. Even if you choose not to work directly with spirits, it's beneficial to your magical practice to at least have a relationship with the *concept* of death and its vital role in the cycle of existence.

Making It Magical

Doing magic in a cemetery doesn't have to be a large-scale affair with pomp and ceremony (in fact, this could attract unwanted attention from people who might not understand your practice). Often, it's a quiet, thoughtful event or a subtle experience with big meaning. Sometimes nothing at all unusual will occur on your walk beyond enjoying the experience, while other times you might feel a distinct poke in the ribs from spirits who want to tell you something. Magical things can happen any time, so you may as well be prepared. The following are some ways to turn an ordinary walk in the cemetery into something more meaningful:

- Remember that respect is important to the land, the spirits, and other people. If you see a funeral or mourners, give them plenty of space. Leave everything exactly as you found it, and, again, don't touch offerings or flowers left by others or in any way disturb a grave. If you plan to work with spirits, do so with gentleness rather than commands.
- When embarking on a cemetery walk, bring a biodegradable offering just in case you need it. This can be a crystal, some dried herbs, or any small thing with personal or magical meaning. An offering is required to express thanks to the spirits when you take any items, such as pebbles or twigs, from the cemetery. Remember not to take anything that is noticeable or causes a disturbance.
- Visit the same graveyard often to create familiarity. Much like the living, the dead are more likely to aid you if they know and like you! Think of it this way: Imagine you start going to a coffee shop at the same time each morning. At first, you don't think much of the other people in the shop, as they are merely strangers passing by. However, over time, you will notice that you see the same people every day. Soon you start to nod hello or exchange words. Eventually, a familiarity develops, and you might even get to know each other. Getting to know spirits can similarly take time and repeated exposure.
- When doing rituals or spells, bring along a protection charm. While you'll find that cemeteries are mostly calm, positive places, there is always the possibility of an unwanted spirit hanging around. You may already have a protection charm of your own, but if not, consider carrying a small amount of salt or a sprig of rosemary. You could also dab some protective essential oil (like frankincense) on your skin prior to your walk.
- Consider the religious elements, if any. If the graveyard is associated with a specific set of beliefs, there's a good chance the spirits there will reflect those values. If possible, learn a

little bit about the religion in question to better understand your experiences there. The magic you're working needs to be compatible with the spirits of the place.

The ability to sense spirits can take practice, especially when it comes to differentiating between imagination and reality. There will be times that you visit a cemetery and don't feel anything meaningful at all, and that's okay. Not everything is an omen or a message, and not every day will contain a spiritual epiphany.

Walking among the Dead

During your stroll, walk comfortably and don't overthink it. Bring your mind into the now. Open up your senses and acknowledge what's there. Be aware of sounds, scents, and what stands out visually. Feel the air on your skin and the dense earth under your shoes. Are there birds or little critters around, and if so, how are they behaving? If your mind wanders, just gently bring it back to your body and senses. By focusing on your physical self, you will slow down the noise in your brain, allowing for receptivity.

Without judgment or force, notice if anything particularly stands out to you, like a specific gravestone, a tree, or maybe even a bench beckoning you to sit down. Follow your gut and let your senses guide you. If a squirrel leads you in a certain direction, go ahead and follow it. If you sit on the bench, look around and pay attention. This is where meaning can be found. It might be something as simple as a ray of sunshine that makes you feel warm and peaceful, or a snippet of overheard conversation with words that

A Little Bit of Magic

THE IMAGE OF AN ANCHOR CARVED INTO A TOMBSTONE REPRESENTS HOPE AND ETERNAL LIFE.

apply to your situation. It's these little things that carry messages for you. If you don't feel much of anything at first, just let it go and try again next time. Attempting to strain meaning out of things that aren't relevant is a tiring exercise in futility. If there is a message meant for you, you will know it.

This receptive, open state is good for magical purposes and also just for simple stress relief. Once you're comfortable walking around the graveyard in this fashion, you can try doing some magic!

Graveyard Divination

This working involves walking in a cemetery while seeking information on a specific issue. Be sure to bring an offering with you as described earlier. This spell is good for when you're wavering over a tough decision or in a situation where you are not being shown the whole truth.

At the entrance to the cemetery, take a moment to whisper your question or concern. Then enter the graveyard and commence walking as described. In your mind, you can explain your concerns to the spirits further as if talking to a friend. (If you do this out loud, you might get some odd glances, but that's up to you!) Maintain your mental presence and just wander. Be aware of any small natural objects that grab your attention or stand out. In keeping with being respectful and minding the law, look for something general that won't disturb any plots, such as a rock, a pine cone, tree bark, a small twig, or even a pinch of dirt. Pick up the object to take it with you, leaving your offering in its place. Mentally or with words, give a sincere thank-you to the spirits who have been listening.

Take the item home and place it in a relevant area. For example, if your issue was relationships, put it in the place where you spend the most time with your partner. For business, put it on your desk, and so on. If it's small enough, you can carry it with you in your pocket as you go about your life. Gently handle the item at least once a day to acknowledge the helpful spirit within it. Be patient, and you will get your answer or resolution as the spirit sees fit. The answer can come at any time, through any source. It might be a mundane occurrence that reveals the information you need in a seemingly very ordinary way or something more mystical, like a dream or vision. Afterward, return the item to the cemetery if possible.

Peaceful Spirit Spell

This spell draws upon the peaceful energy of the cemetery. Only do this spell in a graveyard where you genuinely feel positive vibes. You will need a jar with a lid and an offering.

Find a secluded spot in the cemetery and open the jar. Quiet your thoughts and achieve a mindful state. Be aware of the calm, restful mood of the cemetery. This energy permeates everything in the area. Visualize it as a thin white fog slowly swirling among the trees, lingering over the grass, and caressing the tombstones. It softly covers your skin and mingles with your energy field. This benevolent energy contains peace, mystical knowledge, and the loving guidance of the dead. It holds the comforting surrender of death alongside the rich energy of rebirth. Imagine the jar filling up with this white swirling mist. If you like, you can make the simple statement provided below to the spirits, or if you like something fancier, you can write your own.

Benevolent spirits, I ask for your aid in bringing peace, rest, and healing into my home.

Put the lid on the jar. Leave your offering. Take the jar home, open it, and let the peaceful energy of the cemetery drift out of the jar. Imagine it dispersing into the air and bringing its essence to all it touches.

You can tweak this spell for other purposes by asking the spirits to assist you with bringing love or prosperity into your home.

• • •) • • •

Regardless of whether or not you include cemeteries in your magic, spending time there is a good way to ease stress, get some exercise, and give your day a special little spark of mysticism.

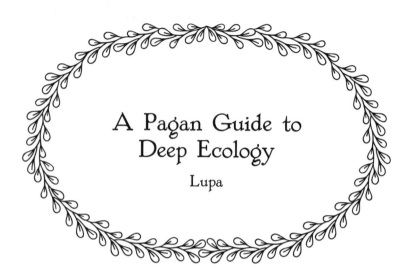

A Pagan Guide to Deep Ecology

Lupa

I was raised Roman Catholic, like many modern Pagans, though this didn't stunt my love of nature. Once I became old enough for critical thinking, I started questioning things that didn't make sense. One of my quandaries was over Genesis 1:26 (KJV): "And God said, Let us make man in our image, after our likeness: and let them have dominion over the fish of the sea, and over the fowl of the air, and over the cattle, and over all the earth, and over every creeping thing that creepeth upon the earth." It gave humanity blanket authority over every other living thing on this planet, and at a time when I was becoming increasingly aware of the environmental destruction we've wrought, it began putting cracks in my childhood faith.

With time, I began seeing how this attitude leaked out of the church and into the secular world. Capitalism's laser focus on growing profits, for example, relies on increasing exploitation of finite resources, with no plans for the future. Any "natural resources" were measured in terms of dollar signs, not ecological value.

These avaricious messages of both religion and economy have so filtered into the mainstream American mindset that many people will argue that nature is there for the taking without ever thinking where that concept came from. While it's understandable that we would prioritize our own species, we're so self-centered that almost everything we've created has been done without considering the negative impact on the rest of the world.

Look at our energy and lighting needs for the past few centuries, for example. It's pretty apparent that in order to extract fossil fuels from the ground you have to destroy an entire ecosystem surrounding the mining or drilling area. We hunted many whale species almost to the point of extinction for the lamp oil made from their blubber. Until relatively recently, very few people questioned the disastrous effects of these practices or seriously looked into better alternatives and solutions.

Why? Because our basic understanding of our place in the world that we've had imprinted in our brains from a young age shows humanity at the very top of a pyramid made up of every other living being. We here in the West are increasingly convinced that we are separate from the rest of nature and therefore can do whatever we want to it. Thankfully, there are antidotes to this ideological toxicity, and I'd like to present one of my favorites: deep ecology.

What Is Deep Ecology?

Imagine that image of a human being standing on top of that ecological pyramid. Now move everyone around until they're all in a circle (and no, humans don't have to be at the top or the center). That's deep ecology in a nutshell. Rather than seeing our species as the pinnacle of evolution, ordained by the Divine to rule over all, deep ecology places us within a greater community of nature in which we are neither better nor worse than other living beings. We are the last remaining human ape, *Homo sapiens*, and our lineage back to the dawn of life is no longer or more important than the lineage of any other species surviving today.

This can be a difficult concept for a lot of people to accept. After all, if you've spent your entire life being reassured again and again of your inherent superiority, suddenly being presented with the idea that you are just one among many might be a bit of a shock. What's important to remember is that you're still special—it's just that other beings are special in their own right.

That specialness can be termed the *intrinsic value* of a being, species, or ecosystem. Simply put, these entities are valuable just for existing and being a part of this world, regardless of what profit

or convenience we can squeeze out of them. This flies in the face of capitalism's focus on the extrinsic value of things: short-term profitability.

More importantly, deep ecology reminds us that every being is dependent on every other being in its ecosystem. It is the diversity of living beings that gives an ecosystem its strength. Each one fills a niche and evolves numerous interrelationships with others. The United States has a particular fondness for rugged individualism, yet this flies in the face of how cooperation helped us survive as a species for hundreds of thousands of years. No matter how alone and off-grid a person may be, they still rely on the clean water, food, and other resources gleaned from the land around them. Hence why so many cultures around the world emphasize gratitude toward nature.

No wonder deep ecology may seem like such a radical concept to those of us in self-centered societies. Yet it's not so different from the worldview of many cultures around the world and throughout history. This doesn't mean we should overly romanticize them, as is often done to Indigenous cultures in the Americas and beyond; after all, every group of humans has its flaws and errors. But at a time when the disasters perpetrated largely by industrialized nations threaten all living beings on Earth, perhaps a paradigm shift is exactly what we need to start turning this behemoth around.

Deep ecology is not without its flaws, of course. It is a very Eurocentric field that tends toward idealism. Its emphasis on "pure," human-free wilderness is at odds with the reality that many protected wilderness areas saw their Indigenous human residents driven out by governmental entities, and that these Indigenous people often traditionally farmed or otherwise tended to the land even if it didn't look like today's intensive agricultural practices. And while "shallow ecology" may be entwined with the environmental destruction we face, the prospect of completely exchanging shallow for deep ideations isn't realistic.

But with criticisms in mind, deep ecology still offers a lot of options for rethinking our relationship with the rest of nature and how our perception affects our choices and actions.

Changing Our Minds

In theory deep ecology should be very Pagan-friendly. After all, many of us base our practices in the natural world. Many of our symbols are drawn straight from the other living beings we share our world with, as well as the land, water, and air. Our deities usually have some aspect of nature that is strongly associated with them. Even the euphemisms used to describe modern Paganism in comparative religious discourse, like "earth religions" or "nature spirituality," reflect that ecological link.

But most modern Pagans do come from a Western, acquisitive background when it comes to nature. Even when we profess to love it and care for it, many still behave within the framework that we can consume without guilt, whether overtly or unconsciously. Look how many of us drop a bunch of money on mass-produced plastic Halloween-themed "witchy décor" at big box stores every fall or fill our gardens with non-native magical herbs and other plants without thinking of the loss of habitat for local wildlife.

Now, these are examples of things we have control over. A lot of our impact on other living beings comes about simply because we have no other options. Few of us have the ability to disconnect ourselves from the massive systems that provide the bulk of the population with water, food, energy, and so on. Moreover, a lot of the discussion over personal carbon footprints and such are ways that the corporations and other entities most at fault for environmental destruction deflect the blame from themselves. That being said, societies are made of individuals, and the best person to start with when trying to spark change is yourself.

The first thing to do is to look at where we've neglected to consider other living beings and their habitats in our actions. Start with your local ecosystem; even in a city you still have to have access to water and air, and your actions almost certainly have an impact on those systems. How developed your area may be also significantly affects what living beings can no longer live there (and which ones have adapted enough to hang on). Try to spend a day taking note of how each choice or action you make affects your immediate ecosystem, including choices made as part of your spirituality. If you can identify specific beings that may be affected, so much the better.

Next, look at the wider-ranging impacts, like how much fuel was burned to bring you your food or to ship an item to you, adding carbon to the atmosphere that affects us all. You may have to do some digging to figure it out, but don't knock yourself out trying to get every single last detail; sometimes you may just have to give it your best guess. Spend another day focusing on these global effects.

As you're examining your choices, notice when you may think things like "We *have* to have this resource even though it destroys ecosystems" or "I really like this food even though I know it has these specific impacts on other living beings." You don't have to leap to a solution immediately; just use these moments as an opportunity to ask yourself how you came to feel that our consumption of these resources was justified. There's a story behind the origin of every one of them that tells an anthropocentric (human-centered) narrative, and I just want you to pick that story apart to see how we got here. This exercise is only meant to increase your awareness of how shallow ecology permeates our lives and worldviews.

Also, *please* don't beat yourself up over every little thing you feel you're doing "wrong." Keep in mind that we're ensnared in massive systems that we're dependent on, which generations of people spent centuries building up and which are largely kept in place by the various entities in power. This is just to break you out of your anthropocentric view of the world, and cultivate awareness of interconnectivity in a way that I find is more effective than "Now, imagine a glowing gold light connecting you to every other soul in the world . . ." That being said, if you're feeling pretty cruddy and depressed about the state of the world and your part in it, you aren't alone and it's completely understandable. Try to approach this thoughtfulness with curiosity and concern rather than hopelessness; just by questioning your worldview, you are taking a step toward being part of the solution!

Taking Action

And now we get into what to do about all of this. Again, you can't save the whole world by yourself, but you can start with yourself. Look at the actions and choices you make day to day, and think of what would need to be done differently in order to carry them out in a more ecologically mindful way that takes other beings into account. Some you won't be able to do anything about, either because they're out of your control (where your water comes from) or not financially viable (buying a house with solar power when you're barely scraping by). Take note of those that you could realistically do something about.

If you're feeling overwhelmed, pick just one of those choices that you could change, and think about what beings you'll be helping by doing so, whether they're in your immediate ecosystem or not. Maybe you'll switch something in your diet to be more sustainable or purchase a spiritual item secondhand rather than brand new (yes, you can cleanse it, and it'll be fine, I promise!). Perhaps instead of buying Halloween knickknacks this fall, you'll instead donate the funds to a nonprofit working to protect endangered species and their habitats. Or you might put some space in your garden aside for a microhabitat made of native plants.

Whatever you do, let it be the symbolic start of moving through life in such a way that you extend your awareness to your entire community, not just the humans. Treat yourself as a constant work in progress; there will always be adjustments to be made as new information arises or your situation changes. Even if you can't change your actions right now, just by cultivating that constant awareness of your impact, you increase the likelihood that you'll make better, more ecologically sound decisions in the future when you have the opportunity.

If you find ways to help others shift their perspectives to ones more in line with deep ecology, so much the better! Don't be a pushy proselytizer; instead, be available if people have questions, and lead by example, not command. Often by walking our talk we open the path for others to explore as well. Not everyone's going to come to the same conclusions about what the best solution may be (just look at how much arguing there is about the most eco-friendly dietary choices!). What's important is that people are really thinking about how to be more collaborative with the rest of our nature community and actively working toward solutions that take everyone into account, not just us humans. These individual changes and actions can add up over time, and often prompt larger, more collective efforts to create a better world.

Handmade from the Heart: A Thoughtful Approach to the Ritual of Gift Giving

Blake Octavian Blair

The giving of gifts is culturally ingrained for many of us. However, many of us also have a desire to move away from the consumerist practices so rampant in modern Western society. The good news is that the custom of gift giving doesn't need to be avoided or eradicated—all that is necessary is an adjustment in approach and mindset. We can achieve this by moving into the mindset of engaging our skills in creation as well as shifting where we spend our money: toward other creators and our local economy. In this way, we still help reduce the amount we feed the consumerist stream of mass-produced items, all while producing what are often higher-quality gifts that actually support your local economy and creative expression more than the mass-produced goods would.

Handmade gifts tend to be inherently more thoughtful. There are two routes to go when it comes to handmade gifts: making something yourself and buying something from an artisan. Either route takes time, planning, effort, and labor on your part and potentially that of others. This is why I personally feel they can have a greater "heart" factor than giving something commercial off the mass-production line. We'll explore both options in this article because while we all possess crafty talents (yes, we all have some talent, even if you still feel like you're searching for yours!), we don't have skills in all areas and we aren't masters of every method of creation. However, this gives us beautiful opportunities to support each other by creating for and buying creations from others in our communities, whether those communities be social or geographical.

Handmade gifts also give us an opportunity to give something meaningful to that person in our lives that "has everything." Some people are at a point where they do not need more mass-produced stuff for stuff's sake. While there are wonderful intangible gift ideas, there are times when we still wish to give a tangible touchstone, but it has to then be meaningful without a doubt. When giving to people in this situation, there is a number of criteria to consider: Is it personally meaningful? Does it represent or symbolize something of personal meaning to the person's life, spiritual path, or identity? Is it useful or functional? Never discount a really nice crafted version of something one uses in every day life. Ask yourself if they'd want it taking up space. If something is thoughtful, of spiritual significance, or is practically useful, normally it is something they would like having around. As we look at gift ideas as our discussion progresses, you'll see that they tend to fulfill one, if not more, of the qualities mentioned here.

Adding Intention, Stitch by Stitch

I have to admit that I myself am the sort that enjoys a practical gift. For many gift-giving occasions, my husband has knit me sweaters. This really checks a lot of boxes for me. It's created by him, by hand, with me in mind, with loving intentions stitch by stitch. That's magic, indeed! Further, there is opportunity to support other local artisans, as he often purchases yarn that was hand dyed by an artisan who is a small business owner and regionally local. In addition, it is often cozier and more well made than any of the commercial sweaters I've ever had. To top it all off, the sweaters are the perfect colors for me. The entire winter I almost live in the sweaters he has hand knit for me. Practical, thoughtful, beautiful, and individualized.

Do you knit, spin, or crochet? If not, check out online tutorials and forums to find walk-throughs and free beginner-level projects. A plethora of inspired handmade gifts await. In addition to being a knitter myself, I'm also a spinner and create hand-spun yarn on my spinning wheels. One year, I gave a fellow fiber artist friend a skein of my hand-spun yarn, along with a set of handmade stitch markers from a local artisan. While this may be a little too much of a DIY gift for some, it was very well received by my friend, an avid knitter, because I custom spun it in her favorite color, and knitting with yarn spun by hand for you is a deliciously different experience than working with another skein of mass-produced commercial yarn. Plus, I was able to spend hours spinning good vibes into it while thinking of my friend. I'm sure you've heard the phrase "to spin a spell"—well, I'm here to tell you that you can, literally!

As is the case with creating gifts via fiber arts media, many handmade gifts are a great route to a more ecological gift as well and lend opportunities to use natural materials. Another good example is gifts made of pottery. Earthen clay transformed into an offering bowl, ritual chalice, or even a coffee cup not only makes a magical gift for a special person, but it also offers a bit of extra grounding effect with the earth element connection of the pottery. If pottery isn't your forte, this is another opportunity to support a local or independent artisan. One of my favorite coffee cups is one my husband gifted me for my birthday, made by an independent artisan, that has the image from a real oak leaf imprinted onto the side and is glazed in lovely woodland greens. Something about a pottery mug crafted with care just makes the morning coffee taste that much better!

Personalized by Path

I'm also a fan of building interfaith bridges with practitioners of differing traditions. It's a personal philosophy of mine that we are stronger working together and celebrating our similarities while respecting our differences. It certainly takes work for all involved but is well worth it. On that note, it can show a vast amount of goodwill to give a friend a gift that has resonance to their spiritual tradition. One of the easiest and most universal ideas is that of handmade candles. Almost every tradition has some use for candles. Beeswax provides a clean and nicely burning natural material. I also find it smells lovely! As a Druid, I have a bit of an affection for the energetic connection to the magic and wisdom of the bees in a beeswax candle. Further, you might be able to obtain wax from a local beekeeper, which helps not only support the local economy but also local pollination! I once received a gift of a specially poured candle from a grove-mate, intended for me to use in my practice as a flamekeeper of Brigid's Eternal Flame. Personal, practical, meaningful, and handmade! One year I also made beeswax votives for a number of my grove elders. For somebody who has everything, a candle is a consumable. They can use it and enjoy it, and it doesn't take up permanent space.

When considering handmade gifts, the ability for customization should not be undervalued. As I've mentioned, the best gifts have personal meaning to the recipient. We have a multitude of opportunities for personalization with handmade items. A great option that also acknowledges the person's spiritual tradition and uses simple natural materials is a wooden altar tile. Two common ways to execute this are painting it and wood burning it. I tend to do the pyrographic version myself (*pyrography* being a fancy

A LITTLE BIT OF MAGIC

Visit local farmers markets to shop for gifts made by local artisans who often vend at these events!

term for woodburned art), but if painting is a forte of yours, by all means, work with your skill set! You'll need to know a bit about the spiritual practices of and symbols that resonate with the person you are creating it for. If you are engaging in creating a handmade gift for someone, you likely know them well enough to already to have sufficient background information for ideas. However, it may not hurt to do a little clever research in advance in stealthy conversation. Remember, the design need not be complicated or elaborate in order to be beautiful, charming, and meaningful. A simple pentacle, Awen, ogham, rune, or other spiritual symbol is just fine, and you can feel free to embellish as much as you want from there.

Woodburned Pentacle

If you'd like to give this particular idea a try, it's quite easy. You will need to gather a few supplies to get started. A woodburning tool can be purchased at almost any craft supply store, but if you don't have access to a shop locally, it can be found online. Woodburning tools get extremely hot, so please handle them with care and practice safety precautions. When the tool is heating, be sure to place it on its stand, on a heatproof surface. Unplug the tool when not in use and leave it on the heatproof surface until fully cooled. For children, I suggest forgoing the woodburning method and instead opting for paint, markers, or colored pencils. Safety first, always.

Found wood also works great for this project. If you have access to fallen tree limbs or trimmings from necessary pruning, you can cut off a disk with a saw. Using found wood can help forge an energetic connection with the spirits of the land as well as reduce the pentacle's carbon footprint, as the supplies didn't have to travel far to reach their destination. Be sure to honor the spirit of the tree who bequeathed its limb to you! You will also want to make sure the wood is thoroughly dried out prior to cutting the disk and starting your creation process.

You will need:
Electric woodburning tool
Wood disk (3 to 4 inches across works well)
Pencil with eraser

Sandpaper (optional)
Transfer paper (optional, sometimes called graphite paper)
Wood finish of your choice (optional)

If the wood disk's surfaces happen to be exceptionally rough or show saw marks, begin by sanding it. It will depend how rough and how deep the saw marks are and how many grits of sandpaper you need to use. Use your best judgment.

The next step is to put your design onto the disk. If you are comfortable with freehanding it directly onto the disk with the pencil, then go ahead. I recommend drawing very lightly, so that anything that needs to be erased during the creation process can be done so easily. If, like me, you're not especially confident drawing freehand directly, you can first draw onto a piece of printer paper, trace a design on tracing paper, or print a design you've laid out on your computer, and then use the transfer paper to transfer the design onto the wood. You simply sandwich the transfer paper between the wood and the paper with the design on it, and then trace over the design with the pencil. You'll want to be sure to hold the disk

and paper steady or securely tape things in place so that they do not shift during the process.

Once your design is on the wooden disk, it is time to burn it in. Simply go over the lines of the design carefully with the woodburning tool. I suggest practicing on some scrap wood first. It can take some adjustment to figure out how fast to move and hard to press to get the effect you desire. However, after just a short bit of practice, you'll be ready. Once you have finished burning the design in, erase any of the light pencil markings that may still be visible.

You can leave it just as it is or put a natural finish on it at this point to help preserve, seal, and condition the wood. There are a number of natural finishes that are a mixture of beeswax and an oil such as tung or linseed. Do follow the instructions of the finish you choose, however. Most you simply wipe on and let soak in. Voilà, you're finished!

Another inspiring twist on this craft that uses similar supplies comes from one of my fellow Druids. She was inspired by the mezuzahs from Jewish tradition. Mezuzahs are small decorated parchment scrolls that contain verses from the Torah and housed inside a small metal or wooden placard-like encasement. These are then nailed inside the doorframe or threshold to the home as a blessing and protective amulet. My friend adapted this by forgoing the scroll, using wood (trees being sacred to Druids), woodburning symbols sacred to Brigid (Celtic goddess of hearth and home) on the front and a prayer on the back, and affixing the small rectangular placard on the inside of the doorway to her home. I was honored to receive the second one she made as a token of our friendship.

Consider Consumables

When in doubt about what to make a person, as mentioned earlier, remember that consumables can be greatly appreciated. Mix a batch of handmade incense for that special mystical person in your life . . . I bet you have a few! Perhaps pair it with some of the aforementioned homemade candles. Also, it may sound cliché, but people really do loved baked goods. I've never seen a tin of cookies refused! Or you can offer to make them dinner in a busy time or time of need and drop off a casserole. Such a gift is twofold: they not only receive the meal but also the gift of the time they'd have spent having to prepare the meal on their own.

Speaking of time, are you short of it? Consider supporting a local coffee roaster for some locally roasted coffee to give that java-loving friend. For an extra luxurious gift, pair it with a locally made pottery mug and a card with a coffee blessing or incantation you wrote yourself.

The year is full of special days that we might commemorate with a gift. We need not abandon this ritual in order to avoid consumerism and to be in line with our ethics. The next time you feel called to the ritual of gift giving, consider the benefits of something hand-made from the heart.

Air Magic

Alchemize Thoughts into Things Using the Five Elements

Tisha Morris

A human being is quite extraordinary if you think about it. We are able to simultaneously be on Earth while also connected to the spirit world. Because we in essence have a foot in each dimension, we are uniquely able to create things from thoughts with intention and action. I can have the desire to have a coffee and just like that I can produce a cup of coffee from my kitchen. Even if I didn't have a coffee maker, I could go to the store and buy one or invent one with makeshift filters and a pour-over container. Humans have obviously thought about coffee in hundreds of different ways. But what about something completely unique to you—a book, a painting, a recipe, a textile, or a song?

The process of creating something out of nothing is the alchemical process that we ourselves are all by-products of and therefore embody within us. To create is to participate in the essence of being alive. This is what nature is busy doing all day too. All beings on earth are part of the creative process, which Taoism refers to as the Five Elements Cycle. The Five Elements Cycle is the interplay of the Five Elements—Water, Wood, Fire, Earth, and Metal—to create and sustain life on earth.

Taoism is an ancient Eastern philosophy that sees the interrelationship of plants, animals, nature, human beings, and even inanimate objects as one, with each being a microcosm of the universe. The *glue*, so to speak, that ties all things together is the Five Elements. Everything consists of some combination of the Five Elements, including ourselves. Simultaneously, when the Five Elements work together in a cycle, they produce the creative cycle, or the alchemical process of turning thoughts into things.

What Are the Five Elements?

When the Five Elements work together, they create a dynamic energy that is the creative process. To understand the process better, it's important to understand the role of each element individually. You can think of each element literally, metaphorically, or symbolically. For example, the Wood element includes what you would think of as wood, such as a tree, but it can also be represented energetically in a variety of ways, including a season, color, shape, and through our personality.

Let's look at how each element presents itself through our own personal energy and personality. As you read the following descriptions, notice if you recognize yourself in one or more of them. We all contain the energy of *all* Five Elements, but we are usually dominant in one or two of them. Also notice if there is one of the descriptions that is definitely *not* you. It may hold the key to unlocking the alchemical process for yourself.

Water Element

The Water element is the Philosopher. They are quiet and typically introverted, and yet so unassuming. They hold a quiet strength. They may seem fragile at times, but they are anything but. They are deeply creative, contemplative, and introspective. They will most likely be the ones to figure out the key to world peace or an invention that saves climate change. It will be up to the other elements, however, to implement it. When out of balance, Water elements can become withdrawn and aloof. They tend to keep their emotions close to them and process slowly before taking action. In Taoism, the Water Element is associated with winter.

Wood Element

The Wood element is the Pioneer. They are the leaders, inventors, seekers, and visionaries. They will take the lead in groups and take action steps to create movement in projects. They can easily vacillate between being introverted and extroverted depending on what a situation calls for. For example, they can work solo on creating a new business or work well with groups. When movement in projects or relationships stalls, the Wood element is quick to become frustrated. Wood elements keep things in forward motion, and their challenge is to know when to contract their energy or take a step back. In Taoism, the Wood element is associated with spring.

Fire Element

The Fire element is the Manifestor. They are high energy and generally extroverted. They are often the life of the party and enjoy life. Similar to a flame, they create the highest expression of energy in the form of enthusiasm and passion. Fire elements provide the fuel in projects in order that they manifest in their highest and truest form. While the idea may have been born with the Water element and the

Wood element provided forward motion, it is the Fire element that brings something to full culmination. When out of balance, the Fire element can become burnt out. Its energy can easily scatter in too many areas without proper focus, which can lead to anxiety. In Taoism, the Fire element is associated with summer.

Earth Element

The Earth element is the Stabilizer. They are the grounding force that keeps the status quo maintained so that change doesn't happen too quickly. The Earth element is the container or stage on which we all get to play. They are highly supportive people that bring harmony to groups and help maintain the peace. Think of the Earth element as the parent that keeps harmony among the children when bickering ensues. They go out of their way to not ruffle feathers. They do not like change and can become controlling if taken to the extreme. Worry is their default emotion, especially when something seems out of their control that could lead to possible change. In Taoism, the Earth element is associated with the equinox points.

Metal Element

The Metal element is the Organizer. They are natural organizers and keep things in check and on schedule. They make great accountants, engineers, scientists, editors, architects, personal assistants, and professional organizers. They are guaranteed to be detail-oriented, focused, and precise in anything they do. They tend to cut to the chase in conversation without the need for embellishments. They also love an orderly environment with even their storage items labeled appropriately. Their imbalance can show up as being obsessive, perfectionist, or overly rigid in their mindsets. They tend to have tunnel vision without the ability to see a bigger picture. In Taoism, the Metal element is associated with autumn.

Did one or more of the elements sound like you? Chances are one of them jumped out and you were able to recognize yourself. Did one of the descriptions not sound like you at all? Our dominant element is usually where we thrive in the creative process, whereas our weak element causes us to stumble, get frustrated, or give up altogether. In the next section, you will learn to utilize all Five Elements to successfully alchemize your ideas into a tangible form.[1]

The Five Elements in the Creative Process

Before we had clocks or calendars, humans had a sense of time by watching the Sun rise and set each day, the Moon cycles each month, and the movement of the planets throughout the year. The passage of time via nature—daily, monthly, annually, along with our own life cycle—is in essence the Five Elements Cycle. We use the Five Elements Cycle in every area of our life, from daily activities, such as exercising and cooking, to major events in our life, including starting a relationship or creating a business. Once you recognize the cycle, you'll see it in everything you do.

As a writer, I use the Five Elements as the template for completing a book. Going from idea to completion of a manuscript is the perfect example of the Five Elements Cycle and can be helpful in not getting overwhelmed with what is a monumental undertaking. As I take you step-by-step through the writing process using the Five Elements as my guide, know that this same process can be used for completing anything you set your mind to.

Like all things creative, a book starts with an idea. The idea phase is the Water phase, where thoughts and ideas drop in seemingly out of thin air. It's the phase in which the veils are the thinnest and you can be a channel from Spirit. Everyone's process for how this happens differs. For example, some people get ideas through meditation, walking in nature, or during dreaming at night. Our best ideas often come when we're not trying to think about them because they come from beyond our physical brain.

The Water phase is also associated with knowing your *why*. In other words, what's driving you to write about or explore a certain

---

1   For a thorough examination of your dominant element and missing element, check out my book *Missing Element, Hidden Strength* (Llewellyn Publications, 2022).

topic or story? Your *why* becomes the river that quietly flows underneath your project and takes you to the end. Your *why* will get you past the doubts and fears along the way. It may feel like your mission or purpose, or something bigger than yourself, because it's the element that's most closely linked to the spirit world.

When you're ready to put your idea onto paper or into your computer, you've officially entered the Wood phase. The Wood phase is when we take the nonphysical idea into some physical form. In Taoism, it's represented by the first buds of spring making themselves visible in the natural world. You can think of it as the beginning of your idea blooming. This can take the form of an outline, the first pages, or simply jotting your ideas down in your journal. The Wood phase helps put structure to the otherwise invisible idea. You can think of it as a map that helps you plot your journey going forward. Once you've worked enough of your idea out on paper, then it's time to enter the Fire phase.

The Fire phase of any creative project is the phase in which you put in most of the work. In terms of writing a book, it's the bulk of the time it takes to actually write the book, or at least write the first draft. The Fire phase is represented by the summer season when the planting season is in full growth. It is in essence the highest point of energy output, which precedes harvest when the energy slows down. You can think of this as the completion of the first draft, at which time you take a break from it. This is the Earth phase. It's the point of the creative process where you take an objective step back to reassess what you've created thus far.

After you've taken a break from your manuscript, it's time to start the editing phase. This is the Metal phase of the creative process, where you go back to make any refinements needed. The energy of the Metal element is such that it cuts back or takes away any excess that may have occurred during the Fire phase. This phase is pertinent to any creative endeavor to fine-tune the final product. Whether creating a book, a product, or a new business, we are alchemists turning thoughts into things through the creative process of the Five Elements.

How You Can Use the Five Elements to Complete Projects

If you've had difficulty getting started with projects, finishing projects, or staying committed to projects, it's likely you've skipped over one of the elements. Now you have the formula for success that you can apply to any creative project. I invite you to use the following worksheet as a step-by-step guide for using the Five Elements to complete your next creative endeavor.

Five Elements Worksheet

Project Title: _____

Step 1: Water—The Idea

What's your why? What's the internal motivation behind what you want to do?

I want to create _____

because I feel passionate about _____

because of my personal experience with _____

_____.

Additional notes for Water phase: _____

_____.

Step 2: Wood—The Plan

What's your plan (e.g., business plan, book outline, blueprint, prototype)?

I will create a plan that includes _____

_____ followed by _____

_____ with a goal of completion by _____.

Additional notes for Wood phase: _____

_____.

Step 3: Fire—The Execution

How much time and energy are you willing to put into it?

I commit to working on _____ for _____ hours/

week for _____ months/years in order to finish _____

_____. *(Repeat for each phase of project.)*

Additional notes for Fire phase: _____

_____.

Step 4: Earth—The Market
Whose problem am I solving and how will I let them know I have a solution?

My target audience or customer is _____

because it meets their need of _____

_____. I will reach them through the marketing channels of

_____ by sharing my

personal story of _____

_____.

Additional notes for Earth phase: _____

_____.

Step 5: Metal—The Adjustments
What changes do I need to make from my original idea, if any?

I need to eliminate or change _____

_____.

I can improve upon _____ if I take out/

change/add _____.

I need to go back to the _____ phase in order to _____

_____.

Additional notes for Metal phase: _____

_____.

The Good Neighbor's Guide to House Cleansing

Diana Rajchel

For those unfamiliar, a house cleansing—or exorcism, as some call it—removes unhealthy-for-you spirits and energies from your home. The practice exists in many cultures, often using the tools available to the people of those regions, such as brooms, cedar bundles, and incense. In the Northern Hemisphere, most house cleansings in the modern day have the same pitfalls and holes in practice regardless of the cleansing tools used just because most people using them are newer to the unintentional errors that can happen with these rituals.

What are those pitfalls? On a practical level, smoke-filled apartments can trigger allergies for neighbors and, over time, may lead to children developing respiratory issues depending on the smoke used. Candles always present a fire hazard. Unless managed well, low-key, unmaintained energy traps can overfill and start spreading through a building. And the seemingly most basic step of a house cleansing is also the most fraught: if you banish a spirit without telling it where to go, it often relocates nearby or returns. Your spiritually cleansed house might mean a haunting for your neighbor.

The practices most Witches use for home cleansing and warding across cultures developed during periods of civilization when people lived farther apart from their neighbors. Animistic cultures also habitually included the input of land, water, plants, and animals in their spiritual plans. Thus, they had the benefit of more allies able to offset unintended results.

Visits from Exorcised Spirits

One of the cooler parts of living in San Francisco is how everyone openly performs their rituals, and the neighbors accept that as normal. If this weren't the case, I might never have been able to figure out what happened!

When my next-door neighbor passed away just before the pandemic, I wasn't surprised when the Chinese-American real estate agent charged with selling the property began holding weekly exorcisms. The bells, chanting, and incense burning every Friday at twilight felt magical. I loved it. What I did not love was the sudden influx of spirits into my house between Friday night and Saturday morning. Yes, I had warning. The volume got so high I couldn't keep up with reinforcing those wards. At first, the intrusions seemed mild, but it got to a point where I couldn't use the bathroom mirror without seeing someone else's face. Not only did I have to redirect spirit traffic every Saturday, but I also had to troubleshoot how someone else's routine exorcism became my problem.

Six months later, I had a relatively nonbelieving acquaintance hire me for metaphysical problem-solving. The issue? My client suspected that the mean next-door neighbor who died early in the pandemic was haunting her house. Sure enough, a reading and an astral scan turned up the spirit best remembered as Ms. Crabapple, and that lady wasn't going anywhere, damn it.

How did Ms. Crabapple get there? The family who purchased her house did what many spiritual people do before moving into a new home: they cleansed, banished, and warded. They wanted peace with the neighbors! As a result, my client's home became the most convenient and familiar place to settle.

In the case of my client, she came from a background where warding meant upgrading to a security camera doorbell. So while she burned prairie sage once in a while to hedge her bets, it never occurred to her that she might need more.

I can't offer empirical data for direct spirit work, but based on anecdotal evidence, I concluded that the same thing happened to the client that happened to me—for different reasons.

Three Key Spiritual Principles

When I perform a house cleansing and follow it with protection, blessing, and additional warding, I operate under the following subsets of spiritual principles. These, to my knowledge, have at best lateral documentation in folklore. If specific Craft traditions also use them, I haven't been exposed to them.

1. The Laws of Hospitality
2. The Laws of Sovereignty
3. The Laws of the Threshold

The Laws of Hospitality

The laws of hospitality hold that so long as an entity does not harm me or mine, it may remain a guest on my property or in my dwelling without fear of harm from me for as long as I allow. This law allows you to hang a metaphysical "no visitors" sign on your home. If a spirit is determined to visit and encounters such a sign, it often inhabits the next nearest space that will have it.

If your neighbor decides to light up a stick of *Artemisia ludoviciana*, open the windows, and chase out Ms. Crabapple, she will flow like water to the next container. The nearest such vessel happened to be my client's house.

The Laws of Sovereignty

Sovereignty means "I am the person with the authority to decide what happens here." The principle serves as a reinforcement to the laws of hospitality. What makes its execution tricky is that the person claiming sovereignty has to feel it. My client, like many women, was socialized to ameliorate and comfort rather than to lay firm boundaries. This weakened the efficacy of her first direct "get out" and made it necessary to hire me to assist with the stubborn spirit.

If an uninvited spirit creeps in where you live, where you rest, where you nourish, then you need to assert that you *are* the authority. Ms. Crabapple, in life, had a reputation for asserting nonconsensual authority on her neighbors, and she planned to continue to do so as a ghost. What finally got the ghost out for my client was claiming her home and her threshold as her sacred territory. I may have encouraged some bellowing. As part of that, she referred Ms. Crabapple to me for afterlife relocation.

The Laws of the Threshold

The issue in my own home came down to a complex matter of thresholds and liminal space unique to San Francisco.

Thresholds are the in-between spaces, such as doors, windows, crevices, and cracks. They belong to no one because they are in-between, and thus you can't claim sovereignty over them. Instead, you have to claim your role as a gatekeeper. The difference between gatekeeper and sovereign is subtle, but once you have a faery poking at things inside your doorway, you'll get a good idea of how

that works. Authority has significant limits when it comes to the in-betweens.

If you claim gatekeeper authority over the threshold of your dwelling, you are given the energy needed to enforce who may come and go from your home via those in-between spaces. That said, certain entities can just hang out in-between, and you can't do much about them except ward their ability to impact as you move through that space. I handle these gaps by hanging tiny brooms and mugwort stems above my doorways.

When I bought my first house, a townhouse in Minneapolis, I felt the jolt of the threshold power come on as soon as I was given the keys. I had only lived in apartments or homes someone else owned prior, so I had no idea that home ownership came with a liminal battery pack. The townhouse still posed some metaphysical challenges because I shared walls with my neighbors. Keeping in harmony with all of them meant that if I reinforced my wards, I reinforced protection for the entire townhouse row, especially since the shared walls formed an additional liminal space that doesn't happen in freestanding homes. Only after my experience with the San Francisco spirit overflow did I understand why my standard practice worked for my townhouse but not for the wall-connected houses in my seaside home.

My wards didn't block the spiritual overflow from the neighbor's exorcism because of how threshold law works: I didn't own my home. My landlord did. He had lived in the house I occupied for forty-five years before I moved in, and even after he moved, he maintained a sense of possession toward the place. I couldn't gatekeep and he didn't care enough to.

Most renters who practice warding are unlikely to experience the issues I did. However, my situation came from a perfect storm most will not encounter. I had a high spiritual population density, a landlord with a sense of possessiveness toward my house but a lack of responsibility toward me, a house next door with no living threshold keeper, and shared walls that created a large liminal space.

The weak command of these brink points in my rental made it very difficult for my wards to stand up to the energetic pummeling that comes with living in a place as gleefully haunted as San Francisco. So I had to corral the incoming spirits by trapping them in water with a modified revocation (think super-energetic vacuum) and then give them a list of places they could relocate to once I had them where they had to listen.

How to Make a Spirit Vacuum Container

Because someone reading this will need to know, here is how you build a spiritual vacuum.

1. Find a clear glass, preferably a beer pilsner, and fill it with water.
2. Cover it with a ceramic plate and flip it upside down—move fast so the water forms a seal on the plate.
3. Set the plate and glass inside a larger metal tray and fill around the plate with sand for an added layer of fire safety. Take an emergency or chime candle—any color will work for this— and cleanse it with a pinch of salt. Tell the candle that when you light it, you need it to bond with the water on the other side of the glass so that it forms a spiritual vacuum. (Glass is a slow-moving liquid, so the transmission works pretty well.)
4. Take a stick lighter and melt the wax on the bottom of the candle just enough so that it will fuse to the bottom of the flipped-over pilsner.
5. As you light the candle, invoke any ancestors, deities, or spirits that you believe are appropriate assistance for removing especially stubborn wandering spirits from your home.
6. Let the candle melt over the glass pilsner. Once the candle is completely melted and snuffs out on its own, pull up a chair and talk with the spirits, with a list of relocation options. Insist that they cannot stay in your home, nor can they just move into your neighbor's home. The following are common places that I suggest to spirits for relocation:

- The ocean, for rebirth
- The afterlife of their cultural origin or religious practice
- Woods, wild areas, and their original natural habitats
- Abandoned buildings where a good haunting will benefit the neighbors

- Dispersal to the elements (works well for ghosts who identify as atheists and are freaked out at having an afterlife)

7. Once the spirits agree to move to a new location, pour the water outdoors and into some soil.

The Amoral of the Story
(It's Just Metaphysical Physics)

These similar yet disparate experiences were caused by people engaging in practices extolled as right and good. That it has a drawback previously not well known is part of the problems and progress of any practice. Seasoned magick workers learn early to consider how our magick ripples through the world, and most beginners learn from their first spell that unintended consequences are part of magick.

The experience that my client and I both had prompted me to audit all my cleansing practices. I looked over multiple common approaches and their impact on those who share walls and liminal space with me. As a result of that assessment, here are a few things to consider when designing your practices.

Incense and Smoke Bundles

In my twenties, I was the ass who set off the smoke detectors, involuntarily cleansed the entire apartment building, and disappointed the police officer hoping for a weed bust. I understand much more about the impact of secondhand smoke now, and I have much-improved respect for artemisias and salvias. I now save smoke bundles for specific occasions: upon moving in, at moving out, and once a year for a deeply spiritual home cleansing. I only use them with all the windows open and a fan blowing the smoke out of the building. If possible, I have at least one air filter running during any smoke cleanse. This does not impact how well the cleansing works.

When I need to move out unhealthy lingering energies outside my annual smoke cleansing, I dust and then wash the surfaces with white vinegar and a tea made from whatever herbs are amenable to helping. Some months, all that's wanted in is a pinch of salt.

Other months, rue, hyssop, and mugwort wind up in my mop water. Switching to a water-based cleansing practice reduces the pollution that comes from smoke.

Candles

I love candles, but I recognize that using them often can lead to smoke and wax buildup. In addition, if my neighbor can smell the paraffin, my candles affect the air quality. Since my neighbors didn't consent to participation in my practices, I now plan for where my spell's physical by-product can reach. In addition to fire safety, I now only burn candles in a room with an air filter, and I try to use soy candles when available because the wax comes from renewable resources that don't affect air quality to the degree of petroleum-based paraffin.

Mirrors

Mirrors have more metaphysical security holes to them than some might expect. An oft-recommended work involves placing mirrors around a property or dwelling to reflect negativity. While that does work for short-term situations, using mirrors long-term causes two

problems. If you have a neighbor continually emoting unhappiness and unhealthiness at you, it turns into a repetitive boomerang situation. The neighbor will feel their negativity returning, and the irritability and aggression can increase. The second problem is that mirrors also serve as spirit passageways. So unless you wash them daily with a colloidal silver solution, you will have a spiritual highway bypass going on in or around your home.

Instead of mirrors, I recommend placing stones in strategic areas. Use crystals well known for grounding, such as hematite or red jasper. If you don't get on well with rocks, set out open jars of vinegar and salt to evaporate unhealthy vibrations. Someone determined to misbehave is still going to misbehave, but by not feeding them back their energy, you can avoid the spiritual version of mad cow disease.

The Takeaway

There is no "away" when we banish, cleanse, or burn. While earlier in history, the "away" part wasn't an issue because of lower population density, these days, we have to consider where energy and spirits go, as they can affect more people faster unless well directed. Because where the energy gets sent affects our dynamic with our neighbors (especially if they didn't get sleep because of our poltergeist), it's important to lay down a "flight plan" before you begin with your cleansing practice. Write down or speak out loud all the places you want the energy to go. Make sure you notify those places—by speaking out loud—that you intend to send them there before you do this. The ocean welcomes all, but she appreciates advance notice.

Even with the best and most knowledgeable practitioners, accidents happen. Magick has aspects of science, but it is neither a perfect art nor science. Give yourself forgiveness, and accept that these mistakes are always part of the continuous work of building a healthy spiritual lifestyle.

Air Magic for Invigorating Your World of Work

Emma Kathryn

It's Sunday night. The last few precious hours of freedom before the working week begins. You should be enjoying this time, relaxing even, but you just can't.

It's started . . .

Perhaps it was a sound or scent (the smell of laundered and ironed cotton is one of mine, harking back to my school days) that triggered the recognition of that feeling. Not the feeling itself, mind. That was already there. Maybe it never went away at all.

If you love your job or at least even enjoy it, or if your work leaves you fulfilled and satisfied, fantastic! It's a great position to be in, having that perfect work-life balance, whatever that may look like for you. But when you don't have that, when it feels like you are living to work and not the other way around, then you'll know what I mean when I talk about the dreaded feeling.

Add to that the rising cost of living and stagnant wage growth due to a variety of factors, including the pandemic, many of us may be feeling somewhat disillusioned with our jobs. And all of that is without even mentioning that we spend a good chunk of our lives at work, so when you look at the picture as a whole, you can begin to see just how big a deal our work is. So if you aren't happy in your job, that's a lot of time spent being unhappy!

Luckily for us, we Witches are used to rolling up our sleeves and changing what no longer serves us. First, though, let us consider for a moment the element of air and how we can tap into its energies to aid and enhance our jobs and careers.

Air is the element that carries scent to our noses and sound to our ears—not to mention we can't live without it! Air is vital for our well-being, just as our careers can play a vital role in our own emotional health and well-being. It invigorates and refreshes and gives energy to new ideas. It aids us in clear communication and in conflict resolution, all-important qualities to have in your professional arsenal. They are all qualities we can use in our magic too, to help make our careers work for us and not the other way around.

As my kickboxing coach used to say, work smarter, not harder!

The Sword Spread

In my book *Witch Life: A Practical Guide to Making Everyday Magical*, I share a number of ways you can use the tarot everyday, and this spread is just one more way of incorporating the tarot into your daily life. By using the tarot in this way, far from becoming a crutch on which you base every decision, instead it becomes a tool that enables you to take the time to consider your options and the opportunities that lie before you and make measured decisions that serve your will.

For this spread you will only need the cards from the suit of swords. Swords represent the element of air and also conflict. While conflict sounds negative, it's worth bearing in mind that conflict is

necessary for growth and that conflict need not always mean negative arguments or fighting. Perhaps most importantly, with conflict comes conflict resolution, a skill that is vital in the workplace and can help get you closer to where you want to be in terms of your career development, whatever that looks like.

When you've separated your cards, give them a good shuffle and lay them out before you in a line. The first card in the line represents you now. The last card represents the final outcome. Turn this card over next.

It's always worth spending some time comparing these two cards before turning over the others. If the last card is of higher value than the first, then you might see this as the kind of progress you want to make, moving forward, but at this point, there's no need to fear—we've got eight more cards to go. If the first card is higher than the last, it might signify a major decision is needed in order for you to move forward.

The cards between the first and the last each represent a conflict that must be overcome or a lesson that must be learned and processed. This is an exercise that can be done over the course of ten days, turning a card each day so that you get a clear focus every day, a challenge to overcome and master or a lesson to be learned and assimilated.

This exercise is worth doing every so often to help guide you as you move forward and toward your own dreams and desired outcomes.

Cooling Breeze Two-Minute Visualization

Have you ever been at work and you're just having one of those days? The boss is making your life hell, your colleagues aren't pulling their weight, and you've got a million things to do and no time to do them. A stress-filled nightmare, and what makes it worse is, if you're anything like me, you end up feeling mad, angry, and bitter. Not a pleasant headspace to be in, made worse by the fact that we can't go anywhere. We're stuck where we are . . . but only physically!

This visualization need only take a couple of minutes, though it can last as long as you need or want. It's designed to give you a bit of breathing space if only for a moment to cool down, refresh, and recharge so that you feel better able to handle the stress of work.

You can do this sitting or standing, anywhere it is safe for you to be for a moment, with your eyes closed.

Relax your breathing but don't try to change the rhythm. Simply let each breath come. Feel your shoulders drop, your jaw unclench, your arms soften. As these feelings of relaxation begin to spread through your body, feel a cool breeze blowing gently on the top of your head. Feel its energy seep into your head. It is cool but not cold—energizing. It feels like taking a long, deep drink of cold water on a hot day. Slowly feel the breeze move lower, onto your face, blowing gently, down to your neck, to your chest, and lower still as it scans your body, moving up and down slowly for as long as you need, filling you with that cool, refreshing energy.

When you are ready, take a deep breath and open your eyes. You can repeat this as often as you like throughout the day or whenever you feel your stress levels begin to rise.

A Honey Spell to Sweeten

Okay, so admittedly no one wants to be the office suck-up, but sometimes the simple truth is a little good fortune or favor with those in command can help grease the wheels to help you achieve your goals. This little sweetening spell is great if you want to build a relationship with a colleague or boss. And it needn't give cause for a moral dilemma either. There's nothing wrong with wanting to build good relationships with your coworkers; it helps make everyone's workaday life a little easier. This is also a good spell if you feel your boss doesn't like you and you want to try every avenue before you address the issue.

You will need:
Any incense
Blue candle
Piece of paper (blue if you wish to use color correspondences)

Blue ink pen
Clean jar
1 tablespoon honey
1 tablespoon lavender
1 dandelion seed head (if out of season, dandelion root or dried
    leaf or flower will suffice)
1 bay leaf

Gather everything you need and if you normally create sacred space before spellcasting, then do so however your tradition or practice dictates. If you are new to the Craft and are unsure what to do, then simply tidy the area and cast a simple circle by walking the boundary of the working area and chanting:

This sacred space I walk and make,
Filled with love and not with hate.
As I will it, so shall it be.
Spirits of this place, hear me!

Next, light your incense to represent the element of air, as well as the blue candle. On the paper, write the name or names of those whom you want to sweeten relations with and fold it up and place it in your jar. Add, the honey and say:

(Names of people),
Sweeten to me, sweeten to me, sweeten to me,
You will.

Add the lavender.

Lavender to soothe former stresses and cool hot heads.

Add the dandelion.

Dandelion to deliver my wishes and will.

Add the bay leaf.

Bay for my success.
My energy and will combine.
My will be done!

Put the lid on the jar and seal with the wax from the blue candle. If it is safe to do so and it is small enough, then you may wish to carry the jar on your person as a charm. If not, then perhaps place in your office or locker. If you are just not comfortable taking it into your workplace, then keep it on your altar, where you can focus your attention and will onto it to further strengthen the spell until you have the desired result.

· · · ☽ · · ·

So there you have it, some of my favorite air-inspired spells and workings to enhance your career and help build the life you want and deserve! Wishing you all the success in your endeavors!

Eggs in Kitchen Magic

Mireille Blacke, MA

Every family has stories that are both amusing and embarrassing to particular family members. One of my family's favorites involves a red-haired, freckle-faced toddler with a penchant for tirelessly racing through her maternal grandparents' home with a cookie in each hand. Over the course of a visit, many cookies would pass through those little hands, to be deposited around the multileveled house and property. You see, this rambunctious toddler only insisted on temporarily *holding* a cookie in each hand as she sped around, instead of actually eating the delicious things. We learned this because her beloved grandmother found stashes of whole, uneaten cookies hidden in various nooks and crannies throughout the home following each and every chaotic, crumb-filled visit.

We also know this because the culprit is still jokingly asked if she wants "one for each hand" any time she's within arm's reach of any cookies at family gatherings. I'll refrain from sharing any of her colorful responses here, but that toddler grew up to have quite a mouth on her. (I confess now the toddler and colorful mouth are both me.)

Perhaps my toddler-size self prophesied that the culinary talents of my Sicilian grandmother, mother, or aunt skipped me and that the only way to hold such gifts in my hands was to literally steal and hide them. It's more likely that I recognized the purloined gems for what they were and, like most wild animals, wanted to store my treasure for a later time, in the event of famine. I didn't yet understand that having a Sicilian grandmother made that possibility very, very unlikely.

It wasn't that my grandmother didn't patiently try to teach me her cooking methods; she did, more than once. Could I follow a recipe? Sure. That was logical and formulaic and appealed to the academic in me. But that was just not how my grandmother worked her culinary magic; her methods were more intuitive.

My ultimate goals were to master her lasagna and eggplant dishes. Ever the realist, my grandmother astutely pointed out, "You have a very strong will, but it's okay if you just learn how to boil an egg." She was quite perceptive, as my professional life took several paths. Eventually, I became a registered dietitian and spent a large part of my career discussing the importance of eggs nutritionally and in healthy eating plans, as well as boiling my fair share of them.

By heritage and education, I knew eggs were versatile, readily available, easy to use, affordable, and nutritious. In perusing the inherited cookbooks and recipes from my grandmother, it was clear that eggs were a staple ingredient across multiple dishes. But I also knew that eggs amounted to more than smart protein sources and delicious omelets. In addition to being useful in a variety of recipes, eggs were historically and multiculturally rich in symbolism and extremely helpful in manifesting magical goals and intentions in kitchen magic.

Cross-culturally, the egg represents fertility, new life, rebirth and resurrection, creation, abundance, and prosperity. The eggshell in particular carries the property of protection and works as a barrier to negativity. While eggs are certainly linked with springtime, Ostara, and Easter, the symbolism stands all year.

With these magical properties in mind, specific Kitchen Witch practices with eggs include cooking magical meals (choosing an intention or goal and selecting ingredients with properties to match), baking magical desserts, and devising several interesting uses for eggshells.

Given the versatility of eggs and that so many baked goods require at least one or two eggs, there are countless combinations of possible intentions to set for magical recipes. (Keep in mind: with magical dishes, multiple intentions are allowed!) Also, it's important to consider that with a term such as *fertility*, you need not limit the meaning to the literal sense of conceiving a child. Also consider its forms of creativity, innovation, and bringing forth new

ideas. Therefore, when adding eggs into a dish, you'll be able to assign its specific magical "job," whether it's "This egg will increase my chances to conceive a child" or "These eggs will increase my creative writing abilities, and I'll write at least thirty pages of my novel a day."

With egg magic, banishing negativity and providing family or household protection are two common goals used in magical recipes. I hope you'll find the following both tasty and useful templates in creating your own kitchen magic recipes.

Recipe for Banishing Negativity

Following is the recipe for my grandmother's Italian cookies, written down in the late 1960s, though my cookie-hoarding antics didn't occur until years after that. These days, you may see similar cookies referred to as "angeletti" Christmas or wedding cookies in mainstream grocery stores or Italian bakeries, typically topped with multicolored sprinkles. For this article's purposes, I've updated the original recipe with kitchen witchery instructions.

One of the egg's main magical properties is banishing negativity, so it makes sense to include eggs in kitchen magic recipes with this overall purpose in mind. To use eggs in my grandmother's cookie recipe to banish negativity, it's important that the rest of this recipe's ingredients fit, or do not hinder, the same magical goal. Most ingredients in traditional and modern recipes will have magical properties or some folklore attributed to them, which you can look up online, as most people do not have this information committed to memory. A quick review of this recipe's ingredients shows that they are compatible with the overall goal of banishing negativity:

Corn Oil: Protection, prosperity, longevity, fertility, abundance
Sugar: Sweetness, love, affection
Egg: Protection, banishing negativity
Wheat (Flour): Abundance, prosperity
Vanilla: Love-drawing, stress relief, restoring vitality
Milk: Protection, prosperity, nurturing
Lemon: Happiness, fulfillment, banishing sorrow/negativity, encouraging innovation/creativity

Because all ovens heat differently in terms of temperature, please note that baking times may vary slightly. Make sure to chill the cookie dough as instructed before baking, as it does make a significant difference in the outcome!

As this recipe's overall magical intention is to banish negativity (removing/decreasing something), it's important to stir counterclockwise when appropriate.

My grandmother's recipe called for teaspoon-size dough balls and yielded close to six dozen cookies! Because these cookies were relatively small compared to today's serving sizes, I modified the recipe to use a tablespoon instead of a teaspoon when measuring out the dough. You'll still end up with a *lot* of cookies—about four dozen!

"One for Each Hand" Italian Cookies to Banish Negativity
For the cookies:
4 eggs
⅔ cup corn oil (canola substitute is okay)
⅔ cup granulated sugar
2 teaspoons vanilla extract

4½ cups all-purpose flour
4 teaspoons baking powder

For the icing:
4 cups confectioner's sugar
3 ounces warm whole milk
2 teaspoons lemon extract

Preheat the oven to 365 degrees Fahrenheit.

In a large bowl, beat eggs, oil, and sugar together, until sugar is dissolved. Visualize the sugar providing a foundation of love and affection into the mixture, the corn oil offering protection, and the eggs banishing all negativity and stress from your life. As you add each egg, say, "I add this egg to banish negativity from the lives of all who eat these cookies. So mote it be."

Add vanilla flavoring. Imagine the vanilla releasing stress and restoring lost energy.

Sift the flour and baking powder together. Add it to the egg mixture gradually until a soft, smooth dough is obtained. When the dough does not cling to the bowl, cover the mixture and place it in the refrigerator for about 1 hour. Take this time to relax, meditate, or focus on releasing negativity from all areas of your life.

Grease and flour a cookie sheet. Using a tablespoon, form little balls from the dough. Place each ball about an inch apart on the cookie sheet, and bake for 15 to 20 minutes, or until nicely browned.

Make a soft white icing of confectioner's sugar and warm milk. Once again, imagine the sugar infusing love and affection, and visualize the milk providing protection.

Add lemon flavoring. As you combine these ingredients to make the icing, acknowledge the separate parts of yourself (positive and negative) that make you unique. Release any part that no longer serves you.

Dip the top of each cookie lightly in icing and set aside until dry. Inhale the comforting scent of the cookies and let them fill you with hope and joy. Know that you or anyone who eats these cookies will feel safe and free from negativity.

Recipe for Family or Household Protection

I have adapted the outstanding sweet potato pudding recipe from actress Jennifer Garner's grandmother, Exie Mae, to imbue the original dish with the magical intention of protecting one's family or household. Since this recipe deals with protection (creating positive change), stir clockwise when appropriate. With the recipe's goal of family or household protection, I've assigned magical duties to the ingredients as follows:

Sweet Potatoes: Connection to ancestors/passed relatives, grounding, nurturing, friendship

Sugar: Sweetness, love, affection

Milk: Prosperity, protection, nurturing

Cinnamon: Luck, healing, enhancing power of recipe's other ingredients

Allspice: Prosperity, luck, healing

Nutmeg: Protection from unwanted energies, stopping gossip, revealing truth

Clove: Protection from negativity, stopping gossip

Egg: Protection from negativity

Salt: Cleansing, purification, protection from negativity

Butter: Maternal ancestral protection, calming, nurturing energy, stress relief

Marshmallows: Protection

Sweet Potato Pudding for Family Protection

4 medium sweet potatoes, peeled and quartered

2½ cups sugar

1¼ cups milk

1 tablespoon ground cinnamon

1 teaspoon ground allspice

½ teaspoon ground nutmeg

¼ teaspoon ground cloves

3 eggs

Salt

3 tablespoons butter

16 ounces mini marshmallows

Preheat the oven to 350 degrees Fahrenheit. Place the sweet potatoes in a large pot of water, cover the pot, and bring it to a boil. Remove the lid, lower the heat to medium, and cook until the potatoes are tender. Drain and place the potatoes in a large bowl.

Mash the potatoes with an electric mixer. As you do this, reflect on your ancestors or relatives who are no longer with you, and respectfully ask them for their protection and support for the living members of your family.

At low speed, add the sugar, milk, cinnamon, allspice, nutmeg, cloves, eggs, and salt to taste, mixing to combine. While you add each ingredient, visualize the sugar drawing love and affection to you and your family, milk bringing prosperity and protection, cinnamon strengthening the recipe and your family, allspice offering luck and healing, nutmeg and clove stopping gossip, eggs adding protection and abundance, and salt offering cleansing and additional protection. When adding the eggs and salt, it's appropriate to say, "I add these eggs and protect my family from harm. I add this salt and cleanse my energy and that of my family. So mote it be."

Butter a 9 × 13-inch casserole dish. As you do so, say, "I butter this dish and call on my ancestors to protect my house and family."

Pour in the mixture. Smooth the top and bake about 45 minutes to 1 hour, until the mixture is set.

Remove the pudding from the oven and cover the top with marshmallows, for additional protection. Change the oven temperature to the broil setting. Cook 3 to 5 minutes, until the marshmallows are brown and fluffy. Makes 6 to 8 servings.

Additional Magical Tips

With any recipe, it's important to focus on your magical intention for the duration of the cooking or baking time, as if the outcome has already happened. Though not always possible, a healthy mindset will yield the best results. Cooking or baking when upset may be detrimental to the outcome of the dish and the kitchen magic. Remember that the emotions and energies that you send into those dishes will transfer to those you feed.

I used some of my grandmother's utensils (wooden spoons, measuring cups) to make the angeletti cookies, to increase my feelings of connection to her while baking. If you're working on a magical goal and find that you could use an infusion of ancestral energy, consider selecting a treasured family recipe or looking through an heirloom cookbook. You may choose to "modernize" some of the other ingredients (e.g., substitute lard with something more heart-healthy) or serving sizes (as with the cookie recipe in this article), but the connection you'll feel to your ancestral tree will be remarkably strong.

You can incorporate the magical properties of eggs into your kitchen magic (and household) even if your recipes don't require them. It's not too difficult to find egg-shaped items, particularly of the metaphysical type, such as thunder eggs (geodes) or crystals and stones in egg-like shapes, that you can place in your kitchen or throughout your home. You can use hand towels, dinnerware, or other meal-related items decorated with eggs throughout the year to include the egg themes into your household and daily life.

A LITTLE BIT OF MAGIC

An easy form of egg magic for self-rejuvenation involves simply salting and eating a single, whole hard-boiled egg on the New Moon.

Cascarilla Eggshell Spell Powder

Based in American folk magic, cascarilla powder is used primarily for protection and purification rituals and spells. It's made by simply grinding washed out and dried eggshells down into a fine powder, typically with a mortar and pestle. The powder is intended for marking magic circles and sigils, used to draw magical seals, and added to incense to remove jinxes, in addition to being used in witch bottles and spell bags.

Also, according to some legends and folklore, tossing eggshells on the roof of your house will protect it from hexes and curses. I don't know about you, but I'll try baking cookies first.

Just as it represents the life cycle across multiple cultures and religions, the egg has been a fundamental ingredient from my earliest childhood memories of family, comfort, and home. In recalling those memories decades later for this article, I accept I'll never be able to cook or bake like my grandmother, but I can proudly share her cookie recipe with others, and perhaps in doing so help them connect with their own long-ago memories of warmth, comfort, or even childlike joy. For those without such memories, I'd like to think there might be shared warmth and comfort regardless.

My grandmother did, after all, steer me toward the wonders of eggs once upon a time, in a much different way than she steered me toward her cookies. Perhaps there's a bit of the tiny, rebellious cookie bandit dwelling in each of us. Even today as a registered dietitian, I proudly carry a keychain that reads, "A balanced diet is a cookie in each hand."

Resources

Meehan, Michaela. "Exie Mae Garner's Sweet Potato Pudding Recipe." Once Upon a Farm. March 11, 2021. https://onceuponafarmorganics .com/blogs/upon-a-blog/sweet-potato-pudding-by-exie-mae-garner.

Wigington, Patti. "Egg Magic and Folklore." Learn Religions. Last modified June 25, 2019. https://www.learnreligions.com/egg-magic-and -folklore-2562457.

Crafting a Personal Devotional Practice

Stephanie Woodfield

In my own practices I treat spells and devotion as very separate. Magic is a tool—technology, if you will. I can use it to manifest my desires and help myself and others succeed in life. I love and enjoy the practice, but that's not the same thing as my devotion. My devotional work, on the other hand, is about connecting to the gods and spirits I worship. It is deeply personal and has evolved as I have grown on my path and will continue to do so. Devotional work can be prayer, offerings, worship, ecstatic dance, and so many other things. It's less formulaic, as spellwork can be, and more free-form. Most importantly, it's our way to commune with the forces in the world that are greater than us, to honor those forces and build deep, meaningful relationships with them. To some that may be gods, ancestors, the fair folk, elementals . . . the list goes on. Of all my practices, devotional work is the one thing that has furthered my spiritual growth and made me feel connected to something greater than myself.

The most beautiful part of Witchcraft is that as a practitioner, you can craft your own unique spiritual practices. It also happens to be one of the most difficult aspects of Witchcraft. It is both an exhilarating idea and a daunting one. Where do we begin? How do we know if we are doing a devotional practice correctly?

Steps to Crafting a Devotional Practice

The thing is I can't give you an exact formula for devotional work. Devotional practices are personal, and you will have to be the one who creates what will work best for you. What I can give you are some things to consider that will help you build your own practice. My book *Dedicant, Devotee, Priest* also outlines other practical information that may be useful in your devotional work.

I find, when creating any sort of practice, it is helpful to break it up into steps. Think of it as a magical formula that will aid you in the creation of your practice. The idea of coming up with something brand new, tailored to your own needs, from whole cloth can at first seem overwhelming. These steps will give you a good starting place to be creative and really think about what your needs are.

Step 1: Whom Are You Connecting To?

The focus of devotional work is to commune with, worship, or build a connection to a force outside of yourself. Deities often have many faces, epithets, or aspects. Which aspect do you want to connect to? You also may want to incorporate languages, items, or offerings that are connected to that deity's culture. These considerations could change the place, time, or way in which you perform the devotion. If I want to do devotion work because I wish to be more grounded, I might want to pick a deity or aspect of that deity that embodies that. Maybe not all aspects of that deity embody that quality.

Step 2: What Is Your Goal?

What is your objective? Do you wish to build a closer relationship with a certain deity? Do you want to cultivate a certain quality or skill? Align your energies to the Divine? Center yourself for the day, or just have a heartfelt chat with deity over coffee? Everyone's goals will be different. This will also likely change at different points in your life as well.

Step 3: How Do You Want the Practice to Make You Feel?

Considering how you want your devotional practice to make you feel is perhaps the most vital step of all. Do I want to feel in awe of the presence of deity? Do I want to feel cleansed, energized, or elated? Once you have an idea of what you want your practice to be and are regularly engaging in it, spend some time after you do your devotional work to consider how you feel. Better? Worse? Full of energy, drained? How I feel after my devotionals is usually the factor that will make me either continue to use that method or switch to something else. In the past I would try devotional practices outlined by others and didn't understand why I didn't feel much of anything afterward. It wasn't that I was doing anything wrong; it just wasn't the practice for me. It didn't give me the feeling I was looking for, so I changed my practices to something that fit me better.

Step 4: How Much Time Do You Have?

Be realistic about how much time you have for devotional work. You aren't a bad Witch if you only have less than five minutes a day or only have time once a week to do your practice. Commit to something that fits with your schedule. Not a morning person? Then don't try to do your devotion in the morning! Only have a few minutes in your car while you sit in the parking lot about to head into work? That's totally fine! Unrealistic goals always fail.

Step 5: Do You Need Any Items to Do the Practice? Will They Cost Anything?

Ideally, the only item you should need is yourself, but incense, libations, and other items may become a part of your devotion. Think about how readily available these items are. What do they cost, if anything? Can you afford them? Think about what purpose they serve and if they can be replaced with something else.

The Lesser Banishing Ritual of the Pentagram

To give you an idea of what these steps might look like in practice, here is a devotional I created using these steps. My goal was to connect more deeply with Hekate and to feel cleansed and centered afterward. I also wanted it to be grounded in something familiar, which in this case was the Lesser Banishing Ritual of the Pentagram. The LBRP is used in ceremonial magic and employs the use of the Hebrew names of God and the names of angels. It is an excellent ritual to use to cleanse a space and to center oneself, and it was also something I used often and was comfortable with. Also, the idea of taking something old and crafting it into a new practice appealed to me. It felt exciting and like a challenge. I also

wanted few items, something I could do with a ritual knife or no items at all. For timing, I chose to do it in the evenings, just when I got home. I am not an early bird. For frequency, I decided on three times a week, as it was doable for my schedule and a number connected to Hekate. This is also not the first version of this devotional. I tried the original one I wrote for a month, noted what felt like it was working and what wasn't, and then made adjustments. After another month of trying my new version, I found other things I decided to change. It took a while before I had it just right, and if you try this practice, you might find other things to change to make it work well for you. Don't be discouraged if your devotional isn't perfect right away. Try things, take notes, make adjustments, and just have fun with the process!

Hekate Lesser Banishing Ritual

Begin by standing with your feet slightly apart. Imagine a brilliant white light descending from your crown. Bring this column of energy all the way down through your body while you take your right hand (or ritual knife if you prefer) and trace it down along your third eye, brow, and sternum while vibrating *ουρανός,* or "sky": *Ouranós* (or-an-ohs).

Continue to draw your hand down the center to your lower body, turning it to point to the floor. See the white light continuing down through your body to your feet as you vibrate *γη,* or "land/soil": *Gi* (yhee).

Draw your hand back upward to your heart, vibrating *ωκεανό',* or "ocean": *Okeanós* (oak-ee-an-os).

Drag your hand from your heart to your right shoulder. See another brilliant ray of light flowing from your heart into your right arm. For this part you will vibrate Hekate's epithets. Vibrate *Apotropaia* (ah-poh-troh-pay-ah), meaning "Averter of Evil."

Drag your hand back across your heart to touch the left shoulder, seeing that brilliant ray of light extending to your left shoulder. Vibrate *Kleidoukhos* (kl-eye-doh-kos), meaning "Key Bearer."

Take a moment to breathe in this light and feel it filling you completely, holding your hands out at either side in goddess pose and vibrating the epithet *Soteira* (soh-tee-era), meaning "Savior."

Instead of turning toward the four quarters as you would in the traditional LBRP, you will be facing only three directions. Imagine these stations as each being about a third of a circle apart from each other. If you picture it as a clock face, you will begin facing 12 o'clock, turn to the right to face 4 o'clock, turn again to face 8 o'clock, then turn once more to face 12 o'clock again. This forms a kind of magical triple crossroads, which were historically sacred to Hekate. Facing 12 o'clock, draw a banishing pentagram in the air (with your finger or knife), then vibrate *Hekate.*

Turn to face 4 o'clock, draw a banishing pentagram in the air, and vibrate the epithet *Enodia* (Eh-no-dee-a), meaning "Of the Crossroads." Turn toward 8 o'clock, draw a banishing pentagram in the air, and vibrate the epithet *Chthonia* (Ka-tho-nee-a), "Of the Earth/Underworld."

Turn toward 12 o'clock, the direction you were when you first started. For this part, see each deity/demigod standing before you as you vibrate their names. They shine with a brilliant light, their strength, power, and protection flowing into you. Vibrate,

Before me, Hecuba!
Behind me, Persephone!
To my right hand, Medea!
To my left hand, Circe!

When you are ready, say,

About me shines the pentagrams,
And within me shines the power of Hekate, Queen of Witches.

Finally, you will repeat the opening segment to finish. Trace your finger or knife down along your third eye, brow, and sternum while vibrating *Ouranós*.

Continue to draw your hand down the center to your lower body, turning it to point to the floor. See the white light continuing down through your body to your feet as you vibrate *Gi*.

Draw your hand back upward to your heart, vibrating *Okeanós*.

Drag your hand from your heart to your right shoulder. See another brilliant ray of light flowing from your heart into your right arm. For this part, you will vibrate Hekate's epithets again, beginning with *Apotropaia*.

Drag your hand back over your heart, across to touch the left shoulder, seeing that brilliant ray of light extending to your left shoulder. Vibrate *Kleidoukhos*.

To end, take a moment to breathe in this light and feel it filling you completely, holding your hands out at either side in goddess pose and vibrating the epithet *Soteira*.

Working with Local Spirits

Olivia Graves

*L*ocal spirits is such a broad term. This can mean anything from the genius loci (the spirit of a place) to plant, animal, and elemental spirits, and of course the dead, to give a few examples. While many are familiar with working with deities (or especially in my background, saints), I've come to find that local spirits are so often brushed aside, as if they don't have anything powerful to offer. The locals are just that: local. They have the knowledge of your area, and many of them have direct influence as well. Think of it this way: Is it easier and more impactful to solve a problem within your community by writing emails and calling the Supreme Court, or by reaching out to your local government officials? Which group will have more direct access to help and more knowledge of what the problem is and how to fix it?

Getting to Know the Locals

Whether you've been in the same home your whole life or you just moved to a new area, take a walk. It doesn't matter if you're living in a city or in the countryside—every area has spirits. You'll notice that some areas will have more than others, some places seem "quieter," and others are bustling. Some you'll find you immediately connect to, while others will be more standoffish and hesitant to engage. Can you point out the land guardian, such as a massive old tree or an animal that seems to watch over the area? Are the water spirits from the creek, pond, or lake active? Are there spirits residing in a building? Is there a cemetery near, where you can introduce yourself to the local dead?

When you are first introducing yourself, do not expect any spirit to immediately want to work with you. Your first priority is building a relationship and knowledge. Begin with these tips in mind:

1. **Just go there.** Take a walk. Exist in the space. Refrain from distractions, even music or podcasts. You want to be fully present and attentive. Feel it out. What does the energy feel like? Can you tell if the spirits are content or not? Are there any spirits that make an impression?

2. **Be consistent.** It's best to choose a place you enjoy going to so you can show up often to familiarize and connect regularly. This is especially helpful when it comes to plant spirits. Watching them grow and shift and change throughout the year will be insightful, especially with plant allies you plan to work with and use in future workings.

3. **Have interest and intent.** It's never a bad idea to bring a used grocery bag to pick up any litter you may spot. This doubles as helpful to your community and my favorite form of offering. If you wish, you can speak aloud, greeting the spirits and saying goodbye. With fauna and flora, do your best to identify the local species. Which are invasive? Which are native? How do they work with each other? With the local dead, dive into your local history and learn about the people who lived there before you, when the city or town was founded, and any local lore it may have. Are there any specific graves that interest you? Who was that person, and what were they like?

4. **Establish the manner of the relationship.** This will most likely be different for each spirit and area. Are you simply wanting to be better connected to the land and area? Are you looking for spirits who will help you with your spells and rituals? Are you hoping for spirits to teach you or guide you in something? Are you okay with a purely transactional relationship (offering/payment for aid)? This is a two-way road, so be sure the spirit wants this type of relationship with you too.

5. **Don't forget your offerings.** Offerings are important, and they can be very simple. Again, this depends on the type of spirits you're looking to work with. Nature and land spirits tend to enjoy offerings of cleaning up trash, tidying areas, planting native species, and simple nature crafts. The local

dead can vary, depending on the person, but some fresh water, picked flowers, a few coins, a small food offering, or a splash of good liquor also doesn't hurt. Don't feel the need to make grand gestures of expensive or fancy offerings every time you show up. Time is also a wonderful offering, as it is the most precious and irreplaceable.

6. **Don't rush.** Take your time getting to know the spirits you have an interest in working with. This (usually) doesn't happen overnight. If you try to rush building this relationship, it will feel forced and your intentions will most likely not be welcomed.

Beginning to Work with the Spirits

How Can You Help Them?

Now that you're a little more familiarized with your area and the spirits within it, I find it's helpful to record your findings in each area. What areas do you like most and why? How does the energy feel? Do you feel the spirits are happy? Content? Quiet? Hesitant? Restless? Upset? If so, do you know what's upsetting them? Figuring out what is upsetting the spirits and helping ease or solve this problem goes a long way. Of course, keep in mind that some problems are bigger and more complex than others.

Know Who to Ask

It is also important that you understand where each spirit's strengths and weaknesses lie. For example, for aid in grounding work, I would ask a land guardian or plant allies over the restless, feisty spirits of the dead from the old cemetery outside town. However, maybe the dead would be more helpful in stirring up some baneful work or a return to sender, while the land guardian or plant allies will probably have less of a bite.

Know the Price

This depends on the kind of relationship you have with the spirits:

Transactional: You give an offering as payment for the help or work a spirit provides.

Neighborly: A good relationship in which a spirit is willing to provide a favor, regardless if an offering is promised or not.

Familiar: Some practitioners have strong relationships with their local spirits. Sometimes the spirits will aid in things such as luck and protection purely out of fondness for the practitioner without being asked to do so. Usually this goes both ways, and the practitioner will provide offerings and rituals for the spirits without any expectations to receive from the spirit.

For the most part, the price will depend on the spirit and what you are asking from the spirit in return.

Simple Charms and Spells Involving Your Local Spirits

I have made these ingredients vague on purpose. Experiment and find what works best for you and the area you live in. Make sure any bones or animal parts are thoroughly and properly cleaned before handling.

Home Protection Charm

Dried native plant leaves, roots, or flowers

Thorns from a local plant

Dirt from a place you feel safe in or from the gates of a cemetery

Dirt from your home

Found bones or pieces of animals or insects that correlate to protection and are native to your area (optional)

Black or red cloth and string

Place all these items in a bag made from the cloth and string, asking each ingredient for protection over your home from ill intentions, curses, evil, mischievous spirits, illness, and bad luck. You may add sigils on paper or embroidered or drawn onto the bag, and anoint the cloth or string with oil if you so choose. Hang this charm above a doorway or bury it at the front and back doors of your home.

Get Things Moving!

This spell is to get a stuck situation moving or get the ball rolling on something such as a job or house hunt, a possible blooming relationship, or spreading the word on your new business and getting exposure to new clients. This spell requires you to have a relationship with a water spirit at a moving body of water, such as a canal, creek, or river. The faster and larger the body of water is, the more impactful the spell. For example, if you want something to happen *now*, despite the results being abrasive and possibly jarring, seek a fast-moving river with white waters, or if you're feeling reckless,

seek a waterfall. If you are wanting something gentle, to ease into a situation, I suggest using something like a creek. Please take care to gather water from a safe access point.

You will need:
Water from said site, with permission from the water spirits. You
   will be returning this.
Ceramic or glass bowl
Corresponding plants, flowers, and items found from your area
Singing bowl and/or a candle (optional)

To execute this spell, you will go to the moving body of water of your choice. I will use a blossoming relationship for this example. I would choose a beautiful creek near my home that has lots of sun and is peaceful, lovely, and warm. It's especially great if I can collect water in the springtime, but it's not needed. Collect native species and found items of your area that correspond to your intent. For this spell, select spring flowers such as lilacs, pink flowers, or leaves of plant allies you know hold loving and romantic energy. Consider seeds if this is a new relationship; buds, berries, and smooth stones are all great options as well. Ask the spirits if you can use some of the water in your working, and let them know you will be returning it.

You may continue this spell at the site or back home at your altar. Pour the water clockwise into the bowl, and speak over it your intent. Place your found items in the water, asking each item, if you have more than one, for its aid and explaining why you chose it specifically for your spell. Once you feel your items are charged, you may charge them with a candle or singing bowl as well if you wish, though this is not needed. Take the water back to the moving body of water, and ask the water spirits to help gain traction and movement in your situation as you safely pour the water back into the creek or river.

Alternatively, this can be used as a banishing spell as well, pouring and working counterclockwise, aided with banishing ingredients and asking the water spirits to sweep away what you wish to banish.

Versatile Witch's Ladder

Use this simple spell for a vast amount of workings, such as attracting clients to a business; attracting wealth, health, peace, and luck; binding; protection; and warding.

You will need:

Cord, string or yarn with a corresponding color to your intent

Large stick that can bear weight or a found antler or bone from a local animal

Found items such as feathers, stalks of plants or picked flowers with the stems, smaller sticks and bones, small rocks or hag stones

Optional: woodburner or paint for sticks and rocks, anointing oils to anoint the sticks, small spell jars to fasten in, dried plants, or a rolled-up paper with intent or sigils written on it

Gather your items. You can make this ladder as short or long and as thin or wide as you wish. Start with tying your cord to the largest stick, antler, or bone you are using. On this main hanging piece you can write, carve, or burn sigils or your intention as well. You may choose to do one cord or multiple. Choosing each item purposefully, tie the feathers, sticks, plants (dried or fresh, though note they will wilt), and any other found items, speaking your intent as you fasten the knots, binding the items into your ladder. Add as much or as little as you wish. Create one long ladder or weave a whole web. Once finished, hang it in your home or business. It is best hung in a main area such as the entryway, living room, or dining room. Thank the local spirits you've included in your ladder.

Guarded Binding

This spell can be used to put a hold on something or someone or to bind two people together.

You will need:

2 sticks wide enough to burn markings on or carve on

Red or black cotton yarn

Stalks, leaves, bones, feathers, or other findings from your area that correspond to your spell

If you are binding a situation, you can carefully woodburn or carve the situation in its simplest form onto one stick (or if you need, you can write on compostable paper and roll it around the stick), and burn or carve binding sigils or commands to the other. Bundle the sticks and any other items you wish to add together, and using the yarn, carefully wind the two sticks, along with any other chosen items, together tightly.

If you are binding a person, I find it helps to create a small poppet with the sticks, adding moss or grass for hair, and carving or burning the name and birthday of the person or fastening a photo to the poppet. Then bundle the other stick with binding symbols or commands and any other items you wish and bind them all together with your yarn.

You will then go to a place where you know protective spirits to be, bury it in a spot where it will not be found, and ask the spirits to guard this binding until you return for it. Depending on your intent, this can be under a land guardian such as a large, old tree, at a crossroads, or it might be at a cemetery. To break the spell, dig up and thank the spirits, leaving an offering. Do not forget where you left this spell.

· · · ☽ · · ·

These are only a few simple ways to work with your local spirits. It's important you spend time with them; get to know their nature, wants, and needs; and commune with them often. Do not ignore the power of local dirt, native plants, local animals, and the local dead. They are all-powerful and have a direct reach into your community and will have a huge impact on your Craft should you choose to work with them, or even if you choose to simply acknowledge them. You can use any knowledge you have in herbalism to create local oils, tinctures, or teas, or kitchen witchery as grand offerings. And remember—the living people in your community are spirits too!

Need Answers? Look Up!: Divination, Augury, and the Air Element

Susan Pesznecker

Like a great many other magical folks, I often find myself turn-ing to divination or augury to help search for answers, find ideas, or reinforce decisions in process. My favorite form of divina-tion is a much-loved tarot deck, but it's often not close by when I need it, or the setting may not feel right. In such cases, my plan B is to look up, literally or metaphorically, into the air.

Let's consider the air element. In today's Pagan traditions, we associate the air element with the sky, the heavens, and their ener-gies and components. We also consider mind, intellect, and Spirit to be aspects of air, in a more esoteric sense. The air element is constantly around us, both visible and invisible, still and moving, protective and potentially dangerous (storms! change!), and always offering inspiration.

Back to divination and augury: What's the difference? With div-ination, we use some sort of concrete tool to find answers: tarot cards, a scrying bowl, runes, a pendulum, and so forth. Augury doesn't use tools but instead looks for insights through naturally occurring omens, movements, and patterns. One might augur with the patterns of waves breaking onshore, the shapes seen in tree bark, or the movement of clouds in the sky.

Why use divination or augury? We can use either or both for several purposes, including the following:

1. To suggest answers to a straightforward question
2. To receive insight or provide guidance for a more complex question or problem
3. To think through the possibilities of an action or path
4. To understand or evaluate ourselves, our thoughts, and our actions more clearly
5. To better understand our relationships with others

Using the air element for divination and augury work is easy: air surrounds us, always there, ready for us to reach out. When using divination, we begin by reflecting on one or more questions—setting our intention for the session—and then we "divine" and do our best to understand what we discover. When working with augury, we open ourselves to the natural world and focus our senses on observation. These observations may be spontaneous or unplanned, as when a natural sign or portent appears, unexpected, in our path. Or we may approach augury with a structured plan, such as engaging intentionally in an afternoon of cloud-watching.

Preparation

In any type of divination or augury, it's essential to be a good observer. Here are some suggestions, and note that observation is equally important when working with runes or cards or when watching clouds:

- Slow down and mentally prepare yourself for a session of heightened awareness, pulling a feeling of centered calm around you like a cloak.
- Open your senses and listen actively, without distraction (leave your digital devices behind or powered off!). Be consciously aware of what you see, hear, feel, and smell.
- As you observe, watch and listen for details and, if possible, take notes—don't assume you'll recall those details later. Use a pencil and paper for note-taking if you can, not a digital device. Neuroscience has shown that writing "by hand" is immensely more effective in how we recall and retain information than typing on a device.
- Draw sketches or maps if needed: for example, sketching the tarot layout you used or the pattern of bird flight in the sky, with the compass directions involved.
- Stay focused. If your mind wanders, bring yourself back on task and renew your focus.

Afterward, take time to reflect actively about the experience. I encourage you to capture a summary via some form of journaling or recording; we'll talk more about this in a bit.

The Air Element and Divination

Tarot work may be applied to any of the four cardinal elements. To work with the air element, we could create a tarot spread and interpret the insights from the cards as air's intellect and spirit. We could create a spread that resembled "air," such as a cloud, balloon, and the like. Or we might simply pull the cards that directly represent air and just work with those. There's an ongoing debate over whether air in the tarot is represented by swords or wands; make your own choice, and whichever it is, be consistent.

Some tarot decks have image details that work directly with air: for example, my favorite deck features clouds, weather, night and day, and birds as elements of each card that add to the interpretation. While the tarot is a hands-on divinatory tool, those natural images add an element of augury to the process.

Another type of air-related divination uses a pendulum. The user dangles a weighted object (pendulum) from a string or cord and observes for movements. The movements themselves—whether in direction, pattern, or intensity—may be meaningful, or the pendulum might be suspended over a "map" or diagram of some kind that lends significance to the movement, as with a planchette on a Ouija board.

Speaking of Ouija boards: with their reliance on mind, spirit, and the etheric veil around us, I definitely consider this a type of air-directed divination. I've heard of a Ouija board being used by a single person, but they're most often used by at least two people or even a group, some with their fingers on the planchette and the others observing. Studies in *Phenomenology and the Cognitive Sciences* and *Consciousness and Cognition* look at the accuracy of results from Ouija sessions: interestingly, the boards seem most effective when used with simple yes-or-no questions, suggesting that the unconscious mind is indeed at play.

The Air Element and Augury

So much of augury is about direct observation. Is the wind blowing? Sitting quietly, what do you see, hear, smell, or even taste? (I always feel like deep Pacific Northwest forests smell and even taste like blackberries.) Do you see patterns in the ways trees are aligned, fallen leaves have arranged themselves, twigs are scattered along a path, or dust has settled in pits and swirls? What do these and other signs mean to you? How or why are they significant? Or are they? A humorous phrase attributed to Freud notes "sometimes a cigar is just a cigar." Not every observation has to be significant.

Watching birds is a common form of natural augury. Augury involving birds (avimancy) may involve watching the direction or pattern of flight for one or more birds, finding feathers on the ground, listening to birdsong or bird calls, observing the arrangement within a fallen bird's nest (much like reading tea leaves, nature style!), or seeing an unusual bird or having one appear at an unexpected time, and those are only a few examples. Augury can likewise be applied to animals of all types. Perhaps you observe a column of ants crossing your path, a pile of scat in an unusual pattern, or a fish jumping as you gaze out over a lake. Each observation must be considered in terms of when and where it appears and what it means to you.

Rocks and minerals are prime targets for augury; lithomancy refers to augury using rocks, minerals, or gems. You might find meaning in stones of certain shapes or colors. A friend of mine looks for heart-shaped stones and always finds they show up at just the right time in her life to carry meaning. Finding an unusual stone in an unexpected place can be important: for example, finding a shiny piece of basalt or a piece of quartz in the midst of a basalt flow. Ditto for petrified rock, fossils, rock carvings, and indigenous items like arrowheads—but please observe these only and *never* remove them. Finding a holey stone, sometimes called a hag stone, may also have significance. Such stones are said to have strong protective qualities, so finding one might suggest a need for extra protection.

For augury of clouds and weather (aeromancy), we have only to step outside. You might observe cloud types, colors, patterns, movements, or colors (nephomancy). You might sit outside (or safely inside) during a storm, noting its sounds, light, intensity, and such. Or you could observe the temperature, direction, and even scent of wind (anemomancy). Watching smoke and its patterns (libanomancy) may provide insights too, as could watching the patterns and structures formed by falling snow or the formation of ice. Skyward spectacles (rainbows, sun dogs, auroras) are always significant.

Don't overlook sound as a manifestation of divination and augury. Many people use auditory props like flute music or drumming to induce a contemplative, meditative, or trance state. Such states free and quiet our minds, preparing us for an intentional session. The sound itself could even become a kind of augury.

And don't forget the heavens! Looking skyward reveals the stars, planets, our Moon, and even the Sun (but please *never* look at the Sun with unprotected eyes!). The appearance of heavenly anomalies (comets, meteors, eclipses) has always been charged with import and meaning, and astrology (astromancy) is one of the oldest known divinatory practices.

Reflecting on Your Results

In order to get the greatest benefit from your divination and augury, I strongly recommend you reflect after each session, creating a quick record of what you did and what you discovered or observed. Do this in whatever way works best for you: a journal (handwritten or digital), a sketchbook with mostly visual images, an audio or video recording, a set of photographs, and so on. Record when and where you had the session, what (if any) tools were used, what you observed or discovered, how you felt, and any thoughts on what it might mean.

Recording your experiences will prove valuable for a number of reasons:

- Writing down your experiences makes you think more analytically about them, and this may help you experience insights or even have an aha moment.
- While a single session might not reveal much, a number of similar sessions over time may allow you to connect the dots and discern patterns.
- Studying your records will give you information about what techniques, tools, and approaches have worked best for you. This is how we fine-tune our practices.
- By recording details, you're effectively archiving your information. This is essential, as it's all too easy to forget small points after even a few days, let alone weeks or months. Most of us want to learn from our magical practices and become even better at them. Recording results is a valuable way to improve.

Here's to your burgeoning skills with divination and augury!

Resources

Anderson, Marc, Kristoffer L. Nielbo, Uffe Schjoedt, Thies Pfeiffer, Andreas Roepstorff, and Jesper Sørensen. "Predictive Minds in Ouija Board Sessions." *Phenomenology and the Cognitive Sciences* 18, no. 6 (2019): 577–88. doi:10.1007/s11097-018-9585-8.

Gauchu, Hélène L., Ronald A. Rensink, and Sidney Fels. "Expression of Nonconscious Knowledge via Ideomotor Actions." *Consciousness and Cognition* 21, no. 2 (2012): 976–82. doi:10.1016/j.concog.2012.01.016.

2024 Almanac

The Date

The date is used in numerological calculations that govern magical rites. Below is a calendar for 2024.

JANUARY
1	2	3	4	5	6
7	8	9	10	11	12	13
14	15	16	17	18	19	20
21	22	23	24	25	26	27
28	29	30	31			

FEBRUARY
				1	2	3
4	5	6	7	8	9	10
11	12	13	14	15	16	17
18	19	20	21	22	23	24
25	26	27	28	29		

MARCH
					1	2
3	4	5	6	7	8	9
10	11	12	13	14	15	16
17	18	19	20	21	22	23
24	25	26	27	28	29	30
31						

APRIL
1	2	3	4	5	6
7	8	9	10	11	12	13
14	15	16	17	18	19	20
21	22	23	24	25	26	27
28	29	30				

MAY
			1	2	3	4
5	6	7	8	9	10	11
12	13	14	15	16	17	18
19	20	21	22	23	24	25
26	27	28	29	30	31	

JUNE
						1
2	3	4	5	6	7	8
9	10	11	12	13	14	15
16	17	18	19	20	21	22
23	24	25	26	27	28	29
30						

JULY
	1	2	3	4	5	6
7	8	9	10	11	12	13
14	15	16	17	18	19	20
21	22	23	24	25	26	27
28	29	30	31			

AUGUST
				1	2	3
4	5	6	7	8	9	10
11	12	13	14	15	16	17
18	19	20	21	22	23	24
25	26	27	28	29	30	31

SEPTEMBER
1	2	3	4	5	6	7
8	9	10	11	12	13	14
15	16	17	18	19	20	21
22	23	24	25	26	27	28
29	30					

OCTOBER
	1	2	3	4	5
6	7	8	9	10	11	12
13	14	15	16	17	18	19
20	21	22	23	24	25	26
27	28	29	30	31		

NOVEMBER
					1	2
3	4	5	6	7	8	9
10	11	12	13	14	15	16
17	18	19	20	21	22	23
24	25	26	27	28	29	30

DECEMBER
1	2	3	4	5	6	7
8	9	10	11	12	13	14
15	16	17	18	19	20	21
22	23	24	25	26	27	28
29	30	31				

The Day

Each day is ruled by a planet that possesses specific magical influences:

MONDAY (MOON): Peace, sleep, healing, compassion, friends, psychic awareness, purification, and fertility.

TUESDAY (MARS): Passion, sex, courage, aggression, and protection.

WEDNESDAY (MERCURY): The conscious mind, study, travel, divination, and wisdom.

THURSDAY (JUPITER): Expansion, money, prosperity, and generosity.

FRIDAY (VENUS): Love, friendship, reconciliation, and beauty.

SATURDAY (SATURN): Longevity, exorcism, endings, homes, and houses.

SUNDAY (SUN): Healing, spirituality, success, strength, and protection.

The Lunar Phase

The lunar phase is important in determining the best times for magic.

THE WAXING MOON (from the New Moon to the Full) is the ideal time for magic to draw things toward you.

THE FULL MOON is the time of greatest power.

THE WANING MOON (from the Full Moon to the New) is a time for study, meditation, and little magical work (except magic designed to banish harmful energies).

The Moon's Sign

The Moon continuously "moves" through the zodiac, from Aries to Pisces. Each sign possesses its own significance.

ARIES: Good for starting things, but lacks staying power. Things occur rapidly, but quickly pass. People tend to be argumentative and assertive.

TAURUS: Things begun now last the longest, tend to increase in value, and become hard to alter. Brings out appreciation for beauty and sensory experience.

GEMINI: Things begun now are easily changed by outside influence. Time for shortcuts, communication, games, and fun.

CANCER: Stimulates emotional rapport between people. Pinpoints need, supports growth and nurturance. Tends to domestic concerns.

LEO: Draws emphasis to the self, central ideas, or institutions, away from connections with others and other emotional needs. People tend to be melodramatic.

VIRGO: Favors accomplishment of details and commands from higher up. Focuses on health, hygiene, and daily schedules.

LIBRA: Favors cooperation, social activities, beautification of surroundings, balance, and partnership.

Scorpio: Increases awareness of psychic power. Precipitates psychic crises and ends connections thoroughly. People tend to brood and become secretive.

Sagittarius: Encourages flights of imagination and confidence. This is an adventurous, philosophical, and athletic Moon sign. Favors expansion and growth.

Capricorn: Develops strong structure. Focus on traditions, responsibilities, and obligations. A good time to set boundaries and rules.

Aquarius: Rebellious energy. Time to break habits and make abrupt changes. Personal freedom and individuality is the focus.

Pisces: The focus is on dreaming, nostalgia, intuition, and psychic impressions. A good time for spiritual or philanthropic activities.

Color and Incense of the Day

The color and incense for the day are based on information from *Personal Alchemy* by Amber Wolfe, and relate to the planet that rules each day. This information can be taken into consideration along with other factors when planning works of magic or when blending magic into mundane life. Please note that the incense selections listed are not hard and fast. See page 264 for a list of color correspondences. If you cannot find or do not like the incense listed for the day, choose a similar scent that appeals to you.

Holidays and Festivals

Holidays and festivals of many cultures, nations, and spiritual practices are listed throughout the year. The exact dates of many ancient festivals are difficult to determine; prevailing data has been used.

Time Zones

The times and dates of all astrological phenomena in this almanac are based on **Eastern Standard Time (EST)**. If you live outside of the Eastern time zone, you will need to make the following adjustments:

PACIFIC STANDARD TIME: Subtract three hours.

MOUNTAIN STANDARD TIME: Subtract two hours.

CENTRAL STANDARD TIME: Subtract one hour.

ALASKA: Subtract four hours.

HAWAII: Subtract five hours.

DAYLIGHT SAVING TIME (ALL ZONES): Add one hour.

Daylight Saving Time begins at 2 am on March 10, 2024, and ends at 2 am on November 3, 2024.

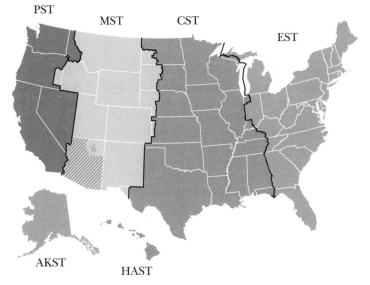

Please refer to a world time zone resource for time adjustments for locations outside the United States.

2024 Sabbats
and Full Moons

January 25	Leo Full Moon 12:54 pm
February 2	Imbolc
February 24	Virgo Full Moon 7:30 am
March 19	Ostara (Spring Equinox)
March 25	Libra Full Moon 3:00 am
April 23	Scorpio Full Moon 7:49 pm
May 1	Beltane
May 23	Sagittarius Full Moon 9:53 am
June 20	Midsummer (Summer Solstice)
June 21	Capricorn Full Moon 9:08 pm
July 21	Capricorn Full Moon 6:17 am
August 1	Lammas
August 19	Aquarius Full Moon 2:26 pm
September 17	Pisces Full Moon 10:34 pm
September 22	Mabon (Fall Equinox)
October 17	Aries Full Moon 7:26 am
October 31	Samhain
November 15	Taurus Full Moon 4:28 pm
December 15	Gemini Full Moon 4:02 am
December 21	Yule (Winter Solstice)

*All times are Eastern Standard Time (EST)
or Eastern Daylight Time (EDT)*

2024 Sabbats in
the Southern Hemisphere

Because Earth's Northern and Southern Hemispheres experience opposite seasons at any given time, the season-based sabbats listed on the previous page and in this almanac section are not correct for those residing south of the equator. Listed here are the Southern Hemisphere sabbat dates for 2024:

February 2	Lammas
March 19	Mabon (Fall Equinox)
May 1	Samhain
June 20	Yule (Winter Solstice)
August 1	Imbolc
September 22	Ostara (Spring Equinox)
November 1	Beltane
December 21	Midsummer (Summer Solstice)

2024 Solar and Lunar Eclipses

Lunar eclipse	March 25, 3:00 am	5° ♎ 07'
Solar eclipse	April 8, 2:21 pm	19° ♈ 24'
Lunar eclipse	September 17, 10:34 pm	25° ♓ 41'
Solar eclipse	October 2, 2:49 pm	10° ♎ 04'

Two- and three-dimentional maps of the visibility range of an eclipse can often be found online leading up to the event. Even if it's not visible in your area, you can still draw on the energy of this astrological phenomenon.

2024 Energetic Forecast
Charlie Rainbow Wolf

This is a busy year in the stars! The overall vibe is one of stability, of growing hard to lay down roots. There's some karmic energy here too, which is interesting considering Pluto's transits! Think back to 2018, your dreams and your aspirations. This is the year to really knuckle down and make them come to pass. It's a year when success is possible, but it won't just fall out of the sky. It will come at the end of diligence, tenacity, and quite a bit of hard work.

Financial matters potentially come to a head in some way this year. Uncalculated risks are, well, risky, but those which have been well researched and proven to be a good speculation could bear fruit. Depending on the circumstances, this might pertain to real-estate or long-term investments. Home improvements are favored.

The tarot card for the year is the Strength card. This doesn't have anything to do with brute force or bravado. In this instance, strength means integrity and courage. Dare to dream, then work hard to make those dreams come true.

The universal number for 2024 in numerology is 8. In astrology, the eighth house is associated with death, inheritance, big business, taxes, financial matters, and life cycles. It's the same in numerology. Pluto is the natural ruler of the eighth house, and Pluto tends to tear down what doesn't work so it can be made better. This is a time for releasing what is no longer viable so that something better can come along—try to hold on to what wants to naturally evolve, and then things could get complicated. As the year unfolds, release what is standing in the way of achieving full potential and simultaneously develop the tenacity to finish what has been started. Be mindful not to become a workaholic or to become distant and alienated from those who offer encouragement and support.

There are four eclipses this year: two solar eclipses and two lunar eclipses. Some of my magical friends say not to do any cer-

emony or ritual during an eclipse because of the power held in the skies at the time, but I find some of my best work is done at eclipses. Focus on self-care during eclipses, rather than what can be done for others—at the end of the day, you cannot tend to them if you're not in peak form, right?

The year opens with a retrograde Mercury—maybe not the best foot to start out on, but fortunately it's only for a few hours. He turns direct on the night of New Year's Day. This is the first of *four* Mercury retrogrades in 2024. His second retrograde starts April 1 and ends April 25. The third is August 5 to August 28, and he finishes the year retrograde November 25 until December 15.

January

The changing of the year means a new calendar, a new numerology cycle, and a chance to start afresh. It's tradition to make a resolution on New Year's Day because it's a whole new vibe. The universal month number is 9, a time for tidying up loose ends and looking ahead. The tarot card for this month is the Hermit, a card bringing a reminder that the answers being sought are already nestled deep in the soul. It's just a case of awakening into them.

The Sun is in Capricorn until January 20, a cardinal earth sign. The Moon is waning as we start the year—a good energy for reflection. The New Moon in Capricorn on the 11th balances the Sun's grounded and rational energy, so look toward practical tasks at this time. The second quarter Moon in Aries on the 17th may give rise to some minor frustrations, because Aries can be so passionate! The Full Moon in Leo on the 25th perpetuates that fiery energy and brings with it creativity and a chance to shine.

February

February 10 marks the Lunar New Year, when we enter the sign of the dragon. Dragon energy symbolizes power and success—qualities that go hand in hand with the universal year number. In

numerology, the universal month is a number 1, a time for independence, new ideas and beginnings, and starting plans and projects. The tarot card for February is the Wheel of Fortune, a card of change. Some of these changes may be unexpected and perhaps a bit of a challenge.

The Sun is in Aquarius until February 18. Aquarius is a fixed air sign, one that is independent and often a bit unconventional. We start the month with the fourth quarter Moon in Scorpio, a good time for introspection. The New Moon in Aquarius on the 9th brings a fresh quality to complement the Aquarian Sun. The second quarter Moon is in Taurus on the 16th, providing a grounding energy as the Sun prepares to enter Pisces. The Full Moon in Virgo on the 24th adds a practical and organized note and creates a time when cooperating with others would be most creative and productive.

March

March 10 sees Daylight Saving Time start, and this is another time when energetic work can be quite powerful. An hour is being lost as American clocks jump forward. Banish anything undesirable at 2 a.m., then put the clocks forward and let the lost hour eat that which has been expelled. The numerological universal month is 2, a number of dualities and one that advises cooperation is often the key to success. The tarot card is Justice, a reminder that what goes around comes around, and to treat people fairly, as you would wish to be treated.

The Sun is in Pisces until March 19, when it enters Aries. Pisces is a mutable water sign whose energy is dreamy and full of creativity. This is the start of the astrological year and marks the spring equinox. March opens with a fourth quarter Moon in Sagittarius, which could create some challenges. It's all just a fleeting thing, though, for the New Moon in Pisces on the 10th will highlight that Piscean idealism. The second quarter Moon in Gemini is a great time to talk out those ideas with someone special, and the Full Moon in Libra on the 25th marks the first lunar eclipse of the year and a time for focusing on balance and harmony.

April

I've always known the first of April as April Fools' Day, but there's nothing frivolous about the way this month starts—Mercury turns retrograde on the 1st! The universal month number is 3, and while this energy is warm and social, there's a caution here not to overdo things; the consequences might be worth more than the enjoyment. The tarot card reflects this, for it is the Hanged Man, a card of vulnerability and sacrifices made in order to find new ways of looking at things. Mercury retrograde ends on the 25th, so next month should see things starting to run more smoothly.

The Sun is in Aries until April 19. Aries is a fixed fire sign, a sign full of passion and vitality. April Fools' Day also sees the first quarter Moon in Capricorn, not a particularly carefree or jovial energy here! The New Moon in Aries on the 8th changes all of that, for this is the first solar eclipse of the year—a total eclipse lasting for nearly four and a half minutes—and magically, it has the potential to be quite powerful. The second quarter Moon in Cancer on the 15th initiates a few days of moodiness, so be aware of that when dealing with others. The Full Moon on the 23rd is in Scorpio; passions may well rise in every sense of the word!

May

In many traditions May Day is the time for celebrating, for rebirth and growth, for fertility and festivities. The numerology for May is the number 4: grounded, stable, but perhaps doing behind-the-scenes work, rather than getting instant gratification or acknowledgement. The tarot card for May is the Death card, a card of transition, an evolution from one phase to the next. It has nothing to do with actual death.

The Sun is in Taurus—a fixed earth sign—until May 20, when it enters Gemini. The Moon is at fourth quarter in Aquarius as May Day dawns, and this energy may be a bit contrary; Aquarius and Taurus are equally stubborn. The New Moon falls on the 7th in Taurus, carrying over that fertile energy. The Full Moon in Sagittarius is on the 23rd, which may well highlight social activities. The month closes with the fourth quarter Moon in Pisces on the 30th, potentially casting a bit of a quiet vibe to any Memorial Day celebrations.

June

June brings us to the longest day and marks the halfway point of the Sun's cycle through the seasons. The universal month numerology for June is the number 5, a social number, one that brings

changes and modifications, some of which could be very beneficial, even if only temporary. The tarot card for June is Temperance. It's a time for balance and patience and for doing things "on purpose" rather than on a whim.

This year the summer solstice falls on June 20 as the Sun enters Cancer. It'll be in Gemini up until then, a mutable air sign of wit, travel, and socializing. The New Moon on the 6th is also in Gemini, so there's a good harmony there for new beginnings. On the 14th, the second quarter Moon in Virgo brings some practicality to what otherwise might be a lack of concentration. The Full Moon in Capricorn on the 21st further grounds that energy and is a good time to meet with others to finalize plans and ideas. The month closes with the fourth quarter Moon in Aries on the 28th, which could give rise to some tactlessness or a bit of self-centered behavior.

July

The tarot card for July is the Devil, but this has nothing to do with demons or other nasties. This is a card that shows where attachment might lie, and carries a reminder that the chains that bind are often self-made and can be undone at any time. The universal month numerology for July is the number 6. The influence of this number advises this month is a good time to put everything in order and be realistic about what can be achieved.

The Sun is in Cancer, a cardinal water sign, until July 22, when it enters Leo. The month opens with a New Moon in Cancer on the 5th, highlighting temperament. Feelings may get easily hurt and emotions may be strong even though they're hidden. The second quarter Moon is in Libra on the 13th, which may help ease any out-of-balance feelings. The Full Moon on the 21st is in Capricorn, and as this is around the time the Sun is entering Leo, there could be a clash of energies here, at least for a few hours. The month closes with the fourth quarter Moon in Taurus, bringing a more practical and harmonious dynamism.

August

There's a pesky Mercury retrograde most of this month, which could bring frustrations. It starts on the 5th and ends on the 28th. The universal month number for August is 7, which is enigmatic at best. Indecision could bring uncertainty about which path to take or which decision to make. Patience is highly advised; let it come together *next* month. The tarot card for August is the Tower, and while this isn't the friendliest looking of cards, it does indicate that some kind of an awakening is possible.

The Sun is in the sign of Leo until the 22nd. Leo is a fixed fire sign. The month opens with the feast of Lammas and the Moon being new in Leo on the 4th. There's a sense of urgency now. The second quarter Moon in Scorpio adds some passion to the proceedings, followed by the Full Moon in Aquarius on the 19th—another good time for ceremony or ritual. The month ends with the fourth quarter Moon in Gemini on the 26th, which may spark impatience as we move into September.

September

Apart from the equinox on the 22nd, September's vibe is fairly quiet too. The universal month number this month is 8, the number of power. This is the number that deals with taking charge and making things happen. The tarot card for September is the Star. Something that's been in the pipeline for a while might just fall into place all of a sudden.

The Sun is in Virgo until the autumnal equinox on the 22nd, when it moves into Libra. Virgo is a hard-working sign and this is in harmony with the universal month number. With the New Moon in Virgo on the 2nd, the start of this month is ideal for sweat equity. The second quarter Moon on the 11th is in Sagittarius, which may bring some distractions. The Full Moon in Pisces on the 17th is a supermoon and a partial lunar eclipse, and it's a perfect time to blend the practicality of Virgo with the creative nebulousness of

Pisces. The month ends with the fourth quarter Moon in Cancer on the 24th; people may be oversensitive about things.

October

The big news in the skies this month is the second solar eclipse of the year, an annular eclipse happening in Libra. This helps bring balance to the energy created by last month's partial lunar eclipse. The universal month number is 9, the number of endings and tidying up loose ends. The tarot card for October is the Moon, heightening intuition but potentially creating some confusion when it comes to seeing things clearly.

October starts with the Sun in Libra, a cardinal air sign. The New Moon in Libra on the 2nd brings the second solar eclipse of the year, one that will last for four minutes. The second quarter in Capricorn on the 10th will help ground those energies. The Full

Moon on the 17th in Aries is another supermoon and a great time for taking positive action. Earth, the Sun, and the Moon will be very close to each other at this time, just missing the chance for another partial lunar eclipse. The fourth quarter Moon on the 24th is in Leo, helping carry that energy and assertiveness into next month.

November

Daylight Saving Time ends at 2 a.m. on the 3rd, and this is another fantastic time to do magic. Work the spell, put the clocks back, then do it again differently. Folding time spells are among my favorites! In numerology, November's universal month number is 1, the number of newness and fresh starts. The tarot card is the Sun, a card of success, of brighter days and happier times. There's another Mercury retrograde at the end of the month, when the planet begins the backward dance on the 25th, and stays there until the middle of next month, stationing direct on December 15.

The Sun is in Scorpio, a fixed water sign, for the first three weeks of November. The New Moon on the 1st in Scorpio adds passion and depth to personal interactions. The second quarter moon on the 9th is in Aquarius, which could bring some discord—or at least a bit of aloofness—to relationships of all kinds. The Full Moon on the 15th is in Taurus, and is the last of the three supermoons this year, a good time for grounding energy and putting it to practical use. The month closes with the fourth quarter Moon in Virgo on the 22nd; there's a good organizational energy here, but people may be quite critical and indifferent at this time.

December

December's energetic highlight is the winter solstice, taking place on the 21st. From now on, the days will lengthen and the nights become shorter—in the Northern Hemisphere, at least! The universal month number for December is both 11 and 2. Eleven is a master number, one that brings tenacity should anything unex-

pected arise. Two is the number of dualities, and while new projects are not particularly recommended, new partnerships to get things done are favored. The tarot card for December is Judgement, a reminder that treating others fairly and behaving with integrity is important when it comes to personal fulfillment.

December starts with the Sun in Sagittarius—a mutable fire sign that brings lots of energy and variety into things—and will stay there until the winter solstice, when it moves into Capricorn. December 1 is also when the New Moon is in Sagittarius, adding a reserved newness to the fiery Sun sign. The second quarter Moon in Pisces on the 8th is a good time for dreaming up new ideas; however, those castles in the air need foundations under them in order to become a reality. The Full Moon in Gemini on the 15th reinforces cooperation, but remember to act on plans, rather than just talk about them. The fourth quarter Moon in Libra is also good for partnerships; however, it is a time to guard against overindulgence or staying with something or someone just to avoid being alone.

The month—and the year—finishes with the New Moon in Capricorn, setting the stage for all those New Year's resolutions once again!

January

1 Monday
New Year's Day • Kwanzaa ends
Waning Moon
Moon phase: Third Quarter
Color: Silver

Moon Sign: Virgo
Incense: Narcissus

2 Tuesday
First Writing Day (Japanese)
Waning Moon
Moon phase: Third Quarter
Color: Gray

Moon Sign: Virgo
Moon enters Libra 7:47 pm
Incense: Cedar

◑ Wednesday
St. Genevieve's Day
Waning Moon
Fourth Quarter 10:30 pm
Color: White

Moon Sign: Libra
Incense: Lavender

4 Thursday
Kamakura Workers' Festival (Japanese)
Waning Moon
Moon phase: Fourth Quarter
Color: Turquoise

Moon Sign: Libra
Incense: Apricot

5 Friday
Bird Day
Waning Moon
Moon phase: Fourth Quarter
Color: Purple

Moon Sign: Libra
Moon enters Scorpio 7:39 am
Incense: Yarrow

6 Saturday
Epiphany
Waning Moon
Moon phase: Fourth Quarter
Color: Blue

Moon Sign: Scorpio
Incense: Sandalwood

7 Sunday
Tricolor Day (Italian)
Waning Moon
Moon phase: Fourth Quarter
Color: Yellow

Moon Sign: Scorpio
Moon enters Sagittarius 4:08 pm
Incense: Frankincense

January

8 **Monday**
Midwives' Day (Bulgarian)
Waning Moon
Moon phase: Fourth Quarter
Color: White

Moon Sign: Sagittarius
Incense: Clary sage

9 **Tuesday**
Feast of the Black Nazarene (Filipino)
Waning Moon
Moon phase: Fourth Quarter
Color: Red

Moon Sign: Sagittarius
Moon enters Capricorn 8:33 pm
Incense: Cinnamon

10 **Wednesday**
Feast of St. Leonie Aviat
Waning Moon
Moon phase: Fourth Quarter
Color: Topaz

Moon Sign: Capricorn
Incense: Lilac

Thursday
Carmentalia (Roman)
Waning Moon
New Moon 6:57 am
Color: Green

Moon Sign: Capricorn
Moon enters Aquarius 10:01 pm
Incense: Balsam

12 **Friday**
Revolution Day (Tanzanian)
Waxing Moon
Moon phase: First Quarter
Color: Pink

Moon Sign: Aquarius
Incense: Mint

13 **Saturday**
Twentieth Day (Norwegian)
Waxing Moon
Moon phase: First Quarter
Color: Brown

Moon Sign: Aquarius
Moon enters Pisces 10:29 pm
Incense: Patchouli

14 **Sunday**
Feast of the Ass (French)
Waxing Moon
Moon phase: First Quarter
Color: Gold

Moon Sign: Pisces
Incense: Almond

15 Monday
Martin Luther King Jr. Day
Waxing Moon
Moon phase: First Quarter
Color: Gray

Moon Sign: Pisces
Moon enters Aries 11:49 pm
Incense: Hyssop

16 Tuesday
Teachers' Day (Thai)
Waxing Moon
Moon phase: First Quarter
Color: Black

Moon Sign: Aries
Incense: Basil

◑ Wednesday
St. Anthony's Day (Mexican)
Waxing Moon
Second Quarter 10:53 pm
Color: Yellow

Moon Sign: Aries
Incense: Bay laurel

18 Thursday
Feast of St. Athanasius
Waxing Moon
Moon phase: Second Quarter
Color: White

Moon Sign: Aries
Moon enters Taurus 3:12 am
Incense: Mulberry

19 Friday
Edgar Allan Poe's birthday
Waxing Moon
Moon phase: Second Quarter
Color: Rose

Moon Sign: Taurus
Incense: Rose

20 Saturday
Vogel Gryff (Swiss)
Waxing Moon
Moon phase: Second Quarter
Color: Indigo

Moon Sign: Taurus
Moon enters Gemini 8:58 am
Sun enters Aquarius 9:07 am
Incense: Magnolia

21 Sunday
St. Agnes's Day
Waxing Moon
Moon phase: Second Quarter
Color: Orange

Moon Sign: Gemini
Incense: Heliotrope

January

22 Monday
St. Vincent's Day (French)
Waxing Moon
Moon phase: Second Quarter
Color: Silver

Moon Sign: Gemini
Moon enters Cancer 4:51 pm
Incense: Lily

23 Tuesday
Feast of St. Ildefonsus
Waxing Moon
Moon phase: Second Quarter
Color: Maroon

Moon Sign: Cancer
Incense: Bayberry

24 Wednesday
Alasitas Fair (Bolivian)
Waxing Moon
Moon phase: Second Quarter
Color: White

Moon Sign: Cancer
Incense: Marjoram

☺ Thursday
Burns Night (Scottish)
Waxing Moon
Full Moon 12:54 pm
Color: Crimson

Moon Sign: Cancer
Moon enters Leo 2:37 am
Incense: Jasmine

26 Friday
Australia Day
Waning Moon
Moon phase: Third Quarter
Color: Coral

Moon Sign: Leo
Incense: Thyme

27 Saturday
Holocaust Remembrance Day
Waning Moon
Moon phase: Third Quarter
Color: Gray

Moon Sign: Leo
Moon enters Virgo 2:11 pm
Incense: Ivy

28 Sunday
St. Charlemagne's Day
Waning Moon
Moon phase: Third Quarter
Color: Amber

Moon Sign: Virgo
Incense: Marigold

January

29 Monday
Feast of St. Gildas
Waning Moon
Moon phase: Third Quarter
Color: Lavender

Moon Sign: Virgo
Incense: Rosemary

30 Tuesday
Martyrs' Day (Indian)
Waning Moon
Moon phase: Third Quarter
Color: Scarlet

Moon Sign: Virgo
Moon enters Libra 3:04 am
Incense: Ylang-ylang

31 Wednesday
Independence Day (Nauru)
Waning Moon
Moon phase: Third Quarter
Color: Brown

Moon Sign: Libra
Incense: Honeysuckle

January Correspondences

Stones: Garnet, moonstone
Animals: Snow goose, owl, bear, wolf
Flowers: Carnation, snowdrop
Deities: Baba Yaga, Enki, Hekate, Loki, Saturn
Zodiac: Capricorn

February Correspondences

Stones: Amethyst, obsidian
Animals: Otter, white cow, snake
Flowers: Violet, primrose
Deities: Brigid, Ea, Ishtar, Isis, Juno, Nut
Zodiac: Aquarius

February

1 Thursday
St. Brigid's Day (Irish)
Waning Moon
Moon phase: Third Quarter
Color: Purple

Moon Sign: Libra
Moon enters Scorpio 3:37 pm
Incense: Myrrh

◑ Friday
Imbolc • Groundhog Day
Waning Moon
Fourth Quarter 6:18 pm
Color: White

Moon Sign: Scorpio
Incense: Violet

3 Saturday
St. Blaise's Day
Waning Moon
Moon phase: Fourth Quarter
Color: Black

Moon Sign: Scorpio
Incense: Rue

4 Sunday
Independence Day (Sri Lankan)
Waning Moon
Moon phase: Fourth Quarter
Color: Gold

Moon Sign: Scorpio
Moon enters Sagittarius 1:28 am
Incense: Eucalyptus

5 Monday
Constitution Day (Mexican)
Waning Moon
Moon phase: Fourth Quarter
Color: Ivory

Moon Sign: Sagittarius
Incense: Neroli

6 Tuesday
Bob Marley's birthday (Jamaican)
Waning Moon
Moon phase: Fourth Quarter
Color: White

Moon Sign: Sagittarius
Moon enters Capricorn 7:08 am
Incense: Geranium

7 Wednesday
Feast of St. Richard the Pilgrim
Waning Moon
Moon phase: Fourth Quarter
Color: Yellow

Moon Sign: Capricorn
Incense: Lilac

8 Thursday

Prešeren Day (Slovenian)
Waning Moon
Moon phase: Fourth Quarter
Color: Green

Moon Sign: Capricorn
Moon enters Aquarius 8:59 am
Incense: Clove

☽ Friday

St. Maron's Day (Lebanese)
Waning Moon
New Moon 5:59 pm
Color: Rose

Moon Sign: Aquarius
Incense: Vanilla

10 Saturday

Lunar New Year (Dragon)
Waxing Moon
Moon phase: First Quarter
Color: Gray

Moon Sign: Aquarius
Moon enters Pisces 8:42 am
Incense: Pine

11 Sunday

National Foundation Day (Japanese)
Waxing Moon
Moon phase: First Quarter
Color: Yellow

Moon Sign: Pisces
Incense: Hyacinth

12 Monday

Abraham Lincoln's birthday
Waxing Moon
Moon phase: First Quarter
Color: Silver

Moon Sign: Pisces
Moon enters Aries 8:26 am
Incense: Clary sage

13 Tuesday

Mardi Gras (Fat Tuesday)
Waxing Moon
Moon phase: First Quarter
Color: Black

Moon Sign: Aries
Incense: Ginger

14 Wednesday

Valentine's Day • Ash Wednesday
Waxing Moon
Moon phase: First Quarter
Color: Topaz

Moon Sign: Aries
Moon enters Taurus 10:02 am
Incense: Marjoram

15 Thursday
Susan B. Anthony Day
Waxing Moon
Moon phase: First Quarter
Color: White

Moon Sign: Taurus
Incense: Nutmeg

Friday
Nichiren's birthday
Waxing Moon
Second Quarter 10:01 am
Color: Purple

Moon Sign: Taurus
Moon enters Gemini 2:39 pm
Incense: Cypress

17 Saturday
Quirinalia (Roman)
Waxing Moon
Moon phase: Second Quarter
Color: Indigo

Moon Sign: Gemini
Incense: Sage

18 Sunday
St. Bernadette's Third Vision
Waxing Moon
Moon phase: Second Quarter
Color: Orange

Moon Sign: Gemini
Sun enters Pisces 11:13 pm
Moon enters Cancer 10:25 pm
Incense: Juniper

19 Monday
Presidents' Day
Waxing Moon
Moon phase: Second Quarter
Color: Gray

Moon Sign: Cancer
Incense: Lily

20 Tuesday
World Day of Social Justice
Waxing Moon
Moon phase: Second Quarter
Color: Maroon

Moon Sign: Cancer
Incense: Cedar

21 Wednesday
Feralia (Roman)
Waxing Moon
Moon phase: Second Quarter
Color: White

Moon Sign: Cancer
Moon enters Leo 8:40 am
Incense: Lavender

February

22 Thursday
Caristia (Roman)
Waxing Moon
Moon phase: Second Quarter
Color: Crimson

Moon Sign: Leo
Incense: Carnation

23 Friday
Mashramani Festival (Guyanan)
Waxing Moon
Moon phase: Second Quarter
Color: Coral

Moon Sign: Leo
Moon enters Virgo 8:38 pm
Incense: Alder

Saturday
Lantern Festival (Chinese)
Waxing Moon
Full Moon 7:30 am
Color: Blue

Moon Sign: Virgo
Incense: Sandalwood

25 Sunday
St. Walburga's Day (German)
Waning Moon
Moon phase: Third Quarter
Color: Yellow

Moon Sign: Virgo
Incense: Almond

26 Monday
Zamboanga Day (Filipino)
Waning Moon
Moon phase: Third Quarter
Color: White

Moon Sign: Virgo
Moon enters Libra 9:29 am
Incense: Rosemary

27 Tuesday
Independence Day (Dominican)
Waning Moon
Moon phase: Third Quarter
Color: Scarlet

Moon Sign: Libra
Incense: Basil

28 Wednesday
Kalevala Day (Finnish)
Waning Moon
Moon phase: Third Quarter
Color: Brown

Moon Sign: Libra
Moon enters Scorpio 10:09 pm
Incense: Honeysuckle

29 **Thursday**
Leap Day
Waning Moon
Moon phase: Third Quarter
Color: Purple

Moon Sign: Scorpio
Incense: Balsam

---

1 **Friday**
Matronalia (Roman)
Waning Moon
Moon phase: Third Quarter
Color: White

Moon Sign: Scorpio
Incense: Orchid

---

2 **Saturday**
Dr. Seuss's birthday
Waning Moon
Moon phase: Third Quarter
Color: Black

Moon Sign: Scorpio
Moon enters Sagittarius 8:56 am
Incense: Ivy

● **Sunday**
Doll Festival (Japanese)
Waning Moon
Fourth Quarter 10:23 am
Color: Gold

Moon Sign: Sagittarius
Incense: Marigold

---

4 **Monday**
St. Casimir's Fair (Lithuanian and Polish)
Waning Moon
Moon phase: Fourth Quarter
Color: Ivory

Moon Sign: Sagittarius
Moon enters Capricorn 4:15 pm
Incense: Narcissus

---

5 **Tuesday**
Navigium Isidis Festival (Roman)
Waning Moon
Moon phase: Fourth Quarter
Color: Red

Moon Sign: Capricorn
Incense: Ylang-ylang

---

6 **Wednesday**
Alamo Day (Texan)
Waning Moon
Moon phase: Fourth Quarter
Color: White

Moon Sign: Capricorn
Moon enters Aquarius 7:38 pm
Incense: Marjoram

March

7 Thursday
Vejovis Festival (Roman)
Waning Moon
Moon phase: Fourth Quarter
Color: Turquoise

Moon Sign: Aquarius
Incense: Jasmine

8 Friday
International Women's Day
Waning Moon
Moon phase: Fourth Quarter
Color: Pink

Moon Sign: Aquarius
Moon enters Pisces 8:03 pm
Incense: Mint

9 Saturday
Teachers' Day (Lebanese)
Waning Moon
Moon phase: Fourth Quarter
Color: Gray

Moon Sign: Pisces
Incense: Sage

Sunday
Ramadan begins at sundown
Waning Moon
New Moon 5:00 am
Color: Amber

Moon Sign: Pisces
Moon enters Aries 8:19 pm
Incense: Hyacinth
Daylight Saving Time begins at 2 am

11 Monday
Johnny Appleseed Day
Waxing Moon
Moon phase: First Quarter
Color: Lavender

Moon Sign: Aries
Incense: Hyssop

12 Tuesday
Girl Scouts' birthday
Waxing Moon
Moon phase: First Quarter
Color: Gray

Moon Sign: Aries
Moon enters Taurus 8:28 pm
Incense: Ginger

13 Wednesday
Feast of St. Leander of Seville
Waxing Moon
Moon phase: First Quarter
Color: Yellow

Moon Sign: Taurus
Incense: Bay laurel

March

14 Thursday
Pi Day
Waxing Moon
Moon phase: First Quarter
Color: White

Moon Sign: Taurus
Moon enters Gemini 11:16 pm
Incense: Clove

15 Friday
Fertility Festival (Japanese)
Waxing Moon
Moon phase: First Quarter
Color: Purple

Moon Sign: Gemini
Incense: Thyme

16 Saturday
St. Urho's Day (Finnish-American)
Waxing Moon
Moon phase: First Quarter
Color: Blue

Moon Sign: Gemini
Incense: Magnolia

◑ Sunday
St. Patrick's Day
Waxing Moon
Second Quarter 12:11 am
Color: Yellow

Moon Sign: Gemini
Moon enters Cancer 5:40 am
Incense: Frankincense

18 Monday
Sheila's Day (Irish)
Waxing Moon
Moon phase: Second Quarter
Color: Silver

Moon Sign: Cancer
Incense: Clary sage

19 Tuesday
Ostara • Spring Equinox
Waxing Moon
Moon phase: Second Quarter
Color: Scarlet

Moon Sign: Cancer
Sun enters Aries 11:06 pm
Moon enters Leo 3:33 pm
Incense: Cinnamon

20 Wednesday
International Day of Happiness
Waxing Moon
Moon phase: Second Quarter
Color: Brown

Moon Sign: Leo
Incense: Lilac

March

21 Thursday
Juarez Day (Mexican)
Waxing Moon
Moon phase: Second Quarter
Color: Purple

Moon Sign: Leo
Incense: Carnation

22 Friday
World Water Day
Waxing Moon
Moon phase: Second Quarter
Color: Coral

Moon Sign: Leo
Moon enters Virgo 3:42 am
Incense: Vanilla

23 Saturday
Purim begins at sundown
Waxing Moon
Moon phase: Second Quarter
Color: Indigo

Moon Sign: Virgo
Incense: Pine

24 Sunday
Palm Sunday
Waxing Moon
Moon phase: Second Quarter
Color: Gold

Moon Sign: Virgo
Moon enters Libra 4:37 pm
Incense: Heliotrope

😊 Monday
Holi begins at sundown (Hindu)
Waxing Moon
Full Moon 3:00 am
Color: Gray

Moon Sign: Libra
Incense: Neroli

26 Tuesday
Prince Kuhio Day (Hawaiian)
Waning Moon
Moon phase: Third Quarter
Color: Black

Moon Sign: Libra
Incense: Bayberry

27 Wednesday
World Theatre Day
Waning Moon
Moon phase: Third Quarter
Color: White

Moon Sign: Libra
Moon enters Scorpio 5:03 am
Incense: Lavender

March

28 Thursday
Weed Appreciation Day
Waning Moon
Moon phase: Third Quarter
Color: Green

Moon Sign: Scorpio
Incense: Mulberry

29 Friday
Good Friday
Waning Moon
Moon phase: Third Quarter
Color: Rose

Moon Sign: Scorpio
Moon enters Sagittarius 3:52 pm
Incense: Alder

30 Saturday
Seward's Day (Alaskan)
Waning Moon
Moon phase: Third Quarter
Color: Brown

Moon Sign: Sagittarius
Incense: Patchouli

31 Sunday
Easter
Waning Moon
Moon phase: Third Quarter
Color: Orange

Moon Sign: Sagittarius
Incense: Eucalyptus

March Correspondences

Stones: Aquamarine, jade, bloodstone, jasper
Animals: Cougar, whale, rabbit, frog
Flowers: Daffodil, narcissus
Deities: Diana, Kwan Yin, Poseidon, Sedna, Yemaya
Zodiac: Pisces

April

☽ **Monday**
All Fools' Day • April Fools' Day
Waning Moon
Fourth Quarter 11:15 pm
Color: White

Moon Sign: Sagittarius
Moon enters Capricorn 12:05 am
Incense: Narcissus

---

2 Tuesday
The Battle of Flowers (French)
Waning Moon
Moon phase: Fourth Quarter
Color: Gray

Moon Sign: Capricorn
Incense: Geranium

---

3 Wednesday
Feast of St. Mary of Egypt
Waning Moon
Moon phase: Fourth Quarter
Color: Topaz

Moon Sign: Capricorn
Moon enters Aquarius 5:08 am
Incense: Marjoram

---

4 Thursday
Tomb-Sweeping Day (Chinese)
Waning Moon
Moon phase: Fourth Quarter
Color: Crimson

Moon Sign: Aquarius
Incense: Myrrh

---

5 Friday
Children's Day (Palestinian)
Waning Moon
Moon phase: Fourth Quarter
Color: Purple

Moon Sign: Aquarius
Moon enters Pisces 7:13 am
Incense: Yarrow

---

6 Saturday
Tartan Day
Waning Moon
Moon phase: Fourth Quarter
Color: Indigo

Moon Sign: Pisces
Incense: Sage

---

7 Sunday
Motherhood and Beauty Day (Armenian)
Waning Moon
Moon phase: Fourth Quarter
Color: Yellow

Moon Sign: Pisces
Moon enters Aries 7:25 am
Incense: Marigold

April

♈

🌙 **Monday**
Hana Matsuri (Japanese)
Waning Moon
New Moon 2:21 pm
Color: Gray

Moon Sign: Aries
Incense: Rosemary

9 Tuesday
Ramadan ends
Waxing Moon
Moon phase: First Quarter
Color: White

Moon Sign: Aries
Moon enters Taurus 7:23 am
Incense: Cinnamon

10 Wednesday
Siblings Day
Waxing Moon
Moon phase: First Quarter
Color: Brown

Moon Sign: Taurus
Incense: Lilac

11 Thursday
Juan Santamaría Day (Costa Rican)
Waxing Moon
Moon phase: First Quarter
Color: Turquoise

Moon Sign: Taurus
Moon enters Gemini 8:59 am
Incense: Nutmeg

12 Friday
Children's Day (Bolivian and Haitian)
Waxing Moon
Moon phase: First Quarter
Color: Rose

Moon Sign: Gemini
Incense: Rose

13 Saturday
Thai New Year (ends April 15)
Waxing Moon
Moon phase: First Quarter
Color: Black

Moon Sign: Gemini
Moon enters Cancer 1:45 pm
Incense: Sandalwood

14 Sunday
Black Day (South Korean)
Waxing Moon
Moon phase: First Quarter
Color: Amber

Moon Sign: Cancer
Incense: Heliotrope

April

☽ Monday
Sechseläuten (Swiss)
Waxing Moon
Second Quarter 3:13 pm
Color: Lavender

Moon Sign: Cancer
Moon enters Leo 10:24 pm
Incense: Lily

16 Tuesday
World Voice Day
Waxing Moon
Moon phase: Second Quarter
Color: Maroon

Moon Sign: Leo
Incense: Cedar

17 Wednesday
Yayoi Matsuri (Japanese)
Waxing Moon
Moon phase: Second Quarter
Color: Yellow

Moon Sign: Leo
Incense: Honeysuckle

18 Thursday
International Day for Monuments and Sites
Waxing Moon
Moon phase: Second Quarter
Color: Purple

Moon Sign: Leo
Moon enters Virgo 10:10 am
Incense: Apricot

19 Friday
Primrose Day (British)
Waxing Moon
Moon phase: Second Quarter
Color: White

Moon Sign: Virgo
Sun enters Taurus 10:00 am
Incense: Violet

20 Saturday
Drum Festival (Japanese)
Waxing Moon
Moon phase: Second Quarter
Color: Gray

Moon Sign: Virgo
Moon enters Libra 11:08 am
Incense: Pine

21 Sunday
Tiradentes Day (Brazilian)
Waxing Moon
Moon phase: Second Quarter
Color: Gold

Moon Sign: Libra
Incense: Almond

April

22 Monday

Passover begins at sundown • Earth Day
Waxing Moon
Moon phase: Second Quarter
Color: Silver

Moon Sign: Libra
Incense: Hyssop

Tuesday

St. George's Day (English)
Waxing Moon
Full Moon 7:49 pm
Color: Black

Moon Sign: Libra
Moon enters Scorpio 11:20 am
Incense: Ginger

24 Wednesday

St. Mark's Eve
Waning Moon
Moon phase: Third Quarter
Color: White

Moon Sign: Scorpio
Incense: Lavender

25 Thursday

Robigalia (Roman)
Waning Moon
Moon phase: Third Quarter
Color: Green

Moon Sign: Scorpio
Moon enters Sagittarius 9:37 pm
Incense: Jasmine

26 Friday

Arbor Day
Waning Moon
Moon phase: Third Quarter
Color: Pink

Moon Sign: Sagittarius
Incense: Cypress

27 Saturday

Freedom Day (South African)
Waning Moon
Moon phase: Third Quarter
Color: Brown

Moon Sign: Sagittarius
Incense: Sage

28 Sunday

Floralia (Roman)
Waning Moon
Moon phase: Third Quarter
Color: Amber

Moon Sign: Sagittarius
Moon enters Capricorn 5:37 am
Incense: Frankincense

April

29 Monday
Showa Day (Japanese)
Waning Moon
Moon phase: Third Quarter
Color: Gray

Moon Sign: Capricorn
Incense: Rosemary

30 Tuesday
Passover ends
Waning Moon
Moon phase: Third Quarter
Color: Red

Moon Sign: Capricorn
Moon enters Aquarius 11:20 am
Incense: Bayberry

April Correspondences

Stones: Beryl, diamond, moonstone
Animals: Falcon, hawk, goat, sheep
Flowers: Sweet pea, daisy
Deities: Ares, Macha, the Morrigan, Ra
Zodiac: Aries

May

○ Wednesday
Beltane • May Day
Waning Moon
Fourth Quarter 7:27 am
Color: Yellow

Moon Sign: Aquarius
Incense: Lilac

---

2 Thursday
National Education Day (Indonesian)
Waning Moon
Moon phase: Fourth Quarter
Color: Purple

Moon Sign: Aquarius
Moon enters Pisces 2:52 pm
Incense: Nutmeg

---

3 Friday
Orthodox Good Friday • Roodmas
Waning Moon
Moon phase: Fourth Quarter
Color: Coral

Moon Sign: Pisces
Incense: Thyme

---

4 Saturday
Star Wars Day
Waning Moon
Moon phase: Fourth Quarter
Color: Blue

Moon Sign: Pisces
Moon enters Aries 4:41 pm
Incense: Ivy

---

5 Sunday
Cinco de Mayo • Orthodox Easter
Waning Moon
Moon phase: Fourth Quarter
Color: Orange

Moon Sign: Aries
Incense: Juniper

---

6 Monday
Martyrs' Day (Lebanese and Syrian)
Waning Moon
Moon phase: Fourth Quarter
Color: Ivory

Moon Sign: Aries
Moon enters Taurus 5:42 pm
Incense: Clary sage

☽ Tuesday
Teacher Appreciation Day
Waning Moon
New Moon 11:22 pm
Color: Gray

Moon Sign: Taurus
Incense: Ylang-ylang

May

8 Wednesday
White Lotus Day (Theosophical)
Waxing Moon
Moon phase: First Quarter
Color: White

Moon Sign: Taurus
Moon enters Gemini 7:20 pm
Incense: Bay laurel

9 Thursday
Lemuria (Roman)
Waxing Moon
Moon phase: First Quarter
Color: Crimson

Moon Sign: Gemini
Incense: Balsam

10 Friday
Independence Day (Romanian)
Waxing Moon
Moon phase: First Quarter
Color: Pink

Moon Sign: Gemini
Moon enters Cancer 11:13 pm
Incense: Rose

11 Saturday
Ukai season opens (Japanese)
Waxing Moon
Moon phase: First Quarter
Color: Brown

Moon Sign: Cancer
Incense: Rue

12 Sunday
Mother's Day
Waxing Moon
Moon phase: First Quarter
Color: Gold

Moon Sign: Cancer
Incense: Hyacinth

13 Monday
Pilgrimage to Fátima (Portuguese)
Waxing Moon
Moon phase: First Quarter
Color: White

Moon Sign: Cancer
Moon enters Leo 6:36 am
Incense: Lily

14 Tuesday
Carabao Festival (Spanish)
Waxing Moon
Moon phase: First Quarter
Color: Scarlet

Moon Sign: Leo
Incense: Basil

May

☽ Wednesday
Festival of St. Dymphna
Waxing Moon
Second Quarter 7:48 am
Color: Brown

Moon Sign: Leo
Moon enters Virgo 5:33 pm
Incense: Honeysuckle

---

16 Thursday
St. Honoratus's Day
Waxing Moon
Moon phase: Second Quarter
Color: Turquoise

Moon Sign: Virgo
Incense: Myrrh

---

17 Friday
Norwegian Constitution Day
Waxing Moon
Moon phase: Second Quarter
Color: Rose

Moon Sign: Virgo
Incense: Mint

---

18 Saturday
Battle of Las Piedras Day (Uruguayan)
Waxing Moon
Moon phase: Second Quarter
Color: Gray

Moon Sign: Virgo
Moon enters Libra 6:23 am
Incense: Patchouli

---

19 Sunday
Mother's Day (Kyrgyzstani)
Waxing Moon
Moon phase: Second Quarter
Color: Amber

Moon Sign: Libra
Incense: Eucalyptus

---

20 Monday
Victoria Day (Canadian)
Waxing Moon
Moon phase: Second Quarter
Color: Gray

Moon Sign: Libra
Sun enters Gemini 8:59 am
Moon enters Scorpio 6:34 pm
Incense: Neroli

---

21 Tuesday
Navy Day (Chilean)
Waxing Moon
Moon phase: Second Quarter
Color: Red

Moon Sign: Scorpio
Incense: Cinnamon

May

22 Wednesday
Harvey Milk Day (Californian)
Waxing Moon
Moon phase: Second Quarter
Color: Topaz

Moon Sign: Scorpio
Incense: Marjoram

☺ Thursday
Tubilustrium (Roman)
Waxing Moon
Full Moon 9:53 am
Color: White

Moon Sign: Scorpio
Moon enters Sagittarius 4:24 am
Incense: Carnation

24 Friday
Education and Culture Day (Bulgarian)
Waning Moon
Moon phase: Third Quarter
Color: Coral

Moon Sign: Sagittarius
Incense: Yarrow

25 Saturday
Missing Children's Day
Waning Moon
Moon phase: Third Quarter
Color: Black

Moon Sign: Sagittarius
Moon enters Capricorn 11:36 am
Incense: Magnolia

26 Sunday
Pepys's Commemoration (English)
Waning Moon
Moon phase: Third Quarter
Color: Orange

Moon Sign: Capricorn
Incense: Marigold

27 Monday
Memorial Day
Waning Moon
Moon phase: Third Quarter
Color: Ivory

Moon Sign: Capricorn
Moon enters Aquarius 4:45 pm
Incense: Hyssop

28 Tuesday
St. Germain's Day
Waning Moon
Moon phase: Third Quarter
Color: White

Moon Sign: Aquarius
Incense: Ginger

May

29 **Wednesday**
Oak Apple Day (English)
Waning Moon
Moon phase: Third Quarter
Color: Brown

Moon Sign: Aquarius
Moon enters Pisces 8:33 pm
Incense: Lavender

 Thursday
Canary Islands Day
Waning Moon
Fourth Quarter 1:13 pm
Color: Green

Moon Sign: Pisces
Incense: Nutmeg

31 **Friday**
Visitation of Mary
Waning Moon
Moon phase: Fourth Quarter
Color: Purple

Moon Sign: Pisces
Moon enters Aries 11:28 pm
Incense: Orchid

May Correspondences

Stones: Agate, emerald, carnelian
Animals: Beaver, cow, elk
Flower: Lily of the valley
Deities: Aphrodite, Dionysus, Gaia, Horus, Osiris
Zodiac: Taurus

June

1 Saturday
Dayak Harvest Festival (Malaysian)
Waning Moon
Moon phase: Fourth Quarter
Color: Blue

Moon Sign: Aries
Incense: Rue

2 Sunday
Republic Day (Italian)
Waning Moon
Moon phase: Fourth Quarter
Color: Gold

Moon Sign: Aries
Incense: Frankincense

3 Monday
Feast of St. Clotilde
Waning Moon
Moon phase: Fourth Quarter
Color: Gray

Moon Sign: Aries
Moon enters Taurus 1:55 am
Incense: Narcissus

4 Tuesday
Flag Day (Estonian)
Waning Moon
Moon phase: Fourth Quarter
Color: Maroon

Moon Sign: Taurus
Incense: Ylang-ylang

5 Wednesday
Constitution Day (Danish)
Waning Moon
Moon phase: Fourth Quarter
Color: Topaz

Moon Sign: Taurus
Moon enters Gemini 4:36 am
Incense: Lilac

☽ Thursday
National Day of Sweden
Waning Moon
New Moon 8:38 am
Color: Crimson

Moon Sign: Gemini
Incense: Clove

7 Friday
Vestalia begins (Roman)
Waxing Moon
Moon phase: First Quarter
Color: White

Moon Sign: Gemini
Moon enters Cancer 8:41 am
Incense: Alder

June

8 Saturday
World Oceans Day
Waxing Moon
Moon phase: First Quarter
Color: Black

Moon Sign: Cancer
Incense: Sage

---

9 Sunday
Heroes' Day (Ugandan)
Waxing Moon
Moon phase: First Quarter
Color: Yellow

Moon Sign: Cancer
Moon enters Leo 3:29 pm
Incense: Hyacinth

---

10 Monday
Portugal Day
Waxing Moon
Moon phase: First Quarter
Color: Lavender

Moon Sign: Leo
Incense: Neroli

---

11 Tuesday
Shavuot begins at sundown
Waxing Moon
Moon phase: First Quarter
Color: Gray

Moon Sign: Leo
Incense: Basil

---

12 Wednesday
Independence Day (Filipino)
Waxing Moon
Moon phase: First Quarter
Color: White

Moon Sign: Leo
Moon enters Virgo 1:39 am
Incense: Marjoram

---

13 Thursday
St. Anthony of Padua's Day
Waxing Moon
Moon phase: First Quarter
Color: Turquoise

Moon Sign: Virgo
Incense: Myrrh

◑ Friday
Flag Day
Waxing Moon
Second Quarter 1:18 am
Color: Rose

Moon Sign: Virgo
Moon enters Libra 2:12 pm
Incense: Cypress

June

15 Saturday

Vestalia ends (Roman)
Waxing Moon
Moon phase: Second Quarter
Color: Indigo

Moon Sign: Libra
Incense: Patchouli

16 Sunday

Father's Day
Waxing Moon
Moon phase: Second Quarter
Color: Orange

Moon Sign: Libra
Incense: Heliotrope

17 Monday

Bunker Hill Day (Massachusetts)
Waxing Moon
Moon phase: Second Quarter
Color: Silver

Moon Sign: Libra
Moon enters Scorpio 2:38 am
Incense: Rosemary

18 Tuesday

Waterloo Day (British)
Waxing Moon
Moon phase: Second Quarter
Color: Black

Moon Sign: Scorpio
Incense: Cedar

19 Wednesday

Juneteenth
Waxing Moon
Moon phase: Second Quarter
Color: Yellow

Moon Sign: Scorpio
Moon enters Sagittarius 12:32 pm
Incense: Lavender

20 Thursday

Litha • Summer Solstice
Waxing Moon
Moon phase: Second Quarter
Color: Green

Moon Sign: Sagittarius
Sun enters Cancer 4:51 pm
Incense: Jasmine

☺ Friday

National Day (Greenlandic)
Waxing Moon
Full Moon 9:08 pm
Color: Pink

Moon Sign: Sagittarius
Moon enters Capricorn 7:08 pm
Incense: Violet

June

22 Saturday
Teachers' Day (El Salvadoran)
Waning Moon
Moon phase: Third Quarter
Color: Gray

Moon Sign: Capricorn
Incense: Ivy

23 Sunday
St. John's Eve
Waning Moon
Moon phase: Third Quarter
Color: Amber

Moon Sign: Capricorn
Moon enters Aquarius 11:14 pm
Incense: Almond

24 Monday
St. John's Day
Waning Moon
Moon phase: Third Quarter
Color: Ivory

Moon Sign: Aquarius
Incense: Lily

25 Tuesday
Fiesta de Santa Orosia (Spanish)
Waning Moon
Moon phase: Third Quarter
Color: Maroon

Moon Sign: Aquarius
Incense: Geranium

26 Wednesday
Pied Piper Day (German)
Waning Moon
Moon phase: Third Quarter
Color: White

Moon Sign: Aquarius
Moon enters Pisces 2:08 am
Incense: Bay laurel

27 Thursday
Seven Sleepers' Day (German)
Waning Moon
Moon phase: Third Quarter
Color: Crimson

Moon Sign: Pisces
Incense: Mulberry

◑ Friday
Stonewall Riots Anniversary
Waning Moon
Fourth Quarter 5:53 pm
Color: Purple

Moon Sign: Pisces
Moon enters Aries 4:52 am
Incense: Vanilla

June

29 Saturday
Haro Wine Battle (Spanish)
Waning Moon
Moon phase: Fourth Quarter
Color: Blue

Moon Sign: Aries
Incense: Pine

30 Sunday
The Burning of the Three Firs (French)
Waning Moon
Moon phase: Fourth Quarter
Color: Gold

Moon Sign: Aries
Moon enters Taurus 8:00 am
Incense: Juniper

June Correspondences

Stones: Pearl, chalcedony, alexandrite
Animals: Deer, eagle, fox
Flower: Rose
Deities: Artemis, Cerridwen, Hermes, Odin
Zodiac: Gemini

July

1 Monday
Canada Day • Tartan Day (Australian)
Waning Moon
Moon phase: Fourth Quarter
Color: Lavender

Moon Sign: Taurus
Incense: Hyssop

---

2 Tuesday
World UFO Day
Waning Moon
Moon phase: Fourth Quarter
Color: Gray

Moon Sign: Taurus
Moon enters Gemini 11:50 am
Incense: Bayberry

---

3 Wednesday
Dog Days of Summer begin
Waning Moon
Moon phase: Fourth Quarter
Color: Brown

Moon Sign: Gemini
Incense: Honeysuckle

---

4 Thursday
Independence Day
Waning Moon
Moon phase: Fourth Quarter
Color: Turquoise

Moon Sign: Gemini
Moon enters Cancer 4:51 pm
Incense: Balsam

☽ Friday
Tynwald Day (Manx)
Waning Moon
New Moon 6:57 pm
Color: Rose

Moon Sign: Cancer
Incense: Mint

---

6 Saturday
San Fermín begins (Spanish)
Waxing Moon
Moon phase: First Quarter
Color: Black

Moon Sign: Cancer
Moon enters Leo 11:56 pm
Incense: Patchouli

---

7 Sunday
Islamic New Year begins at sundown
Waxing Moon
Moon phase: First Quarter
Color: Yellow

Moon Sign: Leo
Incense: Almond

8 Monday

Feast of St. Sunniva
Waxing Moon
Moon phase: First Quarter
Color: White

Moon Sign: Leo
Incense: Clary sage

---

9 Tuesday

Battle of Sempach Day (Swiss)
Waxing Moon
Moon phase: First Quarter
Color: Red

Moon Sign: Leo
Moon enters Virgo 9:48 am
Incense: Cinnamon

---

10 Wednesday

Nicola Tesla Day
Waxing Moon
Moon phase: First Quarter
Color: Topaz

Moon Sign: Virgo
Incense: Lilac

---

11 Thursday

Mongolian Naadam Festival (ends July 13)
Waxing Moon
Moon phase: First Quarter
Color: Purple

Moon Sign: Virgo
Moon enters Libra 10:06 pm
Incense: Apricot

---

12 Friday

Malala Day
Waxing Moon
Moon phase: First Quarter
Color: Coral

Moon Sign: Libra
Incense: Thyme

Saturday

Feast of St. Mildrith
Waxing Moon
Second Quarter 6:49 pm
Color: Blue

Moon Sign: Libra
Incense: Rue

---

14 Sunday

Bastille Day (French)
Waxing Moon
Moon phase: Second Quarter
Color: Amber

Moon Sign: Libra
Moon enters Scorpio 10:53 am
Incense: Eucalyptus

July

15 Monday
St. Swithin's Day
Waxing Moon
Moon phase: Second Quarter
Color: Gray

Moon Sign: Scorpio
Incense: Lily

---

16 Tuesday
Fiesta de la Tirana (Chilean)
Waxing Moon
Moon phase: Second Quarter
Color: Scarlet

Moon Sign: Scorpio
Moon enters Sagittarius 9:25 pm
Incense: Ginger

---

17 Wednesday
Gion Festival first Yamaboko parade
Waxing Moon
Moon phase: Second Quarter
Color: Yellow

Moon Sign: Sagittarius
Incense: Lavender

---

18 Thursday
Nelson Mandela International Day
Waxing Moon
Moon phase: Second Quarter
Color: Turquoise

Moon Sign: Sagittarius
Incense: Carnation

---

19 Friday
Flitch Day (English)
Waxing Moon
Moon phase: Second Quarter
Color: White

Moon Sign: Sagittarius
Moon enters Capricorn 4:14 am
Incense: Rose

---

20 Saturday
Binding of Wreaths (Lithuanian)
Waxing Moon
Moon phase: Second Quarter
Color: Indigo

Moon Sign: Capricorn
Incense: Sandalwood

☺ Sunday
National Day (Belgian)
Waxing Moon
Full Moon 6:17 am
Color: Orange

Moon Sign: Capricorn
Moon enters Aquarius 7:43 am
Incense: Frankincense

July

22 Monday
St. Mary Magdalene's Day
Waning Moon
Moon phase: Third Quarter
Color: Silver

Moon Sign: Aquarius
Sun enters Leo 3:44 am
Incense: Narcissus

23 Tuesday
Mysteries of St. Cristina (Italian)
Waning Moon
Moon phase: Third Quarter
Color: Maroon

Moon Sign: Aquarius
Moon enters Pisces 9:23 am
Incense: Cedar

24 Wednesday
Gion Festival second Yamaboko parade (Japanese)
Waning Moon
Moon phase: Third Quarter
Color: White

Moon Sign: Pisces
Incense: Marjoram

25 Thursday
Illapa Festival (Incan)
Waning Moon
Moon phase: Third Quarter
Color: Crimson

Moon Sign: Pisces
Moon enters Aries 10:52 am
Incense: Mulberry

26 Friday
St. Anne's Day
Waning Moon
Moon phase: Third Quarter
Color: Pink

Moon Sign: Aries
Incense: Orchid

Saturday
Sleepyhead Day (Finnish)
Waning Moon
Fourth Quarter 10:52 pm
Color: Gray

Moon Sign: Aries
Moon enters Taurus 1:23 pm
Incense: Ivy

28 Sunday
Independence Day (Peruvian)
Waning Moon
Moon phase: Fourth Quarter
Color: Gold

Moon Sign: Taurus
Incense: Marigold

July

29 Monday
St. Olaf Festival (Faroese)
Waning Moon
Moon phase: Fourth Quarter
Color: Ivory

Moon Sign: Taurus
Moon enters Gemini 5:28 pm
Incense: Hyssop

30 Tuesday
Micman Festival of St. Ann
Waning Moon
Moon phase: Fourth Quarter
Color: Gray

Moon Sign: Gemini
Incense: Basil

31 Wednesday
Feast of St. Ignatius
Waning Moon
Moon phase: Fourth Quarter
Color: Topaz

Moon Sign: Gemini
Moon enters Cancer 11:19 pm
Incense: Bay laurel

July Correspondences
Stones: Turquoise, ruby
Animals: Dog, loon, woodpecker, salmon
Flowers: Larkspur, water lily
Deities: Danu, Demeter, Luna, Mercury, Parvati
Zodiac: Cancer

August

1 Thursday
Lammas
Waning Moon
Moon phase: Fourth Quarter
Color: Green

Moon Sign: Cancer
Incense: Myrrh

2 Friday
Porcingula (Pecos)
Waning Moon
Moon phase: Fourth Quarter
Color: Rose

Moon Sign: Cancer
Incense: Cypress

3 Saturday
Flag Day (Venezuelan)
Waning Moon
Moon phase: Fourth Quarter
Color: Black

Moon Sign: Cancer
Moon enters Leo 7:10 am
Incense: Rue

Sunday
Constitution Day (Cook Islands)
Waning Moon
New Moon 7:13 am
Color: Yellow

Moon Sign: Leo
Incense: Juniper

5 Monday
Carnival of Bogotá
Waxing Moon
Moon phase: First Quarter
Color: Gray

Moon Sign: Leo
Moon enters Virgo 5:17 pm
Incense: Neroli

6 Tuesday
Hiroshima Peace Memorial Ceremony
Waxing Moon
Moon phase: First Quarter
Color: Black

Moon Sign: Virgo
Incense: Ylang-ylang

7 Wednesday
Republic Day (Ivorian)
Waxing Moon
Moon phase: First Quarter
Color: White

Moon Sign: Virgo
Incense: Lilac

August

8   Thursday
Farmers' Day (Tanzanian)
Waxing Moon
Moon phase: First Quarter
Color: Purple

Moon Sign: Virgo
Moon enters Libra 5:31 am
Incense: Nutmeg

---

9   Friday
Nagasaki Peace Memorial Ceremony
Waxing Moon
Moon phase: First Quarter
Color: Pink

Moon Sign: Libra
Incense: Violet

---

10   Saturday
Qixi Festival (Chinese)
Waxing Moon
Moon phase: First Quarter
Color: Brown

Moon Sign: Libra
Moon enters Scorpio 6:34 pm
Incense: Ivy

---

11   Sunday
Mountain Day (Japanese)
Waxing Moon
Moon phase: First Quarter
Color: Amber

Moon Sign: Scorpio
Incense: Heliotrope

◐   Monday
World Elephant Day
Waxing Moon
Second Quarter 11:19 am
Color: Silver

Moon Sign: Scorpio
Incense: Clary sage

---

13   Tuesday
Women's Day (Tunisian)
Waxing Moon
Moon phase: Second Quarter
Color: White

Moon Sign: Scorpio
Moon enters Sagittarius 6:01 am
Incense: Bayberry

---

14   Wednesday
Independence Day (Pakistani)
Waxing Moon
Moon phase: Second Quarter
Color: Yellow

Moon Sign: Sagittarius
Incense: Lavender

August

15 Thursday
Bon Festival (Japanese)
Waxing Moon
Moon phase: Second Quarter
Color: Crimson

Moon Sign: Sagittarius
Moon enters Capricorn 1:51 pm
Incense: Apricot

16 Friday
Xicolatada (French)
Waxing Moon
Moon phase: Second Quarter
Color: Coral

Moon Sign: Capricorn
Incense: Rose

17 Saturday
Black Cat Appreciation Day
Waxing Moon
Moon phase: Second Quarter
Color: Gray

Moon Sign: Capricorn
Moon enters Aquarius 5:45 pm
Incense: Magnolia

18 Sunday
Ghost Festival (Chinese)
Waxing Moon
Moon phase: Second Quarter
Color: Orange

Moon Sign: Aquarius
Incense: Frankincense

☺ Monday
Vinalia Rustica (Roman)
Waxing Moon
Full Moon 2:26 pm
Color: Lavender

Moon Sign: Aquarius
Moon enters Pisces 6:52 pm
Incense: Lily

20 Tuesday
St. Stephen's Day (Hungarian)
Waning Moon
Moon phase: Third Quarter
Color: Maroon

Moon Sign: Pisces
Incense: Geranium

21 Wednesday
Consualia (Roman)
Waning Moon
Moon phase: Third Quarter
Color: Topaz

Moon Sign: Pisces
Moon enters Aries 7:02 pm
Incense: Honeysuckle

August
♍

22 Thursday
Feast of the Queenship of Mary (English) Moon Sign: Aries
Waning Moon Sun enters Virgo 10:55 am
Moon phase: Third Quarter Incense: Balsam
Color: White

23 Friday
National Day (Romanian) Moon Sign: Aries
Waning Moon Moon enters Taurus 8:00 pm
Moon phase: Third Quarter Incense: Yarrow
Color: Purple

24 Saturday
St. Bartholomew's Day Moon Sign: Taurus
Waning Moon Incense: Patchouli
Moon phase: Third Quarter
Color: Indigo

25 Sunday
Liberation of Paris Moon Sign: Taurus
Waning Moon Moon enters Gemini 11:04 pm
Moon phase: Third Quarter Incense: Almond
Color: Yellow

◑ Monday
Heroes' Day (Namibian) Moon Sign: Gemini
Waning Moon Incense: Rosemary
Fourth Quarter 5:26 am
Color: White

27 Tuesday
Independence Day (Moldovan) Moon Sign: Gemini
Waning Moon Incense: Cedar
Moon phase: Fourth Quarter
Color: Gray

28 Wednesday
St. Augustine's Day Moon Sign: Gemini
Waning Moon Moon enters Cancer 4:47 am
Moon phase: Fourth Quarter Incense: Marjoram
Color: Brown

August

29 Thursday

St. John's Beheading
Waning Moon
Moon phase: Fourth Quarter
Color: Purple

Moon Sign: Cancer
Incense: Jasmine

30 Friday

St. Rose of Lima Day (Peruvian)
Waning Moon
Moon phase: Fourth Quarter
Color: White

Moon Sign: Cancer
Moon enters Leo 1:09 pm
Incense: Alder

31 Saturday

La Tomatina (Valencian)
Waning Moon
Moon phase: Fourth Quarter
Color: Blue

Moon Sign: Leo
Incense: Sandalwood

August Correspondences

Stones: Peridot, carnelian
Animals: Crow, owl, sturgeon
Flowers: Gladiolus, poppy
Deities: Amaterasu, Helios, Sekhmet, Ra
Zodiac: Leo

September

1 Sunday
Wattle Day (Australian)
Waning Moon
Moon phase: Fourth Quarter
Color: Gold

Moon Sign: Leo
Moon enters Virgo 11:48 pm
Incense: Heliotrope

Monday
Labor Day • Labour Day (Canadian)
Waning Moon
New Moon 9:56 pm
Color: Lavender

Moon Sign: Virgo
Incense: Neroli

3 Tuesday
National Feast of San Marino
Waxing Moon
Moon phase: First Quarter
Color: Black

Moon Sign: Virgo
Incense: Ylang-ylang

4 Wednesday
Feast of St. Rosalia
Waxing Moon
Moon phase: First Quarter
Color: White

Moon Sign: Virgo
Moon enters Libra 12:12 pm
Incense: Lavender

5 Thursday
International Day of Charity
Waxing Moon
Moon phase: First Quarter
Color: Green

Moon Sign: Libra
Incense: Clove

6 Friday
Unification Day (Bulgarian)
Waxing Moon
Moon phase: First Quarter
Color: Pink

Moon Sign: Libra
Incense: Vanilla

7 Saturday
Independence Day (Brazilian)
Waxing Moon
Moon phase: First Quarter
Color: Gray

Moon Sign: Libra
Moon enters Scorpio 1:18 am
Incense: Sage

♍

8 **Sunday**
Grandparents' Day
Waxing Moon
Moon phase: First Quarter
Color: Yellow

Moon Sign: Scorpio
Incense: Marigold

9 **Monday**
Remembrance for Herman the Cheruscan (Asatru)
Waxing Moon
Moon phase: First Quarter
Color: Ivory

Moon Sign: Scorpio
Moon enters Sagittarius 1:26 pm
Incense: Narcissus

10 **Tuesday**
National Day (Belizean)
Waxing Moon
Moon phase: First Quarter
Color: White

Moon Sign: Sagittarius
Incense: Cedar

◗ **Wednesday**
Patriot Day
Waxing Moon
Second Quarter 2:06 am
Color: Brown

Moon Sign: Sagittarius
Moon enters Capricorn 10:38 pm
Incense: Bay laurel

12 **Thursday**
Mindfulness Day
Waxing Moon
Moon phase: Second Quarter
Color: Turquoise

Moon Sign: Capricorn
Incense: Carnation

13 **Friday**
The Gods' Banquet
Waxing Moon
Moon phase: Second Quarter
Color: Rose

Moon Sign: Capricorn
Incense: Thyme

14 **Saturday**
Holy Cross Day
Waxing Moon
Moon phase: Second Quarter
Color: Blue

Moon Sign: Capricorn
Moon enters Aquarius 3:53 am
Incense: Pine

September

15 Sunday
International Day of Democracy
Waxing Moon
Moon phase: Second Quarter
Color: Orange

Moon Sign: Aquarius
Incense: Eucalyptus

16 Monday
Independence Day (Mexican)
Waxing Moon
Moon phase: Second Quarter
Color: Silver

Moon Sign: Aquarius
Moon enters Pisces 5:39 am
Incense: Clary sage

Tuesday
Mid-Autumn Festival (Chinese)
Waxing Moon
Full Moon 10:34 pm
Color: Gray

Moon Sign: Pisces
Incense: Ginger

18 Wednesday
World Water Monitoring Day
Waning Moon
Moon phase: Third Quarter
Color: Topaz

Moon Sign: Pisces
Moon enters Aries 5:24 am
Incense: Honeysuckle

19 Thursday
Feast of San Gennaro
Waning Moon
Moon phase: Third Quarter
Color: Crimson

Moon Sign: Aries
Incense: Jasmine

20 Friday
St. Eustace's Day
Waning Moon
Moon phase: Third Quarter
Color: Coral

Moon Sign: Aries
Moon enters Taurus 5:03 am
Incense: Mint

21 Saturday
UN International Day of Peace
Waning Moon
Moon phase: Third Quarter
Color: Black

Moon Sign: Taurus
Incense: Patchouli

September

22 Sunday

Mabon • Fall Equinox
Waning Moon
Moon phase: Third Quarter
Color: Gold

Moon Sign: Taurus
Moon enters Gemini 6:24 am
Sun enters Libra 8:44 am
Incense: Hyacinth

23 Monday

Feast of St. Padre Pio
Waning Moon
Moon phase: Third Quarter
Color: Gray

Moon Sign: Gemini
Incense: Hyssop

◐ Tuesday

Schwenkenfelder Thanksgiving (German-American)
Waning Moon
Fourth Quarter 2:50 pm
Color: Scarlet

Moon Sign: Gemini
Moon enters Cancer 10:50 am
Incense: Cinnamon

25 Wednesday

Doll Memorial Service (Japanese)
Waning Moon
Moon phase: Fourth Quarter
Color: Yellow

Moon Sign: Cancer
Incense: Lilac

26 Thursday

Feast of Santa Justina (Mexican)
Waning Moon
Moon phase: Fourth Quarter
Color: White

Moon Sign: Cancer
Moon enters Leo 6:47 pm
Incense: Mulberry

27 Friday

Meskel (Ethiopian and Eritrean)
Waning Moon
Moon phase: Fourth Quarter
Color: Purple

Moon Sign: Leo
Incense: Cypress

28 Saturday

Confucius's birthday
Waning Moon
Moon phase: Fourth Quarter
Color: Indigo

Moon Sign: Leo
Incense: Ivy

September

29 Sunday

Michaelmas
Waning Moon
Moon phase: Fourth Quarter
Color: Amber

Moon Sign: Leo
Moon enters Virgo 5:42 am
Incense: Juniper

30 Monday

St. Jerome's Day
Waning Moon
Moon phase: Fourth Quarter
Color: White

Moon Sign: Virgo
Incense: Lily

September Correspondences

Stones: Sapphire, sardonyx, zircon
Animals: Bear, stag, fox
Flowers: Aster, morning glory
Deities: Frigg, Hestia, Persephone, Odin
Zodiac: Virgo

October

1 Tuesday
Armed Forces Day (South Korean)
Waning Moon
Moon phase: Fourth Quarter
Color: Red

Moon Sign: Virgo
Moon enters Libra 6:20 pm
Incense: Basil

☽ Wednesday
Rosh Hashanah begins at sundown
Waning Moon
New Moon 2:49 pm
Color: Brown

Moon Sign: Libra
Incense: Marjoram

3 Thursday
German Unity Day
Waxing Moon
Moon phase: First Quarter
Color: Turquoise

Moon Sign: Libra
Incense: Balsam

4 Friday
St. Francis's Day
Waxing Moon
Moon phase: First Quarter
Color: Coral

Moon Sign: Libra
Moon enters Scorpio 7:22 am
Incense: Orchid

5 Saturday
Republic Day (Portuguese)
Waxing Moon
Moon phase: First Quarter
Color: Gray

Moon Sign: Scorpio
Incense: Pine

6 Sunday
German-American Day
Waxing Moon
Moon phase: First Quarter
Color: Orange

Moon Sign: Scorpio
Moon enters Sagittarius 7:34 pm
Incense: Almond

7 Monday
Nagasaki Kunchi Festival (ends Oct. 9)
Waxing Moon
Moon phase: First Quarter
Color: Ivory

Moon Sign: Sagittarius
Incense: Narcissus

October

8   Tuesday
     Arbor Day (Namibian)
     Waxing Moon
     Moon phase: First Quarter
     Color: White

Moon Sign: Sagittarius
Incense: Ylang-ylang

9   Wednesday
     Leif Erikson Day
     Waxing Moon
     Moon phase: First Quarter
     Color: Topaz

Moon Sign: Sagittarius
Moon enters Capricorn 5:38 am
Incense: Bay laurel

◑   Thursday
     Finnish Literature Day
     Waxing Moon
     Second Quarter 2:55 pm
     Color: Purple

Moon Sign: Capricorn
Incense: Apricot

11   Friday
     Yom Kippur begins at sundown
     Waxing Moon
     Moon phase: Second Quarter
     Color: White

Moon Sign: Capricorn
Moon enters Aquarius 12:31 pm
Incense: Mint

12   Saturday
     National Festival of Spain
     Waxing Moon
     Moon phase: Second Quarter
     Color: Brown

Moon Sign: Aquarius
Incense: Sandalwood

13   Sunday
     Fontinalia (Roman)
     Waxing Moon
     Moon phase: Second Quarter
     Color: Gold

Moon Sign: Aquarius
Moon enters Pisces 3:55 pm
Incense: Marigold

14   Monday
     Indigenous Peoples' Day
     Waxing Moon
     Moon phase: Second Quarter
     Color: Silver

Moon Sign: Pisces
Incense: Hyssop

October

15 Tuesday
The October Horse (Roman)
Waxing Moon
Moon phase: Second Quarter
Color: Gray

Moon Sign: Pisces
Moon enters Aries 4:34 pm
Incense: Bayberry

16 Wednesday
Sukkot begins at sundown
Waxing Moon
Moon phase: Second Quarter
Color: White

Moon Sign: Aries
Incense: Lilac

☺ Thursday
Dessalines Day (Haitian)
Waxing Moon
Full Moon 7:26 am
Color: Green

Moon Sign: Aries
Moon enters Taurus 4:00 pm
Incense: Carnation

18 Friday
Feast of St. Luke
Waning Moon
Moon phase: Third Quarter
Color: Rose

Moon Sign: Taurus
Incense: Vanilla

19 Saturday
Mother Teresa Day (Albanian)
Waning Moon
Moon phase: Third Quarter
Color: Blue

Moon Sign: Taurus
Moon enters Gemini 4:07 pm
Incense: Magnolia

20 Sunday
Feast of St. Acca
Waning Moon
Moon phase: Third Quarter
Color: Yellow

Moon Sign: Gemini
Incense: Hyacinth

21 Monday
Apple Day (United Kingdom)
Waning Moon
Moon phase: Third Quarter
Color: White

Moon Sign: Gemini
Moon enters Cancer 6:50 pm
Incense: Rosemary

October

22 Tuesday
Jidai Festival (Japanese)
Waning Moon
Moon phase: Third Quarter
Color: Maroon

Moon Sign: Cancer
Sun enters Scorpio 6:15 pm
Incense: Geranium

23 Wednesday
Sukkot ends
Waning Moon
Moon phase: Third Quarter
Color: Brown

Moon Sign: Cancer
Incense: Lavender

 Thursday
United Nations Day
Waning Moon
Fourth Quarter 4:03 am
Color: Crimson

Moon Sign: Cancer
Moon enters Leo 1:24 am
Incense: Nutmeg

25 Friday
St. Crispin's Day
Waning Moon
Moon phase: Fourth Quarter
Color: Pink

Moon Sign: Leo
Incense: Thyme

26 Saturday
Death of Alfred the Great
Waning Moon
Moon phase: Fourth Quarter
Color: Indigo

Moon Sign: Leo
Moon enters Virgo 11:47 am
Incense: Rue

27 Sunday
Feast of St. Abbán
Waning Moon
Moon phase: Fourth Quarter
Color: Amber

Moon Sign: Virgo
Incense: Frankincense

28 Monday
Ohi Day (Greek)
Waning Moon
Moon phase: Fourth Quarter
Color: Gray

Moon Sign: Virgo
Incense: Neroli

October ♏

29 Tuesday

National Cat Day
Waning Moon
Moon phase: Fourth Quarter
Color: Scarlet

Moon Sign: Virgo
Moon enters Libra 12:30 am
Incense: Ginger

30 Wednesday

John Adams's birthday
Waning Moon
Moon phase: Fourth Quarter
Color: White

Moon Sign: Libra
Incense: Honeysuckle

31 Thursday

Halloween • Samhain
Waning Moon
Moon phase: Fourth Quarter
Color: Purple

Moon Sign: Libra
Moon enters Scorpio 1:29 pm
Incense: Clove

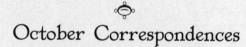

October Correspondences

Stones: Opal, tourmaline
Animals: Bat, rat, crow, raven, dove
Flower: Calendula
Deities: Athena, Cernunnos, Hephaestus,
Shiva, Venus
Zodiac: Libra

November ♏

Friday
All Saints' Day • Día de los Muertos
Waning Moon
New Moon 8:47 am
Color: Coral

Moon Sign: Scorpio
Incense: Cypress

2 **Saturday**
All Souls' Day
Waxing Moon
Moon phase: First Quarter
Color: Black

Moon Sign: Scorpio
Incense: Ivy

3 **Sunday**
Culture Day (Japanese)
Waxing Moon
Moon phase: First Quarter
Color: Yellow

Moon Sign: Scorpio
Moon enters Sagittarius 1:19 am
Incense: Heliotrope
Daylight Saving Time ends at 2 am

4 **Monday**
Mischief Night (British)
Waxing Moon
Moon phase: First Quarter
Color: Ivory

Moon Sign: Sagittarius
Incense: Lily

5 **Tuesday**
Election Day (US)
Waxing Moon
Moon phase: First Quarter
Color: White

Moon Sign: Sagittarius
Moon enters Capricorn 10:17 am
Incense: Cedar

6 **Wednesday**
St. Leonard's Ride (German)
Waxing Moon
Moon phase: First Quarter
Color: Topaz

Moon Sign: Capricorn
Incense: Bay laurel

7 **Thursday**
Feast of St. Willibrord
Waxing Moon
Moon phase: First Quarter
Color: Green

Moon Sign: Capricorn
Moon enters Aquarius 5:58 pm
Incense: Apricot

8 Friday

World Urbanism Day
Waxing Moon
Moon phase: First Quarter
Color: Rose

Moon Sign: Aquarius
Incense: Rose

Saturday

Fateful Day (German)
Waxing Moon
Second Quarter 12:55 am
Color: Gray

Moon Sign: Aquarius
Moon enters Pisces 11:00 pm
Incense: Sage

10 Sunday

Martin Luther's Birthday
Waxing Moon
Moon phase: Second Quarter
Color: Gold

Moon Sign: Pisces
Incense: Eucalyptus

11 Monday

Veterans Day • Remembrance Day (Canadian)
Waxing Moon
Moon phase: Second Quarter
Color: Lavender

Moon Sign: Pisces
Incense: Hyssop

12 Tuesday

Feast Day of San Diego (Tesuque Puebloan)
Waxing Moon
Moon phase: Second Quarter
Color: Black

Moon Sign: Pisces
Moon enters Aries 1:26 am
Incense: Basil

13 Wednesday

Festival of Jupiter
Waxing Moon
Moon phase: Second Quarter
Color: Yellow

Moon Sign: Aries
Incense: Honeysuckle

14 Thursday

Feast of St. Lawrence O'Toole
Waxing Moon
Moon phase: Second Quarter
Color: White

Moon Sign: Aries
Moon enters Taurus 1:59 am
Incense: Jasmine

November

☺ **Friday**
King's Feast (Belgian)
Waxing Moon
Full Moon 4:28 pm
Color: Purple

Moon Sign: Taurus
Incense: Yarrow

---

16 Saturday
St. Margaret of Scotland's Day
Waning Moon
Moon phase: Third Quarter
Color: Blue

Moon Sign: Taurus
Moon enters Gemini 2:09 am
Incense: Rue

---

17 Sunday
Queen Elizabeth's Accession Day
Waning Moon
Moon phase: Third Quarter
Color: Orange

Moon Sign: Gemini
Incense: Juniper

---

18 Monday
Independence Day (Moroccan)
Waning Moon
Moon phase: Third Quarter
Color: Silver

Moon Sign: Gemini
Moon enters Cancer 3:50 am
Incense: Clary sage

---

19 Tuesday
Garifuna Settlement Day (Belizean)
Waning Moon
Moon phase: Third Quarter
Color: Gray

Moon Sign: Cancer
Incense: Cinnamon

---

20 Wednesday
Revolution Day (Mexican)
Waning Moon
Moon phase: Third Quarter
Color: White

Moon Sign: Cancer
Moon enters Leo 8:51 am
Incense: Lilac

---

21 Thursday
Feast of the Presentation of Mary
Waning Moon
Moon phase: Third Quarter
Color: Turquoise

Moon Sign: Leo
Sun enters Sagittarius 2:56 pm
Incense: Nutmeg

November

Friday

Native American Heritage Day
Waning Moon
Fourth Quarter 8:28 pm
Color: Pink

Moon Sign: Leo
Moon enters Virgo 6:01 pm
Incense: Mint

---

23 Saturday

National Adoption Day
Waning Moon
Moon phase: Fourth Quarter
Color: Indigo

Moon Sign: Virgo
Incense: Sandalwood

---

24 Sunday

Evolution Day
Waning Moon
Moon phase: Fourth Quarter
Color: Gold

Moon Sign: Virgo
Incense: Hyacinth

---

25 Monday

Feast of St. Catherine of Alexandria
Waning Moon
Moon phase: Fourth Quarter
Color: Ivory

Moon Sign: Virgo
Moon enters Libra 6:20 am
Incense: Narcissus

---

26 Tuesday

Constitution Day (Indian)
Waning Moon
Moon phase: Fourth Quarter
Color: Scarlet

Moon Sign: Libra
Incense: Ylang-ylang

---

27 Wednesday

Feast of St. Virgilius
Waning Moon
Moon phase: Fourth Quarter
Color: Brown

Moon Sign: Libra
Moon enters Scorpio 7:21 pm
Incense: Marjoram

---

28 Thursday

Thanksgiving Day (US)
Waning Moon
Moon phase: Fourth Quarter
Color: Crimson

Moon Sign: Scorpio
Incense: Balsam

November

29 Friday

William Tubman's birthday (Liberian)
Waning Moon
Moon phase: Fourth Quarter
Color: Rose

Moon Sign: Scorpio
Incense: Vanilla

30 Saturday

St. Andrew's Day (Scottish)
Waning Moon
Moon phase: Fourth Quarter
Color: Blue

Moon Sign: Scorpio
Moon enters Sagittarius 6:53 am
Incense: Pine

November Correspondences

Stones: Citrine, cat's eye, topaz
Animals: Snake, eel, goose, raccoon
Flower: Chrysanthemum
Deities: Anubis, Inanna, Kali, Pluto
Zodiac: Scorpio

December

☽ Sunday

Feast for Death of Aleister Crowley (Thelemic)
Waning Moon
New Moon 1:21 am
Color: Amber

Moon Sign: Sagittarius
Incense: Almond

---

2 Monday

Republic Day (Laotian)
Waxing Moon
Moon phase: First Quarter
Color: Gray

Moon Sign: Sagittarius
Moon enters Capricorn 4:09 pm
Incense: Lily

---

3 Tuesday

St. Francis Xavier's Day
Waxing Moon
Moon phase: First Quarter
Color: Maroon

Moon Sign: Capricorn
Incense: Ginger

---

4 Wednesday

Feasts of Shango and St. Barbara
Waxing Moon
Moon phase: First Quarter
Color: Yellow

Moon Sign: Capricorn
Moon enters Aquarius 11:21 pm
Incense: Lilac

---

5 Thursday

Krampus Night (European)
Waxing Moon
Moon phase: First Quarter
Color: White

Moon Sign: Aquarius
Incense: Myrrh

---

6 Friday

St. Nicholas's Day
Waxing Moon
Moon phase: First Quarter
Color: Coral

Moon Sign: Aquarius
Incense: Orchid

---

7 Saturday

Burning the Devil (Guatemalan)
Waxing Moon
Moon phase: First Quarter
Color: Brown

Moon Sign: Aquarius
Moon enters Pisces 4:49 am
Incense: Sandalwood

December

Sunday
Feast of the Immaculate Conception
Waxing Moon
Second Quarter 10:27 am
Color: Yellow

Moon Sign: Pisces
Incense: Marigold

9 Monday
Anna's Day (Swedish)
Waxing Moon
Moon phase: Second Quarter
Color: White

Moon Sign: Pisces
Moon enters Aries 8:38 am
Incense: Neroli

10 Tuesday
Alfred Nobel Day
Waxing Moon
Moon phase: Second Quarter
Color: Red

Moon Sign: Aries
Incense: Cedar

11 Wednesday
Pilgrimage at Tortugas
Waxing Moon
Moon phase: Second Quarter
Color: Brown

Moon Sign: Aries
Moon enters Taurus 10:55 am
Incense: Honeysuckle

12 Thursday
Fiesta of Our Lady of Guadalupe (Mexican)
Waxing Moon
Moon phase: Second Quarter
Color: Purple

Moon Sign: Taurus
Incense: Carnation

13 Friday
St. Lucy's Day (Scandinavian and Italian)
Waxing Moon
Moon phase: Second Quarter
Color: Rose

Moon Sign: Taurus
Moon enters Gemini 12:22 pm
Incense: Vanilla

14 Saturday
Forty-Seven Ronin Memorial (Japanese)
Waxing Moon
Moon phase: Second Quarter
Color: Gray

Moon Sign: Gemini
Incense: Rue

December

🙂 **Sunday**
Consualia (Roman)
Waxing Moon
Full Moon 4:02 am
Color: Gold

Moon Sign: Gemini
Moon enters Cancer 2:21 pm
Incense: Juniper

---

16 Monday
Las Posadas begin (end Dec. 24)
Waning Moon
Moon phase: Third Quarter
Color: Silver

Moon Sign: Cancer
Incense: Clary sage

---

17 Tuesday
Saturnalia (Roman)
Waning Moon
Moon phase: Third Quarter
Color: Gray

Moon Sign: Cancer
Moon enters Leo 6:39 pm
Incense: Basil

---

18 Wednesday
Feast of the Virgin of Solitude
Waning Moon
Moon phase: Third Quarter
Color: White

Moon Sign: Leo
Incense: Lavender

---

19 Thursday
Opalia (Roman)
Waning Moon
Moon phase: Third Quarter
Color: Turquoise

Moon Sign: Leo
Incense: Mulberry

---

20 Friday
Feast of St. Dominic of Silos
Waning Moon
Moon phase: Third Quarter
Color: Pink

Moon Sign: Leo
Moon enters Virgo 2:37 am
Incense: Mint

---

21 Saturday
Yule • Winter Solstice
Waning Moon
Moon phase: Third Quarter
Color: Blue

Moon Sign: Virgo
Sun enters Capricorn 4:21 am
Incense: Ivy

December

Sunday
Feasts of SS. Chaeremon and Ischyrion
Waning Moon
Fourth Quarter 5:18 pm
Color: Orange

Moon Sign: Virgo
Moon enters Libra 2:08 am
Incense: Frankincense

23 Monday
Larentalia (Roman)
Waning Moon
Moon phase: Fourth Quarter
Color: Lavender

Moon Sign: Libra
Incense: Hyssop

24 Tuesday
Christmas Eve
Waning Moon
Moon phase: Fourth Quarter
Color: White

Moon Sign: Libra
Incense: Cinnamon

25 Wednesday
Christmas Day • Hanukkah begins at sundown (ends 1/2) Moon Sign: Libra
Waning Moon
Moon phase: Fourth Quarter
Color: Topaz

Moon enters Scorpio 3:06 am
Incense: Bay laurel

26 Thursday
Kwanzaa begins • Boxing Day
Waning Moon
Moon phase: Fourth Quarter
Color: Green

Moon Sign: Scorpio
Incense: Balsam

27 Friday
St. Stephen's Day
Waning Moon
Moon phase: Fourth Quarter
Color: White

Moon Sign: Scorpio
Moon enters Sagittarius 2:46 pm
Incense: Rose

28 Saturday
Feast of the Holy Innocents
Waning Moon
Moon phase: Fourth Quarter
Color: Indigo

Moon Sign: Sagittarius
Incense: Pine

December

29 Sunday

Feast of St. Thomas à Becket
Waning Moon
Moon phase: Fourth Quarter
Color: Amber

Moon Sign: Sagittarius
Moon enters Capricorn 11:37 pm
Incense: Heliotrope

Monday

Republic Day (Madagascan)
Waning Moon
New Moon 5:27 pm
Color: Gray

Moon Sign: Capricorn
Incense: Rosemary

31 Tuesday

New Year's Eve
Waxing Moon
Moon phase: First Quarter
Color: Scarlet

Moon Sign: Capricorn
Incense: Bayberry

December Correspondences

Stones: Turquoise, onyx, bloodstone, blue topaz
Animals: Elk, horse, stag, reindeer
Flowers: Narcissus
Deities: Artemis, Jupiter, Rhiannon, Thor
Zodiac: Sagittarius

Fire Magic

Honoring the Fire of Our Ancestral Roots

H. Byron Ballard, MFA

In 2017, I wrote a paper for the Appalachian Studies Association Conference (my professional organization) titled "Gnarly Roots." It traced some of my ancestors' journeys to settle in the southern highlands of Appalachia—the place where I still live and where I've raised my family. My father's side of the family has been here since the 1600s, and my mother's family arrived soon after. They were farmers and shopkeepers, with the occasional stonemason and assorted ne'er-do-wells thrown into the mix.

This land with which I dwell—where my garden hosts an heirloom bean variety called Greasy Cut Shorts and where I drive past the location of my great-grandparents' general store—has seen so many travelers, some who abide and some who stay only for a brief time. The gnarly part of my roots seems to stick into the stony clay soil here—soil that must be amended to grow those heirloom beans. But those roots also answer to the fire of blood and pilgrimage. They hear the call of those distant Border Reivers who left the land between Scotland and England, who left bloody Ulster and made their way through Pennsylvania, finally stopping when they reached the end of the Shenandoah Valley.

Home at last.

The West is only now rekindling the fire of ancestral veneration and is reveling in what can be discovered. We are also grieving for our part in colonization, in enslavement, in forced removals of the ones who were already here when our ancestors—those ragged people who were burning for land, for riches, and, yes, for freedom—arrived. Because of this complicated history, many of us find ancestor veneration too messy, too horrifying to explore. How can we celebrate the lives of such people? How can we escape all that they were?

It is complicated, but it is also filled with nuance and opportunities to think (and feel) both broadly and deeply. We must approach it with eyes and hearts open, with courage as well as compassion. Our ancestors are not one thing, after all. We are all a mix of so many people who came before us—complicated, multidimensional people—as complicated as we are now. Our ancestors had many motivations for the things they did and many influences that came into the decisions they made. When our souls begin to feel the heat of these histories, we begin to learn as much about ourselves as we do about those who came before us.

It is easy now to send in a sample of your genetic-material-filled spit and receive a colorful chart of the places your DNA has been. It isn't accurate, of course, but it gives us a rough idea of the wheres and some of the whens. But it can't tell us the stories of those people, which is why it is best to dig for those wherever the ground seems fertile—talking to relatives, reading old wills and letters, any bits of fact that can add to our understanding of the hows and whys of those faraway people upon whose lives our lives depend.

I teach two classes in ancestor veneration, a beginning one and a more advanced one. The first one is a sweet introduction to the basics: finding the genealogist in your family, if you have one, and asking questions, making a physical space to honor those spirits, and choosing a couple of ancestors you knew to begin your exploration. The second class is more complicated as we look at working with ancestral spirits and how to connect with them in ways that enhance our lives, bring us advice and wisdom, comfort us. That second class is heartrending for many people because they must sometimes come to terms with abuse and shame—and fear, because they remember far too well the terrible great uncles and the hateful father. These are not the places to start nor is it best to start any of this in the darkest of seasons. Let your journey be one of light and learning.

My ancestors—like yours—are a mixed bag of strong-willed characters, some who lived long, some who died young. When I began this work, I started with my beloved and best-known relative, my maternal grandmother. To this day, she is the most helpful of spirits, equal parts loving and encouraging me to do better.

It's best to begin with an ancestor you knew and loved who is now dead. I believe that our ancestors are eager to lend support and give advice, but when starting this sort of practice, it's always easiest to begin with someone you mourn. Often it's a grandparent or parent—the grandma who always made your favorite cookies, the aunt who taught you to play honky-tonk piano. Begin by simply remembering them. If there are still people around who knew them, ask for stories and photographs. You'll be surprised at all the things you may not know about that person you loved so well.

Ancestor Shrine

While your appetite for information is being whetted, set up a simple ancestor shrine. This is usually best inside your house, somewhere on a shelf or table. Many of us share our homes with people who may not understand what we're doing, but don't worry. An ancestor shrine can be a simple thing of beauty—a table that holds a vase with flowers (live or silk), a teacup, a photograph. Or it can be a more elaborate setting that includes mementos of the person with whom you're connecting. I have a chunky ancestor shrine with lots of artifacts, including my grandmother's clip-on sunglasses.

Once you have the shrine set up, it's time to engage with them by offering food and drink. A demitasse cup full of rich, flavorful coffee is a good choice if you're unsure what to offer. But if you remember that your sassy great-aunt loved sweet tea, give her that. And if she loved graham crackers, place one of those on your shrine too. I never leave food on the shrine for longer than overnight. The ancestors take the spiritual nourishment of the offering, and you'll want to make sure to not make an attractive offering for gnats and other insects.

You may choose to burn some sweet smoke—incense or other sacred smoke. If your beloved dad was a smoker, you can use a cigarette or cigar, but I don't like those smells, so I use a smoke blend of my own devising. You may want a particular incense or smoke

mix. Experiment until you have the one that works for you in your venerative practices.

The recipe that I use is based on strong native plants from the southern Appalachian Mountains. Here's my recipe:

Sweet Smoke
Equal parts of the following dried herbs (start with 1 tablespoon each):

Common mugwort (*Artemisia vulgaris*)
Rabbit tobacco (*Pseudognaphalium obtusifolium*)
Mountain mint (*Pycnanthemum virginianum*)

This will burn on a charcoal round in a fireproof bowl. As with any burning material, never leave it unattended.

Spend time at your shrine, thinking about the life of the person you are reaching to, listening to the words, songs, stories that come into your head. You could choose a little notebook to write down memories.

Speak to them, either aloud or in your head, whichever is most comfortable. Remember them on their birthdays, death days, and other special days.

This may be all you wish to do for now. Set up a special place, a shrine of remembrance, and pay attention to it when you feel the call to connect or when you miss the beloved dead and want to spend some time in communion with them. There is no requirement for ancestral veneration—if it calls to you, you may be glad to acknowledge the link.

Candle Meditation

If you want something more intuitive and connective, you can use a candle meditation on a more regular basis. A candle in a protective votive holder can be a literal light to connect with your beloved dead. I've developed the following meditation that can be used when beginning an ancestral connection.

You've chosen an ancestor you knew, one who loved you and whom you also loved. Choose someone who was clever as well as loving, if you can. One of the goals of making this connection is to learn from those who came before, after all. Light the candle on your shrine. Pour a little beverage into the teacup and grab a cup of tea for yourself.

As the candlelight flickers and you sip your tea, call to your mind the person you want to connect with. Remember how they looked, how they smelled, their laugh, their singing. You will benefit from some grounding now, with whichever technique works best for you. And don't forget to keep your breathing deep and steady. Listen with your mind's ear and watch the light of the candle.

When you have spent five or ten minutes at your shrine, you are probably ready to say goodbye and get on with your day. I do this by blowing out the candle and blowing a kiss to the photo of my grandmother. If you have a little notebook, write down your impressions of the meditation and let your mind wander free with memories.

The Fire of Connection

These sacred connections have come naturally to me and you may find the same thing. Please don't save this for Samhain—being in a relationship with your ancestors can enrich your spiritual practice as well as your life experience all year long.

There is no question that we are going through challenging times now, as we reckon with human resilience in the face of cultural and climate change. Finding strength and endurance is a daily chore for so many of us, and it is highly likely that your ancestors went through hard times of their own. Let their wisdom inform and guide you. Remember their stories, and look for the kernels of truth in your family's mythology.

The times of their lives were at least as hard as these that are ours. They bled, they loved, they were filled with fear and longing, they cried, they danced—just as we do. Honoring their gift of life is an honorable thing to do, but connecting to their spirits and listening to their wisdom is a gift that goes both ways. Allow the fire of this connection to inspire and warm you in these cold and disconnected times.

Rites from a Secret Pagan Religion

John Opsopaus, PhD

In 1452 in the mountaintop stronghold of a remote outpost of Byzantium, the most famous philosopher of his age passed away, nearly one hundred years old. He was named George Gemistos, but he called himself Plethon, and his dedicated students compared him to the greatest philosophers of the past, writing "Plato Plotinus Plethon." A trusted counselor to the rulers, he was nevertheless suspected of "Hellenism"—worshipping the ancient Greek gods—and of leading a few select followers down this heretical path. This was a dangerous activity, and some of his contemporaries were cruelly tortured and executed for practicing Paganism.

These suspicions were confirmed by the discovery of Plethon's *Book of Laws* after his death. It contained a complete Pagan theology based on Platonic philosophy, a sacred calendar, and all the rituals and invocations needed for religious practice, even including twenty-seven hymns for various liturgical purposes. All this was based on ancient practice but updated for his time. Although his disciples begged for the book, it fell into the hands of George Scholarios, a fanatical churchman and Plethon's enemy of many years. Scholarios triumphantly reports how he spent four hours ripping out and burning pages, preserving only enough, he bragged, to prove Plethon's crime and to justify his own book burning. He also ordered that if anyone had a copy of the book, they must burn it or they would be excommunicated, but in fact there were no other copies, so far as we know. Fortunately the pages that escaped destruction are the most useful parts for Pagans who want to practice Plethon's religious rituals today.

I should mention how I personally became involved with Plethon's philosophy and religion. I was very excited when C. M. Woodhouse's book, *George Gemistos Plethon: The Last of the Hellenes*, was published in 1986. Here, I thought, was a religion devoted to the Greek gods that was practiced as recently as the Renaissance, but I was disappointed to discover that Woodhouse only summarized the surviving parts of the *Book of Laws* and paraphrased or omitted entirely Plethon's invocations and hymns; there was not enough information to practice the religion. Moreover, there were no English translations of Plethon's book. Therefore, I found other ways to worship the gods based on ancient practice. Over the years, however, I've come to appreciate better the depth of Platonic philosophy and its understanding of the gods, and so I decided to look again at Plethon's philosophical religion. Although there has been recent research on Plethon, there were still no English translations of his book and related texts, and so I decided to make my own translations from Plethon's Greek. These are now published as appendices to my guide to practicing his religion: *The Secret Texts of Hellenic Polytheism: A Practical Guide to the Restored Pagan Religion of George Gemistos Plethon.*

Platonic Theology

As I've mentioned, Plethon's religion is founded on Platonic philosophy. By the sixth century CE, Platonist philosophers, including Plotinus, Porphyry, Iamblichus, and Proclus, had produced the most fully developed Pagan theology in the West. Plethon built on this for his own philosophy of religion and system of religious ritual. He traced his ideas back to Plato and to twenty-seven other ancient sages, including Pythagoras, the Brahmans of India, and the Magi, followers of Zoroaster. Nevertheless, he stated that his religion was not "revealed," but founded on rational and universal philosophical principles.

These principles are taught in the philosophy of Plato and his successors (especially Plotinus and Porphyry). Central to this philosophy are the Platonic Ideas or Forms, which are eternal essences existing independently of the physical world. Numbers provide the best examples of Platonic Ideas. The number 3 for example is outside of space and time. It did not come into being at some time, and it existed before anyone thought of it. It will never cease existing, even if there is no one to think it, even indeed if there is no longer three of any physical thing in existence. If you can grasp this, then you can begin to understand the Platonic Ideas. Moreover, if you understand what the numbers 1, 2, and 3 are, then you also realize that 2 + 1 must equal 3. You don't have to observe anything in the physical world to confirm this, and it cannot be disproved. Moreover, this fact did not become true at some time in the past, nor can it ever cease to be true; it is an eternal truth.

The Platonic Ideas are important because, according to Platonists, the highest gods are Platonic Ideas. Thus, they are eternal and immaterial—that is, outside of time and space. Plethon shows that there are several ranks of divinities with different properties. Highest of all is Zeus, the ultimate principle of unity, by which anything (including the gods) is something. Therefore, he is also called the One Itself and Being Itself. Zeus is in turn the eternal cause of twenty-two supercelestial gods, who are Platonic Ideas outside of time and space. They are the causes of important aspects of our world, including form and matter, identity and difference, motion and rest, the various kinds of immortal souls, the four elements, animals and plants, and so forth. The supercelestial gods are divided into

A LITTLE BIT
OF MAGIC

Plethon died on the same day of the year as Emperor Julian, who briefly restored Paganism in the Roman empire more than a millennium before.

two ranks: the Olympians, who are the causes of everlasting beings, and the Titans or Tartareans, who are the causes of mortal beings. In particular, the Olympians emanate the celestial gods—the gods in the heavens—who exist in space and time but are everlasting (immortal). They manifest as visible celestial bodies: the stars and seven traditional planets. The Olympians also emanate the *daimons*, who inhabit the earth and carry out the gods' intentions. Plethon stresses that all daimons are good, since they are ultimately emanations of Zeus, who is The Good according to Plato. The Titans, who are inferior to the Olympians in power, produce the mortal plants and animals who populate our world. In summary, the orders of gods are as follows:

1. Zeus
2. The twenty-two supercelestial gods
   a. The Olympian gods (Poseidon, Hera, Apollo, Artemis, Pluto, etc.)
   b. The Titans or Tartarean gods (Kronos, Aphrodite, Persephone, etc.)
3. The celestial gods (stars, Helios, Selene, etc.)
4. The daimons

We humans have a unique position in this system, for Plethon explains that we are a joint creation of the Olympians and the Titans. In particular, the Olympian god Pluto is the cause of our immortal soul, and his wife, the Titan Persephone or Kore, creates our mortal body (and the mortal parts of our souls). Therefore, we have a unique and important function: binding together the immortal and mortal parts of existence. Therefore, he explains, we must be regularly reincarnated in order to maintain the unity of existence.

Sacred Calendar

If you are Pagan, then you probably follow the Wheel of the Year and celebrate the quarter and cross-quarter days. Plethon also organizes the holy days according to a sacred calendar determined by the Sun and the Moon, the visible manifestations of the two chief celestial gods, Helios and Selene. The month follows the cycle of the Moon and begins with the New Moon. The year follows the cycle of the Sun, and begins with the New Moon following the winter solstice. As a consequence there are either twelve or thirteen lunar months in each year.

The day in which the conjunction of the Sun and Moon occurs is called Old-and-New because it is the boundary between one month and the next month, which begins at midnight with a holy day called New Moon. These lunar months are either twenty-nine or thirty days long and are divided into four weeks corresponding approximately to the Moon's quarters, each of which ends in a holy day. These holy days are devoted to various deities as follows. The New Moon holy day is devoted to Zeus; the first-quarter holy day is for all the Olympians, but especially Poseidon and Hera; the Full Moon honors all the gods and daimons; the third quarter is for the non-Olympians (the Titans, celestial gods, and daimons); and the end of the month is dedicated to Pluto, Persephone, and the heroes, who jointly care for humankind. On Old-and-New we pray to Zeus and spend some time in introspection, contemplating our mistakes and lapses during the preceding month but also acknowledging and celebrating what we have done well.

The annual holy days are celebrated at the quarters of the year, but they do not occur on the solstices and equinoxes, because the year begins some time after the winter solstice. The various annual celebrations last for several days and are devoted to the gods as follows. The New Year celebrations worship Zeus as the creator and preserver of the universe and the guide of our lives. The first-quarter holy day of the fourth month, which occurs in the spring, is devoted to the Olympians, who are responsible for immortal existence. The Full Moon of the seventh month is a summer celebration for all gods. The third quarter of the tenth month, in autumn, honors the non-Olympian gods (the Titans, celestial gods, and daimons), who together are responsible for mortal existence. The year ends with holy days devoted to Pluto, Persephone, and the heroes.

Threefold Adoration Ritual

Here is a simple ritual that you can do. It is called the Threefold Adoration, and Plethon includes it at the beginning of every religious service.

1. First, kneel on both knees and raise your face, arms, and palms toward the sky. Pray to the Olympian gods, *Oh gods, be propitious!* (or *be kind,* etc.).

2. Next, raise your left knee so that you are kneeling on your right knee and lay your right hand on the earth to acknowledge these gods.

3. Kneel again on both knees, raise your face, arms, and palms, and pray to all the other gods and daimons, *Oh gods, be propitious!*

4. Then lift up your right knee so that you kneel on your left knee, and touch your left hand to the earth to acknowledge these gods.

5. Kneel again on both knees.

6. Raise your face, arms, and palms to the sky and pray, *King Zeus, be propitious!* Then place both hands on the earth and bend down to touch your forehead to the earth.

7. Repeat this adoration of Zeus (step 6) two more times.

Of course, if you have difficulty with kneeling or bowing, then you should do whatever is safe and comfortable for you; Plethon himself says this! The Threefold Adoration was part of the morning, afternoon, and evening worship services recommended by Plethon, but if three times each day is too much, then once a day will do.

Invocation

Plethon's worship services also include quite lengthy invocations to the gods, which you can find in my book, along with shortened versions. According to the Neoplatonic theory of prayer, these help us establish our connection to the gods. Here is a selection, which you can read out loud after the Threefold Adoration (and before the hymn):

O King Zeus, Being Itself, One Itself, Good Itself, you are great, great in reality, and supremely great! Nothing is or has been before you, for you alone are pre-eternal. You are also great, O Lord Poseidon, the greatest and firstborn child of the greatest and first father! You are the second father and second creator of this universe. You are with him, O Queen Hera, mother of the gods within the heavens, leader of the procession into multiplicity of inferior beings. And you other Olympian gods, children of great Zeus, together with Poseidon you create all the immortal beings within the heavens. You are with them, O Lord Pluto, protector of our immortal principle. You too are blessed, O Lord Kronos, eldest of the Tartarean children of Zeus, and you other Titans, who preside over all of mortal nature. And you are blessed, O Lord Helios, and you, O wandering Planets and highest Stars. Last, you too are blessed, O daimons, gods of the last degree, but still infallible and good. May all the blessed gods favorably and kindly accept this prayer! We will follow you in our conduct and actions. With you we will celebrate great Zeus, in which all will find the most perfect and most blessed state. We beseech you to grant the greatest goods possible. Be propitious and preserve us. Govern us in the midst of the All, and grant what you have judged is best for us and also fixed from all eternity.

A Hymn to Chant

Plethon's worship services also include hymns to the gods, and he composed twenty-seven hymns for this purpose. These include hymns that are sung in every service, hymns for each of the thirteen lunar months, hymns for the monthly holy days, and hymns for each of the six secular days of each week. Regardless of what other hymns are sung, Plethon includes the following hymn to Zeus in every worship service:

Zeus, Father, thou Self-Father, eldest Demiurge,
All-Father, King, the highest and most great of all,
Almighty, Unity, Self-Being, and the Good Itself,
who everything has caused from all eternity,
the greatest by thyself, the rest by lesser gods,
all with perfection, to the uttermost degree.
Be kind, protect us, lead us, as in everything,
by thine illustrious children. You entrust them with
our destinies, fulfilled as just they ought to be.

You can chant or sing it after the Threefold Adoration and Invocation. Plethon suggests that we sing the hymn three times on holy days.

Ritual Conclusion

At the end of the ritual, the priest, or whoever is conducting the ritual, proclaims three times, *May King Zeus and all the gods, who as overseers under Zeus have settled our matters, be kind to all of us.* After each proclamation, everyone says, *Be it so!* (or *So mote it be!* if you prefer). This concludes the ritual.

Concluding Remarks

So there you have a simple ritual to worship the Greek gods as taught by Plethon. There is much more to his philosophical religion, which is quite modern, despite being six hundred years old, and it can help us to understand the gods better today. I hope you will find Plethon's philosophical approach to worshipping the Greek gods to be as interesting and worthwhile as I have.

Resources

Opsopaus, John. *The Secret Texts of Hellenic Polytheism*. Woodbury, MN: Llewellyn Publications, 2022.

Woodhouse, C. M. *George Gemistos Plethon: The Last of the Hellenes*. Oxford: Oxford University Press, 1986.

Magical Protection and Warding in the Ozark Mountains

Brandon Weston

In the old days, methods for magical protection would have been an essential part of life for Ozark hillfolk. Survival was constantly on the minds of families in this rough wilderness. Works of protection and warding then became as essential a part of homestead life, as was growing crops, rearing livestock, and living in harmony with nature. This work aimed to protect from both physical and magical maladies, although that separation wouldn't have been made by my ancestors. Even today, traditional healers and magical practitioners in the region will rarely separate illnesses and curses into the "physical" versus "spiritual" or "magical" categories. They take a much more holistic approach to all of life. Wards and amulets figure heavily in the corpus of Ozark folk magic and many times are themselves carefully crafted art pieces that are passed down within families. In many cases, such items can have cleverly disguised purposes, as in one case, when I met a traditional woodworker who carved protective angel statues from sacred trees like the red cedar (*Juniperus virginiana*).

It should be noted that among Ozarkers of the past as well as traditionalists today, you will rarely hear the word *amulet* used, and *ward* is even rarer than that. These are useful designations folklorists and neotraditionalist practitioners use today to better categorize these folk practices. Among the older generations, one is more likely to hear someone say they have a "lucky charm" or "charm," meaning amulet. Old Ozarkers didn't really have specific names for physical objects hung or placed around the home for protection, which I like to call a "ward." In many cases, talking about or giving specific labels to magical procedures or objects was believed to nullify the power of the ritual or item, so in many cases these workings were intentionally never spoken about.

Traditional protective rites and rituals include a number of common ingredients as well as invoked themes within the verbal charms. Ingredients might include certain long-used sacred plants like red cedar, tobacco, oak tree, asafetida (*Ferula assa-foetida*), or buckeye nut (*Aesculus pavia*; or Ohio buckeye, *A. glabra*). This materia magica also includes plant varieties that have thorns, specifically honey locust trees (*Gleditsia triacanthos*), greenbriar vines (*Smilax rotundifolia*), and blackberry canes. These specific plants are often used alongside verbal charms invoking images of swords, knives, and spears intended to stop oncoming sickness or evil before it reaches the individual or their home.

Rituals for magical protection and warding have traditionally been divided by their "targets," such as illnesses, hexes, intruders, spies, natural disasters, as well as just general works for magical protection without any specific target. I will briefly define each of these categories to give you a better understanding of how the workings were categorized by traditional Ozarkers.

Illnesses

This includes both general contagion and specific illnesses. For example, traditionalist healers created wards against "wandering disease," as it was sometimes called, or amulets like the buckeye nut, aimed at warding against arthritis and rheumatism. The protective magic of this category aims at preventing the contagion from entering the body or the home.

Home Ward: Hang black chicken feathers above the exterior doors. Black chickens are used in a number of healing rites and are believed to be able to absorb illnesses without dying, so their feathers have a similar "absorbent" quality.

Personal Amulet: Wear a bag of asafetida around the neck. The stench of the asafetida is believed to be an unstoppable ward against all illnesses.

Hexes

A hex is a malady sent by an outside force. In Ozark folk magic, hexes almost always work through a sympathetic connection made between the hexer and their victim through the use of identifying materials like hair, fingernail clippings, teeth, saliva, blood, and so on. Protective magic of this category aims at actually protecting these identifying materials while still on the person. In one case I observed, a healer fashioned an amulet for a client that would "deaden," or nullify, any materials a hexer might try to retrieve from them. A ward for the home might then work on the basis that it would prevent anything retrieved from out of the home to be used in any hexing rituals against the family.

> *Home Ward:* Hang a horseshoe or cross above the exterior doors (and sometimes the windows). This will magically bless anything taken from the home, thereby nullifying its use in sympathetic hexes.
>
> *Personal Amulet:* Wear a knotted string bracelet as a personal amulet. These bracelets are common among tradition-alists for a variety of needs. A knot is started in a length of ordinary string. Before it is pulled closed, a prayer, blessing, or verbal charm is "blown" through the knot and then caught as the string is pulled tight. This is repeated three, seven, or twelve times.

Intruders

This category includes both physical and otherworldly intrud-ers, although, again, these wouldn't have necessarily been sep-arated by our Ozark ancestors. For many, a human being and a ghost have the same physicality and presence in the world. These protective rites often aimed to strengthen locks on the doors or prevent entities from physically entering into the home itself. Personal amulets could also be used to ward against robbery or even spiritual possession.

Home Ward: "Briar fence" charms are made either from
lengths of greenbriar vines (*Smilax rotundifolia*) or
blackberry canes attached together and hung above the
exterior doors. These wards are usually "expanded" using
verbal charms to become a magical fence that surrounds
the entire house. Thorny vines and plants are used to
magically cut, scratch, or stab intruders before they enter
the home.

Personal Amulet: Small chunks of lightning-struck wood are
sometimes carried as a warding amulet against spiritual
influences, especially possession.

Spies

In addition to general intruders, certain magical rites have also
been traditionally aimed at deterring or "blinding" spying eyes.
More specifically, they prevent another magic user from being able
to look in on your business at any time. This category of protective

warding is often used by healers and magical practitioners themselves. There's a belief here that if someone is able to see the work you are doing for a client, they can undo that work by reversing the ritual procedure. Therefore, it's very important for a practitioner to be able to work in complete secrecy, especially those who are well-known in their communities, because these individuals are known to have many enemies as well as friends.

Home Ward: Charm or enchant mirrors against magical spying. There's an old folk belief that if someone knows the proper method, they can magically spy on a person through any mirror or standing water inside their house. Mirror blessing verses or certain cleaning rituals, like wiping a mirror in three counterclockwise circles, are believed to prevent this sort of magical spying.

Personal Amulet: A necklace made from three plaited strings (or sometimes plaited grapevines) worn around the neck is said to make a person "blurry" to any spying eyes. Ritual bathing using blessed water before one leaves the house is also a very popular method of protection.

Natural Disasters

In the old Ozarks, families were often at the mercy of nature, which is why historically hillfolk have sought a balanced relationship with the land around them. House fires, floods, famine, drought, and all other manner of natural disasters were very real and present worries for hill families. Cunning Ozarkers knew that to control the forces of nature required a power that few possessed, but they were able to develop many different methods to help divert the harm of such disasters or even shift them over just a little bit so that the damage would be lessened.

House Ward: Placing a red ribbon (sometimes blessed with certain verbal charms or prayers) into the oil of an oil lamp is a popular protective measure against house fires, specifically those often caused by oil lamps themselves. There are also traditional charm bags aimed specifically at warding against house fires, usually hung up above a fireplace or sometimes even encased in clay and hung inside the chimney itself.

Personal Amulet: Lightning strikes were once greatly feared, likely more so than they are today. The old adage that lightning never strikes the same spot twice has been traditionally applied to one specific amulet made of a small chunk of wood from a lightning-struck tree, carried in the pocket to prevent a strike. Likewise, carrying oak wood in general, which has long associations with strength, power, lightning, and the planet Jupiter, is a popular Ozark charm against being struck. It's said that even if you are struck with either amulet examples in your pocket, you at least won't be killed.

General Protection

There are many more general methods for magical protection that are aimed at warding against all the previous categories at once. These usually involve repeated ritual measures, such as daily blessings, weekly smoke cleansing of the home, or weekly baths using blessed water. This category can also include travel blessings, of which there are hundreds of varieties, often only used if the individual is going on a long trip somewhere. These rituals might involve blessing the vehicle (or the horse, in the past) with holy water and prayers, or even by smoking them with protective plants like red cedar (*Juniperus virginiana*) and tobacco.

Home Ward: Regular or semiregular smoking of the house as a protective measure. Traditionally, red cedar, tobacco, or a mixture of the two is used for this purpose. Both of these plants have deep associations in the Ozarks with cleansing all manner of evil and illnesses as well as offering a protective barrier. Both the inside and outside of

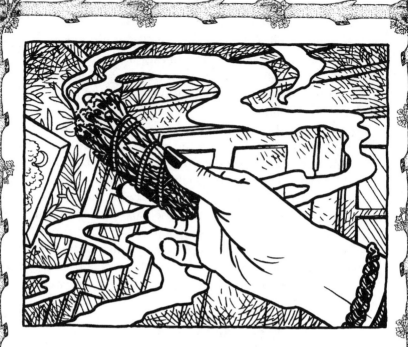

the home can be smoke cleansed. The traditional ritual procedure is to begin at the front door and work in a counterclockwise circle three times through the inside, or around the outside perimeter, of the home.

Personal Amulet: These might include carrying lucky amulets like silver dimes, rabbit's feet, buckeye or nutmeg nuts, or five-finger grass (a.k.a. "cinquefoil," *Potentilla* spp.). This category can also include personal rituals for protection, such as certain "shield" prayers, verbal charms, and Bible verses aimed at offering a protective layer of power around a person.

In the Ozarks today, we often have very different needs when it comes to our protection work, but it's interesting to see how so many of these needs are a part of some deep, primal connection within our human natures. We're still afraid of the unknown, whether that is a mysterious illness, a thief waiting in the shadows to break into our homes, or a mischievous ghost rapping in our walls. The protective rites I've collected and those that feature as a part of my own work fall into two main categories with many specific examples underneath those. Much of Ozark folk magic, even in a modern setting among neotraditionalists, is still based on a case-by-case basis, and rituals are commonly altered and changed to fit an individual's needs.

Active Warding

Rites within this category usually figure as a part of a regular schedule of "magical maintenance," as I like to call it, often alongside other works like cleansing. For example, an individual might recite a protective prayer or verbal charm upon rising in the morning to protect themselves throughout the day. Or a practitioner might encircle their home with sacred smoke (usually red cedar or tobacco) on a weekly basis to maintain their protective wards. The "active" quality denotes preventative measures or reactionary work, which aims for protection in the moment rather than leaving a lasting, renewable effect.

Three Briar Charm

This charm is to be recited as soon as one wakes up from sleeping. In order to protect yourself from all malign forces during the day, recite this charm three times with your eyes closed, facing the east, with your right hand covering your right eye and your left hand covering the left eye:

With my words I tie three briar vines together. Three rings surround me like three thorny fences. Be a wall around me! Be a guard around me! Be a hedge around me! Let none that mean me harm pass this fence, and let those who try be scratched, be cut, be clawed apart until there's nothing left! Let this fence stand until all the stars fall from the heavens above.

While this charm has traditionally been used as a part of a daily practice, it is also beneficial for use specifically before traveling or if you are journeying into a dangerous situation.

A Water Shield

Use this shield alongside your daily bath. This shielding bath ritual is best used in the morning before you begin your day but will also serve you well at any time. Repeat this charm three times over your bathwater as it fills the tub, or while you are showering:

In the east there is a silver spring. I draw water before the Sun shines. I draw water before the Sun rises. Three pails of water at dawn. From head to toe, from toe to head, may I be covered. Blessed water flow over me three times. Silvery water, silvery armor. Against all evil. From now until I bathe again.

Then continue with your bath or shower.

Passive Warding

Unlike active warding, passive protective magic aims at creating objects that will sustain a magical charge for a long duration. Rituals within this category are most often used when creating personal amulets or wards for the home, vehicle, and so on. These magical objects are imbued with power and a purpose upon creation. The effects of the ward then last a certain duration before the object needs to be ritually recharged again.

A Pocket Amulet

This amulet can be used for constant protection against all ills and evils. On a New Moon in Aries or Leo, take a whole nutmeg or buckeye nut and carve your first, middle, and last initials on the surface of the nut with a knife or nail. Repeat this verbal charm three times, blowing across the surface of the nut after each recitation:

In the east there is a mountain. On the mountain there is a tree. On that tree there grows a golden nut. With holy hands I pick this nut and put it in my pocket. Seven angels guide me. Seven angels guard me. Seven angels walk along the road with me.

Place the nut in a small cloth bag and carry it in your pocket.

This amulet needs to be recharged every New Moon by repeating the charm and blowing action above three additional times. So long as the amulet remains charged, it shall be your constant friend.

Red Cedar House Ward

Use this ward to protect a home from Full Moon to Full Moon. On a Full Moon in Taurus, take three sprigs of red cedar and tie them together with red ribbon or string using three knots. You can make a bundle like this for each of the exterior doors to your home, however many you might have. Make all your bundles at the same time. Repeat this verbal charm over all your bundles then sprinkle each three times with salt water.

In the east there is a mountain. On the mountain there grows a red cedar tree as wide as the ground and as tall as the sky. I pluck three branches. I pluck three rings of white fire. A flame on every doorway. Against all evil! Against all sickness! Until the world crumbles away.

Hang your bundles above the doorway, on the outside or inside of the home.

Recharge this ward every Full Moon. Mix together a small amount of salt water. Stir the water three times clockwise with the index finger of your right hand, and then sprinkle it on the ward to recharge it.

Practical Uncrossing Spells 101

Mickie Mueller

In the life of any magical person, sometimes things get weird. You might fall under a string of bad luck, events that seem unconnected, but after a while, you start to get suspicious that something has gone asunder in your world and you're not sure why. Maybe you've noticed an oppressive energy and you're having trouble seeing the good things around you. You've found yourself crossed.

The term *star-crossed* first appears in Shakespeare's *Romeo and Juliet,* meaning to be "thwarted by a malign star." Stars aren't the only energies that can create a crossed condition. Being crossed means having opposition, something standing in your way. We see magical remedies to being crossed shared by spellcasters, most famously in Hoodoo, Rootwork, Conjure, Palo, and Brujería. These magical traditions have served their communities for decades, removing all kinds of obstacles with uncrossing spells. It's an accurate description for the wide range of energetic maladies that can happen to anyone. The umbrella of a crossed condition can include but is not limited to being hexed, cursed, under the evil eye, or jinxed, either by purposeful malicious spellcasting or by absorbing ill will from others who are not spellcasters. We feel the effects but don't know the origin, which is why "crossed" is appropriate, because it's a blanket term for any of these situations. This might sound scary, but there's no need to panic. We have more power *over our own energy* than anyone else does, so solving this problem once you've identified it isn't too hard. Being fearful about it can make matters worse, so stand in your power. I've got your back with several practical spells to choose from that use items you probably have at home or can easily access. Take a deep breath—you've got this!

When Is Uncrossing Needed?

Sometimes you might find yourself surrounded by energies that are running against you. You might feel stuck, like there are obstacles at every turn or that everything you try to accomplish is harder than trudging through wet cement. One or two negative experiences don't necessarily mean that you're cursed. It's important to remember that not everything will go our way. If you stub your toe, that might just be because you weren't paying attention or someone moved the end table. However, if you stub your toe and break your favorite coffee cup, a bird flies into your windshield, an important communication is misconstrued, your internet goes out, your protective jewelry breaks or goes missing or gets tarnished overnight, you feel physically drained and you can't find a medical reason for it . . . you might be dealing with a blocked condition. Watch for patterns of things going awry and unusual circumstances behind them. Every problem you have is not a crossed condition—most of the time, it isn't. Finally, you can do some quick divination to check in with the energy around you and confirm that you are, in fact, crossed.

It's also important to remember that sometimes a situation that seems bad in the moment can turn out to be beneficial in the long term. Missed flights, running late on the highway, and dinner plans getting canceled can all seem frustrating, but they might turn out to have kept you out of a bad situation. Don't assume that everything that goes wrong in your life is because there's a metaphysical cloud hanging over you. It's just not the case.

A crossed condition can happen in lots of ways. Occasionally someone is sending harmful energy your way on purpose, like a hex or curse, but that's much rarer than people think. If you haven't gotten on someone's bad side, or if you have but they don't have the skills or resources to attempt purposeful casting against you, then that's probably not the case. More often these things happen completely by accident. People may feel jealousy toward you and you're picking that up. Maybe you are forced into situations where you're spending time with people who wish you ill in their hearts, and you absorb that in your subconscious and your energy field. Your lofty neighbor might not like your witchy awesomeness and glare out the window with bad intentions whenever they see you. These aren't people casting actual spells but sending unintentional psychic attacks. Their repeated energy can build up and leave you feeling stuck from it, especially if you've been busy and forgotten to keep up your magical wards and cleansing protocols.

We can even curse ourselves! Too much negative self-talk, ruminating, or focusing on problems that are out of your control can manifest into a low-key self-cast curse, leaving you feeling stuck and heavy. You can use any or all of these methods to break up that stagnant blocked energy and get you back on track.

There are different schools of thought, but I never worry about waiting for a certain phase of the Moon or day of the week for this kind of magic. I usually do it as soon as I've confirmed that it's needed and then repeat on the next Tuesday during the waning Moon. These kinds of spells are very personal and deal with your own energy, so the most important thing is that it's the right time for you.

Lemon and Salt Uncrossing Spell

There are many versions of this spell out there, and this is my version, I like to adjust spells that I find to fit my own practice. I first

encountered this spell in a book from the seventies by Al G. Manning. Most people I have shared either the original or my version
with have had fast results, so I wanted to share mine with you here.

You will need:
1 lemon
About 1 cup salt (Cheap table salt is fine.)

Using a sharp kitchen knife, cut the ends off the lemon. Then
cut the lemon into 5 wagon wheels. Pour ½ cup salt onto a small
plate and arrange the slices of lemon in a circle on top of the salt.
Using your finger or the tip of the knife blade, trace a five-pointed
star in the air above the lemons with each slice of lemon representing a point of the star. Then trace a circle around the lemons to
bring power into the lemon. Imagine the harmful energy around
you in every area in your life as you hold your open hands over the
lemon, and, using multiple downward sweeping gestures, pull the
baneful energy into the lemon. As you do so, repeat this chant until
you feel all the offending energy is trapped:

> *All sour energies, you can't resist.*
> *Your hold over me shall now untwist.*
> *Drawn to this lemon like a moth to flame,*
> *Bound here by my will, trapped and lame.*

Next, pour more salt liberally all over the lemon slices, sealing
in the blocking energy in the lemons. As you do so, repeat this incantation to seal it in:

> *I am unblocked! I am unblocked!*
> *I seal you in with blessed salt!*
> *No escape for you foul energy.*
> *As this lemon dries up, so am I free!*

Leave the plate somewhere it won't be disturbed, and as the
lemon dries, the harmful energy will be destroyed. If the lemons

mold instead of drying out, repeat the spell. Once this spell is complete, I like to dump the materials into a brown paper bag and throw it away on garbage day. Some people might prefer to toss the bag of remnants in a gas station trash can.

Clearing and Uncrossing Candle

This is another one of my favorites. It uses clearing and uncrossing herbs that are found in most kitchens. You can add a few from your witch's apothecary if you have them, but it's not necessary for this spell to be successful. This is a flexible method that you can adjust according to what you have on hand. You can use several white tealight candles, with one in every room in your home, or use a taper, jar, or pillar candle and burn it all the way down in the center of your home.

Use any or all of the following kitchen herbs: cayenne, garlic, black pepper, salt, dill, mint, rosemary, coffee, and cloves.

Add any of these witch's apothecary herbs if you have them: hyssop, rue, angelica, and ground High John the Conqueror root.

Add a pinch of each herb to a small dish as you repeat the words *clearing and uncrossing* over and over. This charges the mix and tells each herb which of its attributes you are requesting. Mix all your herbs together. Anoint your candle with an uncrossing oil of your choice or use plain olive oil. Then sprinkle the herbs on the candle or roll the candle in them depending on what candle you've chosen. With the candle before you, focus on the feeling of being crossed, think about all the hardship it's caused, and imagine pulling the oppressive energy into a ball between your hands. Imagine that feeling pouring out of your hands and into the candle or candles. The herbs and your intention will pull it in like a magnet and hold it there. Now light them, and as the candle burns down, the oppressive energy that has been weighing you down will dissipate and burn away.

Simple Egg Cleansing

There are many ways to use an egg to divine whether you've been crossed or to prevent psychic attack, and these are found in many folk traditions across the world often performed by a grandmother

in the kitchen. This is a very simple version that can be used by anyone, but it may be easier to get help with this one.

Pass the egg through incense smoke; I like frankincense, sandalwood, or dragon's blood for this. Next you can cleanse it with a bottle of spring water or water blessed under the Full Moon and pat it dry. Take some deep breaths and get yourself into a calm headspace. Begin to pass the egg over your body, going in a downward direction. Starting at your crown, go down the spine and down to the floor. Repeat, moving counterclockwise around your body, face, arms, legs, chest, groin, and feet, imagining the egg absorbing any energy that is not wanted. Once finished, you can flush the broken egg (without the shell) down the toilet, take it to a public trash can in a brown paper bag, or bury it in the ground.

Energy Cleansing Bath

Even if you only do one of these uncrossing spells, I highly recommend that you follow it up with this easy energy clearing bath. To a warm bath add 1 cup Epsom salt, lavender, chamomile, and lemon slices. You can tie up the lavender and chamomile in a cloth, but an easy Kitchen Witch hack is a lavender chamomile tea bag. If all you can find is a calming tea with lavender, chamomile, and other herbs, look those herbs up—they're probably all good for protection and cleansing, so you can use that. I usually burn some sandalwood or frankincense incense and play energy-clearing music on my device. This is a practice that lifts your spirits and leaves you ready to face life again. No bathtub? You can put the mix in a bottle and pour it over yourself in the shower.

I suggest that once your energy is cleared, you do a good house cleansing and recharge any wards that you have in place. If you don't have magical wards in your home, consider adding a few at this time. There's no need to be fearful of a crossed condition, if it happens, take matters into your own hands and you'll be back on track in no time.

Resources

Bird, Stephanie Rose. *365 Days of Hoodoo: Daily Rootwork, Mojo & Conjuration.* Woodbury, MN: Llewellyn Publications, 2015.

Manning, Al G. *Helping Yourself with White Witchcraft.* Parker Publishing NY, 1972.

Rasbold, Katrina. *Uncrossing: Identify, Cleanse, and Heal from Hexes, Curses, and Psychic Attack.* Woodbury, MN: Llewellyn Publications, 2021.

Magical Cookery

Tudorbeth

As a daughter of generations of master chefs, I was taught the power of food at an early age. The transference of energy from the earth to the food source and then through to us was paramount to our overall health, and the process involved was fundamental in the delivery of that energy. Vegetables were never to be overcooked. Indeed some were eaten almost raw or firm to the bite—as chefs call it, *al dente*. Yet the cooking process was revered and respected as a crucial part of a magical path, one that covered correspondences and the Divine in its application. Magical cookery was the first lesson of the Craft, touching every part of our lives and fundamental to human existence.

First and foremost, our food comes from the earth, whether it is grown in the fields or gardens, grazes on the land, or swims in the oceans. Everything we consume has been kissed by Gaia, the Mother Goddess, our Earth. Celestially, it is also blessed by Father Sun, and these two powerful parents infuse their energy into the food we consume. Therefore, the cookery process becomes paramount in honoring that food without destroying it. Moreover, from the very beginning of human existence, we began to acknowledge this power within the food we consumed. We made connections between the various food groups and the planets, to the times of the year, to days of the week, and so on. Everything is connected to one another, and all flows like one giant circle: the earth, Sun, food, humans, animals, and back to the earth again.

Food Correspondences

Herbs, vegetables, fruit, grains, and fish and meat all have connections to something else. Since ancient times, humans, including Greek philosophers and ancient Egyptian teachers, have grouped foods according to their specific planetary correspondence:

Sun: Orange, pumpkin, lemon
Moon: Pear, lettuce, plaice, lemon sole
Mercury: Raspberry, carrot, shrimp
Venus: Apple, potato, oyster
Mars: Pineapple, hot spices, onion
Jupiter: Blueberry, asparagus, maple syrup
Saturn: Coconut, beetroot, shellfish
Uranus: Rhubarb, bean sprouts, artichokes
Neptune: Melon, mushrooms, haddock
Pluto: Pomegranates, Jerusalem artichokes, cod

This connection between the food we eat and its ability to enhance our mind, body, and spirit was fundamental in the development of specific roles within society, hence the cook becoming a very important person in the household. In addition, as our adventurous spirit took hold and we explored new lands, our tastes widened—the discovery of the cocoa bean, for example, and its magic contained within became a part of universal appeal.

The magic of chocolate and its place within the correspondences of life is just one tiny example. Chocolate is brown or white; it is sweet; it is happiness; it can be used in a spell for positivity; and depending on its color, it can be used on a Monday or Saturday. It can be used in a ritual, predominately an autumn ritual such as Mabon, with apples, which are the traditional fruit of this first festival of the season. The energy contained within chocolate and the power and mystery derived from it compose an echo of its past, and with all foods, the knowledge and reverence of what we are eating is paramount.

The Journey of Food

The journey of food is the journey of our planet as it travels around the Sun, and we need to respect that. We can do that very easily by eating foods that are in season. You would not expect to eat fresh, local spring onions in December or strawberries in February if you lived in the Northern Hemisphere.

This simple act of eating the foods the Mother Goddess gives to us at that time is a sign of respect, and that knowledge and reverence for our food is so important in living the magical life. The Earth gives us foods that we need at that particular time of the year for our health. Think about the autumn harvest and the abundance of food that is readily available. It is there for a reason: Gaia is getting stocked up for the coming winter, and the very molecular structure of these fruits and vegetables will keep us healthy through the cold, damp months. Rosehip syrup and elderberry rob are laden with nutrients that ward off cold and flu, which are prevalent in winter months, while those foods naturally found in

the spring are ideal for making tonics and meals that help to clear out our sluggish winter gut and detox us from the cold months. Spring foods give us the energy and zest to start a new year fresh and cleaned from within.

Cleansing the Magical Kitchen

How many of us find ourselves congregating in the kitchen having a heart-to-heart? This room of a house that for thousands of years contained the living, breathing fire of the family upon which to cook is a source of power. The energy within this room is sacred and flows into the food and meal we cook for our families. For millennia humans have lived, worked, and even slept in this sacred space. Although we no longer need to sleep in the kitchen or by the fire to keep warm on long winter nights, we still adhere to its life-giving energy, and we need to respect the power contained within.

If you are beginning to cook or create spells within the kitchen, always be respectful of the power contained within this room. I always cleanse and consecrate it if I am beginning a specific type of cooking—for example, during the canning season when making jam and chutney.

Before you begin with all your delicious magic, clean and prepare the kitchen area. Mix water, salt, and a handful of rosemary or sage leaves in a spray bottle and spritz the kitchen. As you do, say these words:

Fresh and clean here
Kitchen magic throughout the year

Then go about your magical cooking, manifesting all that energy and intent in every dish you make. I perform this at least four times a year, usually during the changing of seasons or when a particular event is coming up, just to boost the energy in the room and cleanse it from anything magical I've done.

Magical Meals

There are certain meals throughout the year that represent the earth and nature itself. One of the main meals is Thanksgiving, and like the English harvest festival, it is not only a celebration devoted to food in thanks for the year's crops. It also represents family and friends coming together via food.

While Christmas was traditionally twelve days of constant feasts, these meals represented the foods available at that time of year, each with their own symbolism and magic attached to them. From the pumpkin pie to the chestnut stuffing, they are all manifestations of the power of Mother Earth. The spring meals and celebrations during Easter and Ostara are also gifts of Gaia and represent the new life we see around us through the imagery of the Easter eggs, which are incredibly symbolic of our magical past. Eggs contain so much energy, and when added to any meal, they increase the magical power of that dish. Eggs represent fertility, protection, new beginnings, and good luck, so they are wonderful additions to any spell of positivity.

As the Wheel of the Year turns, we embrace the summer, and one of the most important and abundant festivals is Midsummer, when the foods and their powerful magic are plentiful. Cooking with these ingredients somehow ignites the dish with a power of its own. Further, it is also a time of recognizing that magical cookery is not just about the main meal made with these foods but also the accompaniments as well. The appetizers, sides, desserts, and drinks all have manifestations of power within them.

This menu is an example of a powerful and magical Midsummer meal:

Starters: June soup, salmon mayonnaise, lobster salad
Main: Roast chicken with watercress garnish, new potatoes, fresh seasonal vegetables, French beans in butter, vegetable salad, cucumber sandwiches, salmon, fresh coleslaw
Dessert: Eton mess, cherry water ice, beetroot cake
Drinks: Coffee, Midsummer tea, currant water

Cherry Water Ice

Cherry water ice is the embodiment of summer. Red ripe cherries are full of the Sun's power and energy, and their color symbolizes the fire of summer and the energy of love. The ice represents winter, and

Midsummer is the direct opposite of Midwinter. Therefore, in one dish we are recognizing and respecting the turning of the wheel, and although we are ripe with the fullness of love and summer, we are also aware of the coming winter.

Making this dish calls for patience when preparing the cherries. Slice them in half to remove the stone, each half representing half the year: one is summer, and the other half is winter.

You will need:
2 cups cherries
½ cup sugar
4 cups water
1 tablespoon lemon juice

Remove all stones and stalks from the cherries, then pound them or put them in a blender until they are fine. Pour the blended cherry mixture into a pan along with the water and sugar and bring it to a boil. Remove from heat and cool before pouring into a plastic container and freezing for 2 hours. After 2 hours, take out and stir the mixture a couple of times before putting it back in the freezer for another 5 hours. Make it the night before for a special occasion. Serve in little bowls or glasses.

Magical Bread

In all these magical meals throughout the year in whatever culture or religion you adhere to, there is something that accompanies every one, and that is bread. Bread is one of the most staple foods in all cultures from time immemorial. The different styles of bread, including plaited and horn-shaped loaves common at harvest festivals around the world, carry with them the echoes of fertility beliefs from our ancient past. Bread in all cultures has so many beliefs and superstitions surrounding it that it becomes a part of our spiritual psyche. The following are several such superstitions:

- Never cut a loaf from both sides, or you will be unlucky.
- Always refuse the last slice if you are unmarried because otherwise you will remain single.
- Hang a fresh loaf from the ceiling on Maundy Thursday to protect the family from illness.
- Do not eat too much bread, as it will give you a hairy chest.

Bread plays a crucial role in Christianity, representing the body of Christ, and allows believers to connect spiritually with God through the act of transubstantiation. In Christian tradition the "sin-eater" would take responsibility of the sins of someone recently deceased by consuming a glass of milk or ale and a loaf of bread that had been in contact with the dead body. In Witchcraft and many Pagan paths, the symbolic power of bread plays a key part in our Lammas or Lughnasadh festivals.

Lammas bread was cooked with magic and love and given out to friends and family. On Lammas, it was customary to offer not only the first fruits but also a baked product such as bread or biscuits. Demeter is the Greek goddess of the harvest, which we often associate with wheat, oats, and barley. In some parts of the world, it was custom on Lammas to make gingerbread.

Lammas Gingerbread

1 cup plain flour
¼ teaspoon baking soda
1 teaspoon ground ginger
½ cup butter
½ cup brown sugar

Sieve flour, baking soda, and ginger in a bowl. Then rub in the butter and add sugar. Line a shallow baking tin with greaseproof paper and press the mixture into it. Bake in a moderate oven at 350 degrees Fahrenheit for about 30 minutes. Take out the pan and leave it to cool before taking a piece and leaving it as an offering to Demeter or the harvest deity in your tradition on your altar, giving thanks for the harvest and the passing of the year.

Lammas Spell

As you place the gingerbread on your altar for the deity, say these words:

Mother Earth, hear me now.
Thank you for your gifts all year.
Lammas brings first harvest.
First fruits are the best.
I offer the finest bread
To keep the winter fully fed.

Then cut pieces of the gingerbread and give them to friends and family, but always leave one piece for the harvest deity during the festival of Lammas.

Water Magic

Rainbow Magic

Natalie Zaman

My friend Jennifer had rainbow hair. It really suited her. When we were younger, she was a bleach blonde, but the colorful tresses she donned later in life were a true reflection of her personality and path: tarot reader, crystal healer, reiki master. She literally left a trail of light wherever she went. Before Jennifer and I ever met, rainbows were a part of my life: chasing rainbows, gold at the end of the rainbow, somewhere over the rainbow . . . I grew up in the era of Lisa Frank stickers, Robin Williams in rainbow suspenders, and curvy disco lettering in rainbow hues. Jen and I were of an age and shared a love of rainbow nostalgia.

Sadly, Jennifer developed several serious health issues as the years went by. When she passed into Spirit, too soon, she left a Jennifer-size hole—but one that was filled with the brilliance she brought to everything she did. Now she *is* the reiki, and she showed me this, literally. I'm not a happy flier, but the day Jen died, I had to get on a plane. Shortly after takeoff, as we were flying over Newark, I looked out the window . . . and there was a rainbow! Immediately, I thought of Jen—how could I not? The flight path out of Newark Liberty International took us over several bodies of water, and as I watched, the rainbow seemed to widen and blur so that it looked like a person walking next to the plane! I'd never seen anything like that before, and afterward, I wished that I had taken my phone out and taken a photo of it, but I was too absorbed in the moment. I'm sure it was Jennifer. It would be just like her to do something like that. And while that sign let me know that my friend would always be with me, it was bittersweet, as rainbows often are.

I admit I was a bit disappointed when I looked up the root of the word *rainbow*. It derives from the Old English *regnboga*, *regn* meaning "rain," and *boga*, "bent"—not the romantic tie-in I was hoping for. But it does explain the science (and Jen was a fan of science). When light from the Sun enters a raindrop—which is round rather than tear-shaped—it slows down and bends. The water drop acts as a prism, splitting the light into the seven colors of which it's made. But that isn't exactly accurate. Have you ever seen a pale rainbow? Or a double rainbow, where one arc seems a little more pastel-hued than the other? Rainbows are actually made of many more colors than the seven standard. We get glimpses of some of them when the conditions are right. Also, rainbows form circles, not arcs. Most of the time our vantage point only allows us to see a span of colors across the sky. But from a different position—usually higher up—a full circle can be seen (which gives the whole concept of the "rainbow bridge" a more eternal and cyclical slant to its meaning!).

I'm sure the speed at which we were traveling, clouds, shadows, and the amount of moisture and light in the air can explain what I saw from my airplane seat. But just because something can be explained by science does not make it less of a miracle or a message. The ritual crafts and ideas that follow are a small tribute to Jennifer's life and light and to the miracle of the rainbow. It is a symbol that means so much to so many:

- The calm after the storm—indeed, the beauty that is the result of the storm
- The literal incredible lightness of being
- The embodiment of self-esteem and self-worth

Rainbows are the bridges that connect worlds. They are ribbons of inclusivity, slides of joy, and curtains of light. However you chose to invoke the magic of the rainbow, remember that you are the reiki, as we all are.

Rainbow Bridge

We often think of the rainbow bridge as that nebulous yet colorful path our pets take to the next life—one that we'll take one day and be reunited with them. It's a bridge of hope and joyful anticipation, a path of transition and change that brings light to the darkness. Of course, as the saying goes, the only constant in life is change. Building a rainbow bridge may help ease the anxiety of any transition. Use this simple ritual craft to construct a bridge from your present to whatever it is you are waiting for, manifesting, or hoping to achieve.

You will need:

9 smooth stones, 7 of which should be close to the same size. The remaining 2 should be larger, and large enough to write at least 1 word on each with chalk.

Red, orange, yellow, green, blue, indigo, and violet paint (use opaque paint—poster or acrylic paint may work best)

Sealant for the paint, if needed or wanted

Chalk

Clean and clear a space to do this working; the creation of this tool is just as sacred as when you will put it to work! Paint each of the 7 smaller stones in a rainbow color and seal them if needed. Rainbow magic is, at least in part, color magic. As you're painting, visualize each stone taking in the energy of the color you are giving it:

Red: Passion
Orange: Creativity
Yellow: Positivity
Green: Growth and healing
Blue: Peace
Indigo: Mysticism
Violet: Memory

Color symbolism can be very personal and carries different meaning depending on an individual's culture, beliefs, and experiences. The traits listed above are suggestions. Visualize the energy these colors give to you!

When you are ready to do this ritual craft (which can be adapted to suit your needs), clean and clear the space again and ground. You may want to consider building the bridge on your altar or in a place where it will not be disturbed and you can refer to it when you need to.

Write the word *now* on one of the larger stones and place it in front of you on a flat surface. Think about where you are at the present moment. This is hard: try to think of it without judgment or without editorializing it with feelings. Try to see it for what it is.

Next, think about what you want to manifest. See it in your mind as if it already happened. If you can, try feeling as if it already happened. Pay attention to your body—did you relax, sit up, or stand a little straighter? Are you less stressed? Write one word that represents this manifestation on the other stone, and place it on the flat surface, but at a distance from the first stone.

Now build the bridge to connect the present to the manifestation. One at a time, place the rainbow stones in order (red, orange, yellow, green, blue, indigo, and violet), so that they lead from the "present" stone to the "manifestation" stone. As you lay each down, think of the color of the stone and the attribute of that color; each will assist in processing the changes that *must* occur so that you can get from one place to another. For example, red imparts the confidence to move forward boldly. Orange inspires creativity to solve problems. Yellow helps you think positively. Green promotes growth. Blue relieves stress. Indigo reminds you that there are other powers at work that you might not be able to see, protecting and guiding you as you go. And violet reminds you of how far you've come. You can do this work in one session, or it can be built into Moon magic: begin building your rainbow bridge at the New Moon, and set a rainbow stone in place every couple of days (or whenever it feels right to you) over the two weeks leading up to the Full Moon.

Keep the bridge in place until what you want to manifest comes to pass. When you disassemble the bridge, do so with thoughts of gratitude. Cleanse the stones with water and salt and store them until you need to use them again.

Rainbow Rocks

You can paint stones to resemble a rainbow, but there are stones and crystals that have naturally occurring rainbow hues and inclusions. Carry one in your pocket or wear one for an easy-peasy way to have your very own rainbow (and its attendant magic) with you wherever you go.

Stone	Qualities
Opal	Intensifies all with which it comes in contact, promotes creativity and psychic visions
Rainbow Quartz	Cleansing, clears blockages
Rainbow Moonstone	Brings balance, builds confidence
Abalone	Promotes peace and love

Rainbow Obsidian	Absorbs negativity, alleviates pain and stress
Bismuth	Helps achieve goals
Labradorite	Reenergizes, spiritual healing
Ammonite	Protective, relieves trauma

Magic for a Rainy Day

You never know where a rainbow will turn up. Most of the time, they're a pleasant surprise—the "sign" you've been looking for. Sometimes the best kind of magic or ritual happens serendipitously. When the rain starts to fall, keep these ideas in mind to make some magic on a moment's notice:

- Do your magical working, manifestation, meditation, or affirmation during a storm and then under or in sight of a rainbow to imbibe its power.
- Cleanse stones and tools (when appropriate) in the rain, and then charge them with rainbow light, which will bring both light and color energy to whatever you lay in its sight or path. You don't necessarily need a rain-rainbow for rainbow light. Ever look through a window only to see a rainbow "shadow" beaming through? Use this light for charging!
- If practical and safe to do so, find the end of a rainbow. This is a magical experience, even if it's just something you can see. The first time I saw the end of a rainbow, I was driving down a two-lane highway, and the rainbow fell like a curtain in the two lanes next to the ones I was driving in. Imagine driving through such a gateway!

Rainbow Ritual Tent

As discussed previously, part of rainbow magic is color magic, and while each individual color is important, it's equally important to remember that—especially as a rainbow—they are connected and work together; bands overlap and each one effects all the others. Working under or in the presence of a rainbow brings its energy to whatever you are doing. A rainbow ritual tent will create a space where you can always work "under the rainbow" and utilize all of its benefits.

When you create this ritual tent, remember you are creating sacred space. Again, clean and clear a space and ground before you being crafting. Just as with the components of the rainbow bridge, the tent is a tool for which the making is as meaningful as its use.

You will need:

Full-sized Hula-Hoop (You need a large and sturdy ring—if you don't have a Hula-Hoop handy, try using recycled wire clothes hangers to form one.)

70–80-inch-long strips of fabric (sari fabric works beautifully if you have access to it!), ribbon, or yarn in red, orange, yellow, green, blue, indigo, and violet. You want equal amounts of each color to cover the entire hula hoop.

24-inch strips of fabric in red, orange, yellow, green, blue, indigo, and violet. These strips will be used for hanging the tent and will need to be weight bearing. If the material you've used is light in weight, you may want to double up on it or use a different material.

Beads or small bells (optional)

To make the tent, tie your material of choice around the ring with a knot at the top. Start with red, and then change to the orange, yellow, green, blue, indigo, and violet, repeating until the ring is filled. The bulk of the material should hang down, and your knotting should create a "fringe" around the hoop. Take your time and try to keep the fringe length as well as the longer lengths of material that hang down even. (You can always trim both the fringe at the top and the length at the bottom if needed.) Don't pack the ring too tightly, as you'll need space for the material you'll use to create the hanging apparatus.

Position the 24-inch strips of material around the ring. You can use one of each color or several to give the tent a more "pavilion" look at the top. Tie each strip to the ring, using the same method: one end will add to the fringe around the ring while leaving as much length as possible on the other. When all the colors are incorporated, bring the longer free ends together, adjusting the length of the individual strands so that the tent hangs evenly. Knot the strands together—your tent is now ready to hang!

Depending on the materials you've used, your tent can be used both indoors and outdoors (in good weather!). If you have beads and bells, select random strips of material and tie them to the longer ends. This will weigh some of the strips down a bit and control movement if you use the tent in a breezy spot.

Your rainbow ritual tent can be used as a single-person meditation space or as a canopy over a larger area. The strips of fabric can be spread out or tied up to accommodate a small gathering. Once in place, add beach blankets or towels and pillows to soften up seating and create a comfortable and welcoming space. Visit the tent to recharge and ground, to divine, or as ritual space.

May you always see a rainbow when you need to—and even when you don't!

Resources

Evers, Jennie. "Rainbow: A Rainbow Is a Multicolored Arc Made by Light Striking Water Droplets." National Geographic Resource Library. May 20, 2022. https://education.nationalgeographic.org/resource/rainbow.

Melody. *Love Is in the Earth: A Kaleidoscope of Crystals: The Reference Book Describing the Metaphysical Properties of the Mineral Kingdom.* Wheat Ridge, CO: Earth-Love Publishing House, 1995.

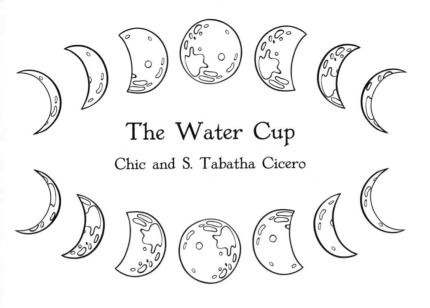

The Water Cup

Chic and S. Tabatha Cicero

Magicians and philosophers of the ancient world gifted us with the knowledge of the four magical elements: fire, water, air, and earth. These elements are not simply the physical substances that have the same names. Instead, they are regarded as realms, kingdoms, or divisions of nature. They are the basic categories of existence and modes of action, the building blocks of everything in the universe.

The magical element of water is much more than its physical counterpart of liquid matter composed of hydrogen and oxygen molecules. In magic, water is the essence of the Divine Feminine as well as the great unfathomable and mysterious well of wisdom contained within the subconscious mind. In short, water symbolizes the infinite realm of possibilities, which precede all forms and all creation. It is limitless and immortal—the waters of creation. Water represents receptiveness, responsiveness, creativity, fluidity, fertility, sustenance, nourishment, transmutation, regeneration, and reproduction. Water governs pleasure, social interactions, emotions, and all liquid physical matter. The direction attributed to water is west.

This transformative element has long been essential in magic, although the vessel that contains it has taken many shapes and forms.

The cleansing nature of water makes it the perfect symbol for ritual purification. In the ancient world, vessels used to contain the sacred purifying water took many forms: vases, bowls, cups, seashells, and even cupped hands. The Mesopotamians used a type of short-necked, round-bodied vase called the *hegallu*, meaning "abundance," as a symbol of fertility and bounty. Egyptian priests and priestesses took ritual baths before performing religious rites; they stood in shallow basins as water was poured over their heads from a vessel called a *nemset* jar, which was associated with the breath of the goddess Isis.

In the Eleusinian Mysteries of ancient Greece, an officer called the *Hydranos,* also called the "Purifier of the Mysteries," ritually cleansed the initiates by sprinkling them with water or by pouring water on them from a bowl. This practice would later evolve into the Christian rite of baptism.

Another implement associated with water was the cauldron. In ancient times the cauldron served as an essential piece of equipment in Celtic households and was a source of nourishment. Cauldrons were also used for washing, bathing, and other chores. Over time it became a magical symbol of transformation and regeneration.

The cauldron has long been used as a symbol of the Goddess in Pagan practice. Celtic mythology is full of accounts of deities who possessed magical cauldrons. The cauldron of the Dagda (the Irish Good God or All-Father) was one of the four treasures of the Tuatha Dé Danann, a race of supernatural beings in Irish mythology. This cauldron was named *Undry* and was said to be bottomless, providing an endless supply of food for any number of people. The sea god Manannán mac Lir was said to own a cauldron of regeneration. The Welsh goddess Cerridwen possessed a cauldron that she used to brew a potion that bestowed wisdom and inspiration. In one legend the goddess gives the mighty warrior god Bran the Blessed a cauldron with the magical power to resurrect dead warriors. The cauldron of Dyrnwch the Giant (the cauldron of Tyrnog), considered one of the thirteen treasures of Britain, had the power to discriminate between cowards and heroes. And finally the Welsh poem "Preiddeu Annwn" from the fourteenth-century *Book of Taliesin* describes King Arthur's quest for a magical cauldron rimmed with pearls and warmed by the breath of nine maidens. The legend of the Holy Grail, the Sacred Cup of the Last Supper used to collect the blood of Christ after the crucifixion and said to have miraculous powers of regeneration, is likely descended from these narratives.

A LITTLE BIT
OF MAGIC

We were once asked to fix a broken glass Water Cup owned by Israel Regardie. A small group of us worked slowly to reconstruct it, gluing the pieces back together, like archaeologists working on a piece of ancient pottery!

During the nineteenth century occult revival, the tarot suit of cups became associated with *Briah*, the creative, archangelic world of the Qabalists, as well as *Heh*, the second letter of the holy and unfathomable name of God known as the Tetragrammaton (YHVH), a letter also associated with water and the Divine Feminine.

In Wicca and Witchcraft, the cup or chalice is an essential symbol of the female principle, the Great Mother, receptivity, and the element of water. It is also used to hold wine that is ritually blessed and passed around the circle.

The Golden Dawn system of magic calls for at least three cups that are used in ritual: (1) the Cup of the Stolistes used to purify the temple, (2) the Chalice of Wine used in the Mystic Repast, and (3) the Water Cup of the Adept, which is covered in symbols and used to represent the element of water in all magical workings involving the four elements.

The Fire Wand, Water Cup, Air Dagger, and Earth Pentacle compose the Four Elemental Tools (sometimes called the Elemental Weapons) of the Golden Dawn Adept. They represent the tarot symbols of the Divine Name YHVH and have a strong bond between them. Even if you intend to use only one of these four tools, the others should always be present in order to reflect the holistic nature of the Divine Universe.

According to Golden Dawn tradition, the Water Cup could be adapted from any convenient smooth glass cup with a bowl shaped somewhat like a crocus or lotus flower. Magicians often created

them by pasting eight petals constructed out of paper around the bowl of the cup. The resulting design resembled cups shown in the art of the ancient Egyptians. The petals were painted in bright blue and edged with orange. Divine Hebrew names and sigils, along with the magician's name, were painted on the petals in orange before it was consecrated.

A Personalized Water Cup

The Water Cup is one implement that you can create from any store-bought cup or chalice. Since it will be your *personalized* magical tool, it can be any style of vessel that you choose—a wine chalice or goblet, stemmed or stemless. It can be tall and elegant like a wineglass or short and stout like a brandy snifter. Some traditions may even prefer that it be in the form of a tankard or a shallow bowl. Most importantly, the implement needs to *speak* to your personal conception of watery energy.

In the early Golden Dawn days, it was common for initiates to make their Water Cups out of any convenient glass cup as indicated in the order's documents. However, we've seen far too many glass cups, painstakingly covered in symbols, be dropped and broken, shattered to bits. We much prefer that students use a more durable cup made from wood or metal.

Keep in mind that water is one of the strongest forces on earth; it can wear down mountains and cut rivers into valleys. Water accidentally left overnight in a wooden Water Cup can crack it. Also, wooden Water Cups are sometimes painted inside as well as outside, and water can get underneath the paint and ruin the finish. So if you intend to put water in your Water Cup, use a metal cup.

"Why would you not use water in the Water Cup?" you might ask. Well, why would you not put your Fire Wand in the fire? These implements are intended to represent the subtle forces and divine powers behind the elements. So, while there is an affinity and correspondence between the candle flame and the Fire Wand, it is not necessary to physically join them together. The same is true for the Water Cup, which is why Golden Dawn magicians often use a separate cup, the Cup of the Stolistes, to hold consecrated water for preliminary purifications, while the Water Cup is used to embody the Divine Powers that rule over water.

After you choose an appropriate cup, determine what type of paint you need to use. For a wooden cup, a water-based acrylic is best. If you want to add Golden Dawn–style lotus petals, cut them out of a supple piece of leather and glue them to the cup with a strong white craft glue. After the glued petals have had time to dry, add a couple coats of white acrylic primer.

If your cup is metal, you may need to apply an oil-based primer before you add your water-based paint, because it is hard for latex paint to hold on to a metal surface. An oil-based spray-paint primer works well for this and protects against rust and chipping. Then apply your water-based acyclic paint.

Next, determine what symbolism you would like to add to your cup. If you want to follow Golden Dawn teachings, you can make a traditional Water Cup as described in Israel Regardie's book *The Golden Dawn*. Or you can add water symbolism that speaks to you personally, making for a more unique magical implement. The following table provides a list of names, symbols, and materials that you can draw upon for this purpose.

Correspondences of Water	
Godname of Water	El, "God"
Archangel of Water	Gabriel
Angel of Water	Taliahad
Ruler of Water	Tharsis
Zodiac Signs	Cancer, Scorpio, Pisces
Tarot Cards	The Hanged Man (with the Chariot, Death, and the Moon for the Signs)
Hebrew Letters	*Heh* (as a group) with *Cheth*, *Nun*, and *Qoph* for the Signs
Planets	Jupiter, Mercury, Luna
Colors of the Signs	Cancer: yellow-orange; Scorpio: blue-green; Pisces: red-violet
Angel of Water Signs	Chankel
Sephiroth	Binah, Chesed, Hod
Deities of Water	Abzu, Enki, Enilulu, Nammu, Anuket, Hapi, Khnum, Nephthys, Nu, Satet, Sobek, Tefnut, Poseidon, Neptune, Llyr, Oceanus, Amphitrite, Galatea, Thetis, Triton, Danu, Manannán mac Lir, Njord, Freya
Animals	Fish, dolphins, eagle, crab, scorpion, starfish
Symbols	Inverted triangle, pyramid, cup, cauldron, rain-drops, waved lines, curvy lines, swirls, seashells, mermaid
Metals	Copper, silver
Woods	Birch, willow, poplar, elm, rowan, sandalwood, tamarisk
Gemstones	Pearl, aquamarine, agate, beryl, coral, moon-stone, sapphire, azurite, jade, mother-of-pearl, lapis lazuli, blue calcite, tourmaline, selenite, sodalite, sugilite, celestite, chalcedony
Fabrics	Silk, satin, taffeta

Choose whatever symbols and names of power you want to adorn your Water Cup. You may paint the bulk of the cup blue, since that is the primary color associated with water. You can also paint some of the added symbolism in orange, since orange is the "flashing" or complementary color to blue. Alternative colors associated with water include silver, silver-white, sea green, and gray.

For a cup that includes the astrological water triplicity, you can include petals painted in the colors of Cancer (a yellow-orange background with the symbol of the sign in flashing blue-violet), Scorpio (a blue-green petal with the symbol in flashing red-orange), and Pisces (a red-violet petal ornamented with flashing yellow-green symbol). You may wish to add the name of the angel *Chankel,* which comes from the Hebrew letters associated with the three water signs (*Cheh, Nun,* and *Qoph*) with the divine suffix *-el,* indicating the angel is "of God."

Water is the element of creativity and inspiration, so feel free to add whatever colors and symbols inspire you. Add your magical name to establish an etheric connection between you and your cup.

Finish the painted portions of the cup by spraying on a couple coats of non-yellowing acrylic lacquer, taking care to cover any gemstones or delicate symbolism with painter's tape if desired. Once the finish coat is completely dry, gently remove the tape. If you don't want to use lacquer, brush on a couple of coats of clear-drying acrylic gloss gel medium. When the Water Cup is finished, it is ready to be consecrated.

Simple Consecration Ritual for Your Water Cup

Prepare your sacred space for ritual work. If you don't have a dedicated temple space that faces east, not to worry! Any tabletop, desktop, or dresser top can be cleared and transformed into a temporary altar for consecrating your Water Cup. Cover your altar with a blue cloth to resonate with the energies of water. Since orange is the flashing color complement to blue, your work will be enhanced by placing a circle of orange twine, cord, or ribbon at the center of the blue altar-cloth. Have ready a lighter and an incense stick that corresponds to water, such as sandalwood, myrrh, or jasmine. Place a blue candle outside and to the right of the orange circle, on the side farthest away from you at the upper right of the altar top. (An LED candle can be used if safety concerns are an issue.) Place a plain silver chalice (or bowl) half-filled with water outside and to the left of the orange circle, balancing the candle at the upper left of the altar top. Keep a blue linen or silk bag nearby for wrapping your cup. Place your new Water Cup in the center of the orange circle.

Mentally and psychically prepare yourself by sitting or standing at the altar (your choice) at the outset of the ceremony. Start with slow, focused rhythmic breathing to relax the mind and let any stress or physical tension evaporate. Inhale slowly to the count of one, then exhale slowly to the count of two. This will lead your awareness inward and strengthen your connection with the energies of the Divine.

Take a short pause and then begin a course of breathing known in yoga as *Ujjayi,* meaning "victorious breath." This form of pranayama breath control is also called "Ocean Breath" due to the sound it makes. (Some have also said it sounds a bit like Darth Vader from Star Wars!) Inhale deeply through both nostrils until your lungs are full of air. Hold your breath for a second or two, then exhale slowly through your nose while constricting the muscles in the back of your throat. You should feel the exhalation on the roof of your mouth, and it will sound like ocean waves crashing onto the shore. Repeat this breath about twenty times, then relax and let your breathing return to normal.

Stand before the altar and light the incense. Begin to vibrate or intone the Western equivalent to the Eastern mantra *OM,* which is "IAO," pronounced ee-ah-oh in slow, long syllables. It refers to a triad of Egyptian deities (Isis, Apophis, and Osiris) who represent the cycle of life, death, and rebirth. As you vibrate the name, visualize the figure of an inverted triangle, the traditional Western symbol of water, in blue with its apex pointed downward (toward you).

> **A LITTLE BIT OF MAGIC**
>
> The phrase "Elemental Weapons" hearkens back to when a main duty of a magician was to perform apotropaic magic. However, "weapons" does not present an accurate picture of how they are used in Golden Dawn tradition.

Take up the plain silver cup or bowl of water and use it to trace the lines of this triangle clockwise directly over your Water Cup starting from the bottom point, moving clockwise. While tracing the first line, inhale deeply then slowly vibrate "eee." When tracing the second line, intone "aahh." Trace the third line and vibrate "oohh." Trace the triangle and intone the name five times for the number of Spirit. After this, gently dip your index figure in

the water and trace the triangle on the side of the Water Cup that faces you. There is no need to soak the cup! Use just a little water that will evaporate quickly and not hurt the cup's finish.

Hold the plain silver cup or bowl of water above the Water Cup and say,

The heaven is above and the earth is beneath. And between the Light and the Darkness, the energies vibrate. I call upon the Divine Source of All, by the Majesty of the Divine and fiery Name of Power EL, the Archangel of Water GABRIEL, the Angel TALIAHAD, the Triad Angel CHANKEL, and the ruler THARSIS to bestow this present day and hour, and confirm their mystic and potent influence upon this Water Cup, which I hereby dedicate to purity and occult work, and may its grasp strengthen me in the work of the Magic of Light! May it aid me in all things that require wisdom, creativity, regeneration, receptivity, subconscious inspiration, and fluidic energy!

Visualize a glory of light surrounding your Water Cup, consecrating it with divine light and the waters of creation. Take some time to dedicate your Water Cup to any personal deity who embodies the sacredness of water. Allow as much time as you need before thanking any gods, goddesses, or angels invoked. When finished, wrap your consecrated Water Cup in the blue cloth. Finally, extinguish the candle and end the ceremony.

The time and energy that you spend crafting your Water Cup will serve you well. A skillfully designed cup will become a focus for your inner creativity as well as a catalyst for developing your psychic faculties and awareness. It will become a wellspring for divine inspiration and wisdom. For water is the mirror of nature.

Resources

Cicero, Chic, and Sandra Tabatha Cicero. *The Babylonian Tarot.* Woodbury MN: Llewellyn Publications, 2006.

Forrest, Isidora. *Isis Magic: Cultivating a Relationship with the Goddess of 10,000 Names.* Portland, OR: Abiegnus House, 2013.

Greer, John Michael. *The New Encyclopedia of the Occult.* St. Paul, MN: Llewellyn Publications, 2003.

Regardie, Israel. *The Golden Dawn.* 7th Ed. Woodbury MN: Llewellyn Publications, 2015.

_____. *How to Make and Use Talismans.* London: The Aquarian Press, 1972.

Magical Infusions

Suzanne Ress

An infusion results when herbs, barks, flowers, fruits, and other ingredients are steeped, leaving their essences in hot or cold liquid, which can then be used either by ingestion or as an external splash, a bath, a tonic, and so on. Some herbal teas are considered infusions, as long as they do not contain tea leaves. In general, infusions need more steeping time than herbal teas: they may sometimes take days or even months to make. What makes an infusion magical is the combination of ingredients and the maker's intent, plus the ritual to charge it.

Infusions can be philters, which are any potion with magical power. Infusions can also be potions, but only if they are intended to be drunk. If an infusion is not intended for drinking, don't drink it.

We'll begin with the basics on the best ingredients for magical infusions and walk through the creation of ten infusions for different intentions.

Infusion Ingredients

These ingredients are common and accessible, offering a variety of approaches to personalized potion-making:

- Herbs, fresh or dried
- Flowers, fresh or dried
- Spices, salt, sugar
- Roots (garlic, ginger, turmeric, onion, horseradish)
- Berries, fresh or dried
- Nuts, green or mature
- Tree bark (cinnamon, willow, birch, sumac)
- Metal objects: nail, coin, chain, ring
- Insects, dead only
- Seeds and seed pods

- Fingernails, hairs, fur, feathers, leather, bone
- Rocks, stones, shells, crystals
- Air (breath, smoke, wind, salt air, forest air, night air, petrichor)
- Mushrooms, fresh or dried

Water

Tap water and bottled water are best avoided, as are any dubious-looking waters that contain scum or algae. For any infusion that is intended to be imbibed, the water should be allowed to settle, so that impurities sink to the bottom, and then purified by boiling for one full minute. Usually, the purification process is part of the charging ritual. Don't use water purification tablets, as these add chemicals that will change the composition of your water.

Seawater is great for infusions, especially ones that will not be drunk. Just make sure to use it fresh.

Any water, from any source, that you collect should be in a clear glass jar, preferably a heatproof mason jar with a lid. Recommended waters include rainwater (storm, soft, downpour), frozen

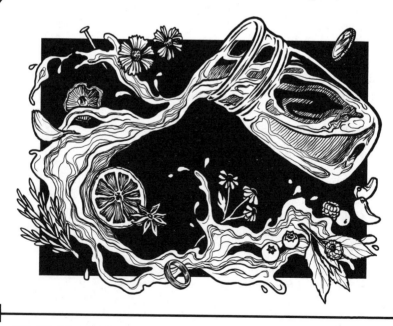

water (snow or ice, melted), groundwater (spring or well), running water (stream, river, brook), still water (pond, lake, puddle), and salt water (ocean or sea).

Oils

Purchase oils for infusions in small amounts, as many, especially nut and seed oils, will not remain fresh for very long. Once they lose their freshness, they take on a rancid odor that will ruin your infusion. When choosing an oil for an infusion, take into account the odor of the oil itself and try to stay away from oils with very strong odors, like coconut, unless its smell blends harmoniously with your other ingredients. Olive oil is the most versatile, and has a long shelf life. Use a good-quality virgin olive oil with a mild scent. Shea is also a good choice but much more costly. Steer away from mass-produced corn, peanut, and vegetable oils, and any oil in a plastic bottle.

Recommended oils include olive, jojoba, almond, walnut, hazelnut, avocado, coconut, shea, sesame, and sunflower.

Alcohol

If you are mainly interested in the scents, flavors, and powers of the other ingredients, use a neutral base, like grain alcohol, vodka, or gin for your potion. If you desire a magical philter that is milder and more drinkable, use wine, port, brandy, and the like.

Recommended alcohols include grain alcohol (96 percent), vodka, gin, wine, port, and brandy.

Honey

There are hundreds of different wildflower and monofloral honeys available. The best ones for magical infusions will be light in color, liquid, and clear, such as these: clover, acacia, tupelo, light wildflower, and orange blossom. One of the benefits of making a magical infusion with honey is that it will last a long time without needing refrigeration.

Vinegars

Depending on what you are infusing, you can use any of these: apple cider vinegar, red wine vinegar, white wine vinegar, rice vinegar, and balsamic vinegar (seldom). Balsamic vinegar can be used only in certain very potent infusions.

Other Liquids

If you choose to employ milk or cream from animals or plants, it must be made fresh and used up quickly.

Charging

When ready to charge your magical infusions, consider using any of the following, or a combination thereof: time, sunlight, moonlight, darkness, earth, fire, and water.

Magical Infusion Recipes

Magic Philter to Strengthen a Bond (for Lovers)

On the afternoon of the Full Moon in June collect 2 cups of fresh spring water in a glass mason jar. Gather the following ingredients:

2 handfuls fresh red or pink rose petals
8 lavender blossoms
8 fresh cherries, stemmed and pitted
2 whole cloves
2 fresh basil leaves
1-inch piece fresh angelica root, sliced vertically into 2 pieces
Red candle

Heat the fresh spring water in a nonreactive metal, Pyrex, or enamel pan over a fire (this can be a gas stove fire). Stand before the heating water and focus on it, picturing two lovers together, holding and caressing each other. As the water heats, so should the passion between the lovers in your mind's eye. Let the water reach a full boil, and boil it for 1 full minute, then take it off the fire. Place the fresh flowers and petals, fruit, leaves, and spices into the glass mason jar you collected the water in, thinking of each item as

a different kind of kiss or caress as you put it in. Close the jar's lid, and leave the philter to infuse and cool for 2 hours.

Light a red candle at moonrise. Strain the philter. The lovers should each be served a goblet of this infusion with 1 teaspoon of honey added. Make a toast to the love bond while gazing into each other's eyes over the flame of the red candle.

Infusion to Bathe in for Wealth
1 teaspoon crushed dried mint leaves
½ cup whole fresh basil leaves
1-inch piece fresh ginger root, peeled and chopped
⅓ cup olive oil
1 tablespoon shea oil
Green candle
Shiny coins (or metal or chocolate coins wrapped in gold foil)

On the night of a New Moon, place the herbs and ginger root into a glass jar. Pour the oils over all, pressing the leaves down with a silver spoon so that everything is covered. Close the jar and wrap it in a green cloth; a bandanna will serve.

After 2 weeks, in the evening, draw yourself a bath. Strain the herbs from the infused oil and add it to the bathwater. Light a green candle on a heatproof dish, and surround the candle with shiny coins. Get into the bath and visualize yourself bathing in money. Do not use soap. Stay there soaking until the water grows tepid or cool, then step out of the bath and stand in the candlelight while you air dry.

Household Protection Infusion
Obtain a glass mason jar of sea or ocean water on a sunny morning. Add the following to it, one at a time:

1 sprig sea lavender
1 bay leaf
1 clove garlic, peeled
1 purple-toned shell

Close the jar and leave it in the sunshine to infuse for the rest of the day. Once the Sun has set, walk around outside the house with the jar, and, using your right hand, douse all corners of the house, in front of the doors, and at the foot of any steps.

Special Vinegar for Longevity

Obtain 3 cups (750 ml) of a good-quality red wine vinegar. On a sunny day in late spring and wearing a straw hat or a sun bonnet, stroll around your herb garden with a pair of silver snippers or a white-handled knife. Carry a basket on your arm or a paper sack, and walk slowly, enjoying the birdsong and the flittering pollinators. Carefully cut a few sprigs each of the following herbs, and put them gently into the basket:

Rue
Sage
Mint
Wormwood
Rosemary
Lavender flowers
Old man

Obtain a pretty clear or colored glass vinegar bottle, liter- or quart-size. Tear the herb sprigs into smaller, but not very small, pieces, and stuff them into the bottle, one by one, pushing them down with the fingers of your right hand if necessary. As you do this, imagine yourself to be very much older than you are, and very spry. Then add these:

1-inch piece cinnamon bark
Small piece of a whole nutmeg
4 whole cloves
1 peeled garlic clove

Using a funnel, carefully pour in the red wine vinegar. Close the bottle with a cork, and put it in a cool, dark place to infuse for three

months. When the infusion is ready, use it regularly on salads and vegetables and even sparingly in meat dishes.

Infused Honey for Prophetic Dreams

1 palmful of dried tiny rosebuds
1 teaspoon dried lemon thyme
1 tablespoon dried chamomile flowers
½ teaspoon dried diced angelica root
1 pound good-quality clear light liquid honey

On the night of the New Moon, go to a quiet and lonely place and gently stir the flowers and herbs into the honey using a tiny silver spoon (like one you would use to feed a baby). Close the honey into a glass jar and leave it in a cool, dark, undisturbed place for 1 month. After the allotted infusing time, this magical honey may be used, 1 teaspoon at a time, stirred into a cup of freshly brewed chamomile tea, to be drunk before retiring.

Walnut Liqueur for Psychic Power at Yule

4 whole green walnuts, in their hulls
4 small leaf sprigs fresh horehound
2 cups grain alcohol
1½ cups fresh spring water
1½ cups light honey or sugar

On St. John's Day, June 24, go to where walnut trees grow and pluck four fresh green hulls with unripe nuts from a low branch. From your herb garden or elsewhere, use a white-handled or other magically charged knife to cut four small leaf sprigs of fresh horehound. Using a large kitchen knife, cut each green walnut into 3 pieces, and put them into a large glass mason jar. Add the horehound. Pour the alcohol overall and screw on the lid. Put the jar away into a dark, cool pantry for 3 months, and leave it undisturbed. The alcohol will turn green, then nearly black.

Just after the autumn equinox, make up a syrup. Mix the spring water with the light honey or sugar in a nonreactive metal, Pyrex, or ceramic pan. Bring it slowly to a boil over a fire, stirring and watching it. Do not let it boil, but just before it does, and as soon as you see that the sugar or honey has completely dissolved, take it off the fire. Let it cool to room temperature.

Strain the walnuts and horehound out of the alcohol. Blend together the syrup and the alcohol, and use a funnel to pour it into an attractive glass bottle. Close with a cork, and put it away in a dark cool place until Yule. This liqueur should be savored at the end of a holiday meal, in small amounts and in good company.

Birch Bark Infusion for Fertility

This will be most effective in autumn, between Mabon and Yule.

Obtain 2 cups of clean rainwater from a heavy downpour, in a large glass mason jar. Bring the water to a boil in a nonreactive pan on a fire. Stand and watch the water until it boils, and let it boil for 1 full minute, visualizing it as the same water that recently poured down heavily from the sky to hydrate the earth and all living things. Take it off the fire and add the following:

1-inch square piece cleaned birch bark
1 dried fig
10 fresh pomegranate seeds

Cover the jar and let it steep for 10 minutes, then strain. Drink ½ cup each morning for 4 mornings. Store in the refrigerator between uses.

Milky White Healing Infusion

Obtain a small bunch of dried yerba santa or borage tied with a white string or ribbon, and use this to smoke cleanse the area where you will prepare the infusion. While it is still smoking, place the bundle on a heatproof dish in such a way that the smoke will drift over your infusion as it's being made.

You will need 1 cup whole raw cow's or goat's milk or any freshly made nondairy milk. Heat it gently in a glass pitcher set into a bath of simmering water, over a fire. Allow it to get quite warm, but not to simmer or boil. Take it off the fire. Into a large white or blue ceramic mug put ¼ cup crushed fresh raspberries. Pour the warmed milk over. Stir in 1 teaspoon clear light honey, and add a sprinkle of ground cinnamon. Light a white candle, and look into its flame as you slowly drink the infusion. Visualize yourself glowing with vibrant good health and wellness.

Hex-Breaking Bath Infusion

On a rainy day when the Moon is waxing, preferably between Midsummer and Yule, collect a mason jar full of rain, and leave it outside, uncovered, on the night of the Full Moon.

Late in the day, after the night of the Full Moon, prepare the bath oil infusion. Into a red glass bottle put the following:

1 dried hot pepper
6 black peppercorns
2 peeled garlic cloves
Piece of broken chain
1 tablespoon jojoba oil

Funnel the charged rainwater into the bottle, place the bottle into a brown paper lunch bag, and leave it to infuse for 3 days in a dark, cool place. After 3 days have elapsed, remove the bottle from the bag, but keep the bag for further use. Then using a funnel, add the jojoba oil. Shake well.

Draw your bath. Light 1 small black votive candle in a fireproof dish near your bath. Strain the entire infusion into your bathwater, reserving the peppers, garlic, and chain rolled up tightly in the brown lunch bag. Soak in the bath until the candle burns out.

The next day, dig a hole far from your home, and bury the lunch bag packet containing the peppers, garlic, and chain.

Potion to Mend Discord

Sometimes friends or relatives get blocked into a state of inexplicable discord. To remedy this sort of blockage, try this infusion.

Using an electric coffee grinder, grind up a tiny piece of cinnamon bark with the thoroughly clean fingernail and toenail clippings from one of the people stuck in the blockage.

Obtain a quart of quickly moving brook water in a large glass mason jar. Let the water sit for several hours so that dirt, sand, and grit will settle at the bottom.

Play some happy music that appeals to you, something that makes you feel that all is right with the world. While this music is playing, carefully pour the water (leaving behind any sediment) into a non-reactive metal, Pyrex, or ceramic pan, and set it on the fire. Watch it as it comes to a boil and think harmonious thoughts. Let it boil 1 full minute, then take it off the fire and put it aside to cool.

At an opportune time, use this water (boiled a second time) in a French-press coffee maker to brew a pot of coffee. To the coffee grounds, add the ground fingernails and toenails and the cinnamon.

When the coffee is ready, a cup of it should be served to each of the two involved in the blockage, with their consent. Offer cream and sugar if desired. This infusion can be repeated several times, until all discord melts magically away.

Pathworking into the Shadow

Sasha Graham

The active imagination of a Witch is one of her greatest tools. It is as boundless as the universe itself. We honor our power by honing magical skills and gifts. It doesn't matter what outer circumstances look like. We may be held down and repressed and have the odds stacked against us. A Witch is always free to make magic because it exists inside of her.

Witches walk between worlds. It is what we do. Baby Witches are born into the kaleidoscopic mystery of life. We cultivate a unique path as we tend to the unique talents embroidered into the fabric of the soul. The work of Witchcraft calls for us to navigate the external world as well as the inner sanctum of the self, psyche, and body as a humming conduit of power. This is what stokes our supernatural essence.

Shadow work is powerful energy. It requires deep soul diving into mysterious valleys miles beneath the surface of the psyche. Imagine sinking into the depths to discover a valley of plateaus, caves, and tidal currents. Deep inside these caves, you discover where you have stored away all sorts of forgotten, hidden things.

If you could gaze at stored hopes, dreams, and desires, locked away, what would you see? Would you observe yourself being loved, cherished, and adored before you or someone else told you you didn't deserve it? Would you see yourself dancing before you decided you weren't good enough? Can you find yourself radiating incandescent power before it was beaten out of you?

The Shadow is the storehouse where we place anything we don't want to acknowledge about the self. This includes bad behavior we'd rather ignore and justify. Shadow work is not about throwing the world into chaos. It does not advocate a bacchanalian "anything goes" attitude. It is a careful examination of what is repressed inside the self. The Shadow contains good qualities, repressed talents, and potentials. Shadow work rips away the veil blocking us from seeing and honoring the true self.

The occult axiom "As above, so below" states what is true for the world is true for you. What is true for you is true for the world. Understand this on a simple level by recalling how joyful the world feels when you are feeling full of happiness and contentment. By contrast, the world is dismal and depressing when you are in a state of duress and pain.

The Rider-Waite-Smith tarot Magician gives us a visual cue to this remarkable truth. The Magician points one finger toward the sky (above) and channels energy into earth (below). Would evil people feel the need to harm others if they felt a deep sense of happiness? What we feel on the inside is what we project on the outside. No act is insignificant. We heal the world when we heal ourselves. This is the heart of Shadow work.

Tarot's Devil card is the foreboding gatekeeper who traps your power under lock and key. The Devil card's power comes from the inner need to control the self and others. The more a person is out of alignment with the authentic self (symbolized by the High Priestess card) the stronger the Devil's power becomes. Pathworking into this card will release bonds you have involuntarily placed on the self.

Pathworking into the Shadow with tarot helps release this power. It transforms energy you've been using against yourself and others. Outrage dissolves into pleasure, negative relationships drift away, a sense of peace is cultivated, and the world is transformed.

Pathworking is a specific operation created by late-nineteenth-century occultists inside the Hermetic Order of the Golden Dawn and the group's offshoots. It is the process of mentally and astrally projecting oneself around the Kabalistic Tree of Life using tarot and the active imagination.

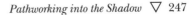

The Tree of Life is a mystical diagram expressing the way in which a thing, impulse, or intelligence moves from the invisible world to manifest in the visible world. Nineteenth-century occultists placed tarot snuggly on top of the Tree of Life because its structure aligns perfectly with the different parts of the tree. *Pathworking* is a term specifically used to navigate the Tree of Life's paths and will guide the Witch from point A to point B. The Devil card rests on path 26 inside the tree. The path extends between a point called Splendor (*Hod*) and a point called Beauty (*Tiphereth*) when working up the tree to gain spiritual insight.

The terms *active imagination* and *shadow self* were both coined by Swiss psychologist Carl Jung. He defined the Shadow as the deep place where known yet repressed ideas, desires, and impulses are stored away inside the psyche. He described the active imagination as what is used when an object like a mandala or tarot card is selected and focused on. The practitioner follows this focal point to discover where it goes. The practitioner, at a certain point, does not control what is observed but participates in an experience. Doing so, they recover lost pieces of themselves and gather information and insight. The same process occurs during guided meditation, which should not to be confused with mindful meditation. Mindful meditation focuses on observing the nature and clearing the mind. Each process uses the active imagination, but a guided meditation is a fluid experience. It is led by another person or set up in advance by the solo practitioner.

Prepare for pathworking into the Shadow by reading the process a few times and answering these Shadow journaling questions:

- The current thing that bothers me most and makes me angry about someone (or a group of people) right now is . . .
- I do the exact same thing as this person (or group) when I . . .
- The thing I desire more than anything but have never allowed myself to do is . . .
- If I were truly free, I would . . .

Answer the questions in the form of a writing blurt. Compose a stream-of-conscious answer, without any thought about spelling or punctuation. Set a timer to write nonstop for three to five minutes. Do not stop moving your pen. If you run out of things to say, write, "I have more to say, I have more to say . . ."

Pathworking

Prepare the body, space, and mind. Take a cleansing shower or saltwater bath. Clear the mind by focusing on the sound of your breath. Move to a quiet space where you won't be disturbed. Wear comfortable clothing. Close your eyes.

Imagine a space called Hod/Spendor. This is where creativity cusps into the material world. Visualize your favorite creative and sensual space. How does it look and sound? Imagine a real thing you have created that you once imagined in your mind's eye. It may be a cake, a child, a garden, or a work project. Recall imagining it before it was real. How did it feel when you conceived it? Where were you in your mind when you imagined it? Linger in this space of creativity as long as feels appropriate. Consider what new create projects you are bringing through. When you are ready to move on, a closed door appears before you.

If you work with a spirit or animal guide, you may request their company before you open the door. Open the door and move into the Devil card.

Use a soft gaze into the card, or if you are quite familiar with the image, bring the Devil card to your mind's eye. Can you feel the heat of brimstone? Do you hear the fire crackling? What does the dark lair smell like? What do the chained figures say or do? Will you interact with them? Can you free them from their chains? What message do they have for you? Move deeply into the card. Touch the Devil figure. What does he feel like? Does he scare you or make you laugh?

Explore every facet of the card until the Devil presents you with a key. You stick this key into his belly button and he deflates like a balloon. Everything falls away and a second doorway appears where the Devil sat. Move through this door into a pulsating space of freedom, possibility, and beauty. This is Beauty/Tiphereth. Feel yourself pulsating with love, reaching out like the branches of a tree above and below you. What does it look like? How does it feel?

Exit the pathwork when you are ready to return. Record the experience in your journal.

. . . ☽ . . .

Shadow work is a lifelong process. It never ends because we are ever shifting and evolving. If you are interested in working with a tarot deck specifically created for Shadow work, you might enjoy the *Dark Wood Tarot* created by me and illustrated by Abigail Larson. Best of luck in your adventure. The world needs your magic now more than ever!

Yoga for Sleep

Elizabeth Barrette

Yoga is an ancient discipline for body, mind, and spirit. It can be performed in many ways and for diverse purposes, alone or in groups. Today there are yoga studios specializing in dozens of different physical styles and metaphysical approaches. Vinyasa focuses on poses, pranayama features breathwork, and kundalini is all about energy. Hot yoga and cold yoga deal in different temperatures. Jivamukti yoga has a vegetarian philosophy. Restorative yoga helps the mind and body wind down after a long, hard day.

Among the most popular purposes for home yoga practice is improving sleep. A hectic world often makes sleep elusive, but everyone needs plenty of sleep to meet their obligations. Of the styles mentioned above, Restorative yoga is the closest to this, but it's not necessarily meant for night—just the end of the working day.

Yoga for sleep is the last thing you do before bed, or in some cases, actually in bed. There are two branches of this: soothing asanas and yoga nidra. Soothing asanas are postures that loosen and relax the body, sometimes with meditations that encourage the mind to follow. Yoga nidra is a more advanced mental practice, sometimes called "yogic sleep."

Along with yoga for sleep, pay attention to sleep hygiene. This is a set of principles and practices designed to increase things that help sleep and decrease things that undermine sleep. Examples include the following:

- If you wear sleep clothes, ensure they are comfortable. Yoga clothes and sleep clothes resemble each other because they meet similar needs.
- Keep the room temperature pleasantly moderate by your standards, not too warm or too cool.

- Check to see that your bed, pillow, and bedding are comfortable and not so old they cause problems.
- Avoid blue light or daylight at least an hour before sleep, as these send signals to stay awake. If you can't avoid electronic devices altogether, check whether yours has an "evening" mode that reduces the troublesome blue light.
- Remove distractions such as a television, computer, or phone from your bedroom. Also get rid of anything that makes unpleasant noise or lights. If you need an alarm clock, get a "sunrise clock" with a gradual wake-up function.
- Avoid body-altering substances like caffeine or alcohol in the later part of the day. Some yoga disciplines eliminate these and other such items completely. Ayurvedic dietary principles aim to balance body, mind, and spirit; these are worth considering if you find yoga helpful.

Soothing Asanas

Asanas are yoga poses. They work physically by stretching and relaxing the muscles. They work mystically by changing the orientation of energy centers in the body relative to each other. Different sources advise holding a pose for different lengths of time. For beginners, try to hold each one for a few breaths. Experienced yogis may hold a pose for several minutes or more.

There are many different asanas, from the simple to the challenging to the intricate. They can be sorted into groups based on their functions: opening and closing asanas, invigorating and relaxing ones, and so on. Another way is to sort them by orientation or shape: vertical, horizontal, or inverted; seated, two-legged, or one-legged. For sleep, consider the wide variety of asanas that are classed as relaxing or soothing:

> *Apanasana (Knees to Chest):* Stretches the spine and improves blood circulation; brings comfort and peace. Lie on your back, feet together, arms at your sides, and breathe deeply. As you exhale, bend your knees and bring them to your

chest, clasping your arms around your lower legs. Release your back muscles and lengthen your spine into the curve. As you inhale, release your legs to lie flat again.

Ardha Uttanasana (Standing Half-Forward Wall Bend): Gently lengthens the spine and stimulates the abdominal organs for better digestion. A less challenging variation of Uttanasana (Standing Forward Bend), this uses a wall for support. Start a foot away from the wall, feet slightly apart. Lean forward to place your palms on the wall. Step back to straighten your spine. Try to get your arms and torso parallel to the floor, adjusting stance as necessary. Finally, walk back toward the wall to straighten up.

Balasana (Child Pose): Good for easing dizziness or anxiety; stretches the hips and legs; calms the mind and body. Kneel with knees together, seat touching heels, arms along sides with palms up. Push forward and down until your forehead reaches the mat, with hands pointing behind you. Your body should form a ball like a baby in the womb. Feel your

breath along your back, lengthening your spine. Then straighten up. This pose often combines with Sasangasana (Hare Pose).

Bitilasana (Cow Pose): Helpful for making the spine flexible and massaging internal organs to improve digestion; aids blood circulation and brings calm. Balance on your hands and knees, hands below shoulders, knees below hips. As you inhale, bring your head and tailbone up like a relaxed cow. Pull your shoulder blades together and hollow your back toward the yoga mat to stretch your spine. As you exhale, lower your head and flatten your back like a table. This pose commonly combines with Marjaryasana (Cat Pose).

Dirga Pranayama (Three-Part Breath): Slows breathing, grounds body, and focuses attention. Sit in a comfortable position, eyes closed, left hand over navel, right hand on right side of ribs. Relax your body and breathe naturally. Feel your belly rise and fall as your ribs expand and contract. Concentrate on your breath as you inhale, hold briefly, then exhale.

Makarasana (Crocodile Pose): Good for easing lung problems and relaxing the nervous system. Lie on your front, legs together, toes pointed away from your body. Fold your forearms in front of you and rest your forehead on them. Breathe slowly and deeply. This pose has numerous variations. One that works well in combination with the head-on-forearms version is stretching up to support yourself on your elbows with your chin resting on your hands. Going back and forth between these loosens the spine and upper body.

Marjaryasana (Cat Pose): Good for improving flexibility and digestion; stretches the spine. Balance on your hands and knees, hands below shoulders, knees below hips. As you exhale, tilt your head and hips down, arching your back like an upset cat and spreading your shoulder blades to stretch your spine. As you inhale, lift your head and flatten your back like a table. This pose commonly combines with Bitilasana (Cow Pose).

Matsya Kridasana (Flapping Fish Pose): Stimulates digestion; relaxes perineum and nerves in legs, relieving sciatic and other pain caused by pressure on lower nerves. Lie on your front, fingers laced under your head. Keeping your right leg straight and relaxed, bend your left leg to bring your knee toward your chest. Tilt your left elbow toward your left knee and rest the right side of your head on your right arm. Relax into this position, which is common for side sleepers. Then return to your belly, and reverse the position to stretch your other side by bringing your right knee toward your chest.

Padmasana (Lotus Pose): Good for easing menstrual cramps and childbirth; improves posture, aligns chakras, and awakens consciousness. Sit with spine erect. Bend your right knee and place the foot on your left thigh, sole up, close to your hip. Repeat with your left foot on your right thigh. Press your palms together in front of your sternum in the Anjali mudra, or "prayer position," for mindfulness of the moment. Keep your spine straight, through the back of your head, chin dipped slightly down. Relax, breathing slowly and evenly.

This pose has many variations. Ardha Padmasana (Half Lotus) places one foot on the opposite thigh. Sukhasana (Easy Pose) merely bends the knees and crosses the ankles. You can choose from many mudras (hand positions) too. To make the Gyan mudra for knowledge, touch thumb and forefinger, resting backs of hands on knees. Dyana mudra for enlightenment: place right hand flat in left hand with palms up, touch thumbs above palms, and rest backs of hands in lap. Mushti mudra for processing strong emotions: close fists with thumbs over ring fingers, pressing fronts of fists together over chest.

Paschimottanasana (Seated Forward Bend): Good for easing insomnia and menstrual or menopausal complaints; lifts mood and calms mind. Sit with legs straight together, toes

pointed up. Lean forward to grasp feet, bending head to touch legs. Breathe and stretch. Then sit up.

Sasangasana (Hare Pose): Improves circulation and adrenal response; promotes humility; stretches spine and arms. For this variation, kneel with knees together, seat touching heels, hands at sides. Lean forward, stretching arms in front with palms down like the ears of a hare. Push forward and down until your forehead reaches the mat. Feel your breath along your back, lengthening your spine and extending your arms. Then straighten up. This pose often combines with Balasana (Child Pose).

Savasana (Corpse Pose): Calms nervous system and aligns chakras; reduces headaches, stress, and anxiety. Lie on your back with your arms at your sides, breathing freely. Relax and focus on how limp and heavy your body feels.

Uttanasana (Standing Forward Bend): Stimulates abdominal muscles and filter organs; helps insomnia, lung problems, and sinus issues. Stand with feet apart, knees slightly bent. Exhale as you lean forward, pressing your hands to the mat. Inhale as you straighten, bringing your arms to your sides.

Uttanpadasana (Raised Leg Pose): Good for relieving gas or constipation; strengthens abdominal, uterine, and lower back muscles. Lie on your back with legs straight together, arms at sides, palms down. Keeping legs straight together, lift them as far as you comfortably can. Hold for a moment, then lower them.

Viparita Karani (Legs-up-the-Wall Pose): Drains fluid and improves circulation to relieve swollen legs or feet; releases tension from back; aids sleep and digestion. Lie on the yoga mat near a wall and prop your feet vertically against the wall, using your hands to adjust position. Relax, loosening your leg and back muscles. To end, bend your knees and push away from the wall.

As you can see from these examples, many poses have multiple variations and different names. If the first version you try doesn't feel right, try others until you find asanas that work for you. Modify as needed to accommodate the body you have. Evening isn't the time for strenuous poses anyway; save those for midday sessions.

Evening Routines

Evening routines help prepare the mind and body for sleep. Repetition and familiarity improve the effectiveness, so try to find a routine you like enough to stick with it. Note that it helps to balance evening routines with morning routines. This is one reason why variations on Salute to the Sun are so popular. So let's consider how to assemble a matching Salute to the Moon routine.

You can create a floor routine and a bed routine with different asanas. Choose poses that flow well and end in a resting pose. The last asana for bed should match your preferred sleep position. Back sleepers use Savasana. Side sleepers use Matsya Kridasana. Front sleepers use Makarasana.

> *Floor Routine:* Ardha Uttanasana (Standing Half-Forward Wall
> Bend), Uttanasana (Standing Forward Bend), Bitilasana (Cow
> Pose), Marjaryasana (Cat Pose), Paschimottanasana (Seated
> Forward Bend), Viparita Karani (Legs-up-the-Wall Pose)
> *Bed Routine for Back Sleepers:* Padmasana (Lotus Pose) with
> Dirga Pranayama (Three-Part Breath), Apanasana (Knees
> to Chest), Uttanpadasana (Raised Leg Pose), Savasana
> (Corpse Pose)
> *Bed Routine for Front or Side Sleepers:* Padmasana (Lotus Pose)
> with Dirga Pranayama (Three-Part Breath), Sasangasana
> (Hare Pose), Balasana (Child Pose), Makarasana (Crocodile Pose) or Matsya Kridasana (Flapping Fish Pose)

Yoga Nidra

Yoga nidra is a practice of concentrated rest. Descriptions vary about whether it is a type of deep sleep that is conscious or a meditative state between waking and sleeping. Compare this with hypna-gogia, the state between wakefulness and sleep when falling asleep, or hypnopompia, the state between sleep and wakefulness when waking up. If you can learn to stop in that middle state and extend it, the experience is delightful—but it's slippery and takes practice to maintain. Quite possibly, different people experience variations on what can happen with yoga nidra. However, it is generally de-scribed as deeply relaxing. Many people find that a short period of yoga nidra delivers as much rest as a much longer period of ordinary sleep.

Often yoga nidra is practiced as guided meditation. If this ap-peals to you, there are many scripts and recordings you can use, available in books or online. You might even find a yoga studio offering yoga nidra, although it's not among the most common styles. However, you can also do it on your own. This approach just takes more focus; it can be challenging to find your way into

relaxation without help. But if a voice just winds you up, then try it without.

An advantage of yoga nidra is that it tends to be beneficial whether you succeed or not. If you do it right, you get the meditative state. If you can't get there, the most common result is that you fall asleep the usual way—which, if you're trying to beat insomnia, is a great result anyhow. For this reason, yoga nidra is typically done in Savasana. If you don't sleep well on your back, choose a different asana that better resembles your preferred sleep position, such as Makarasana for front sleepers or Matsya Kridasana for side sleepers.

Begin by lying down in a comfortable pose. Think about why you want to practice yoga nidra. Set a goal in your mind, such as peaceful rest. Pay attention to each body part in turn, from your feet to your legs, your torso, your arms, and finally your head. If you find your attention drifting, that's common. Just bring it back to the last place and keep going from there. Next, shift your attention from your body parts to your breath. Deep, slow breaths help you relax. As you sink deeper into yoga nidra, your awareness of body and mind fades. Try to keep focused on your personal goal as your thoughts drift farther apart. To end the session, bring your attention back to your body. It's okay if you fall asleep, though.

Conclusion

Yoga is one of the best ways to improve sleep. It helps some physical and mental issues that can make sleep difficult. It boosts mystical awareness and control of energies. Even if you don't achieve the mental and metaphysical benefits the first few times you try, the physical benefits carry through. Yoga doesn't cost anything to do, and while expert guidance or materials are helpful, they aren't essential. There are so many different poses, routines, and techniques that there's something for almost everyone. Give it a try, and you'll soon find your way to sweet dreams.

Bless Your Meds

Raechel Henderson

I'm a Witch. I cast spells and talk to animals and read tarot; I also live with mental health issues for which I take several medications. I experience both a physical and spiritual side of my depression and anxiety. To that end, I bless my medications so that they address both of those sides. Doing so seems a natural extension of my belief in science and magic. The two can work together, in harmony, to address the totality of a person.

It is important to understand that magic is not meant to be a replacement for modern medicine. The two address different aspects of illness. Magic deals with the metaphysical and spiritual symptoms of disease. Medicine takes care of the physical cause of the disease. All the information that follows is meant to be used in conjunction with taking medication.

Any medication can be blessed, from your over-the-counter painkillers to your chemotherapy drugs. Medications that you take only occasionally (painkillers, allergy meds, etc.) can be blessed verbally. A simple "Work quickly to dull this pain" when taking an aspirin for a headache is often effective on many levels. The blessing reminds

the painkiller what it is meant to do: it is affirming, out loud, that the pain will go away, and it prepares your own body for the pain relief to come.

You can get more elaborate, from writing sigils on your medicine bottles to full-fledged astrologically timed rituals. Using a blue marker or pen, write a rune like Sowilo 𝍣 or Uruz 𝍢 for healing and health or Elhaz 𝍡 or Ingwaz ◇ for protection. You can also make a bindrune or two to mark your medication. If you are dealing with depression or mental health issues, use a yellow pen, and if your medication is for fertility or reproductive issues, use green. Instead of a rune, you can create a sigil as well. Make one from the phrase "I am healthy" or "I am well" or some other affirmation.

Crystals, coming as they do from the earth, have strong connections to healing magic. Charging crystals with healing intentions and then setting them near your medications will help bless them. Keep the crystals dusted and recharge them on occasion (such as when you get refills) to keep the energy flowing. Some crystals that are well suited for this work include these:

- Amethyst for anxiety, depression, and other mental health issues
- Carnelian for fertility issues
- Garnet for helping regulate menstrual cycles and for reproductive disorders
- Hematite for blood issues
- Jasper for anything related to cancer
- Quartz as a general all-purpose healing stone

Healing herbs can be used not only to deal with symptoms of illness (such as drinking a tea from thyme to soothe a sore throat) but also in blessing medications as well. Spell pouches stuffed with healing herbs such as allspice, cinnamon, almonds, and barley can be tucked in the drawer where you keep your medicine. Cotton has healing properties as well, so adding a couple of drops of eucalyptus, lavender, or mint essential oil to a cotton ball can serve the same purpose. Or burn myrrh incense and waft your medication through the smoke to bless it and add the healing properties of the herb to it.

Don't feel limited to only herbs and crystals, though. Poppets have been used for centuries in healing magic. You can easily make one from green cloth. Instead of stuffing, place your medicine inside the poppet when you aren't using it. Or give the poppet a pocket in which you can store your pill bottles. The poppet holds the medicine safely and contributes its protective energies to your healing.

The Sun is associated with health and healing, so time any ritual blessings during the day. Rituals performed in the morning with the rising Sun are for increasing health, noon for sustaining health, and afternoon for diminishing disease and illness. This is especially helpful for charging crystals, herbs, or your medications. Setting them out for even a few minutes in the sunlight can charge them with the Sun's healing energies.

Don't forget your ancestors. Maybe you had doctors and nurses among your relatives. Maybe your ancestral line had a culture of herbal and spiritual medicine. You can call upon them to help bless your modern medications. If you don't know of anyone in your family who had a connection to healing, or if you are estranged or otherwise cutting off bloodlines, you can look to deities, folk heroes, and historical figures to call on.

Most every pantheon has a deity associated with healing or medicine. Take some time to identify that god or goddess in your own practice and get to know them. You could set up a small altar in your medicine cabinet with a picture of the deity behind or next to your medicines. This will keep them at the forefront of your mind when you are reaching for your medication.

Below is a brief, nonexhaustive list of deities from various cultures and religious paths. If you decide to work with any of them, do the legwork and research them, especially if they come from a culture outside of your own. Read any myths or legends related to them, and find out what goes into their worship, their symbols, and their correspondences. In short, start to forge a relationship with the deity. This is someone you are going to call on to bless your medications, so it behooves you to show respect to them by getting to know them before doing so.

- Airmed, an Irish goddess of healing
- Apollo, a Greek god of healing
- Bao Sheng Da Di, a Chinese god of healing
- Caboyaran and Akasi, two of several deities of healing found in Filipino religions
- Eir, a Norse goddess of healing
- Ixtlilton, an Aztec god of medicine
- Sekhmet, an Egyptian goddess of healing and medicine

Finally, consider using your empty pill bottles to aid in your health. They can be used for jar spells, filled with crystals, herbs, and other items and then placed in your bathroom. Whenever you notice the bottle, give it a good shake and say, "My body, mind, and spirit are healing."

As Witches, we know that there are some problems that need to be addressed in multiple ways. The human body is a complex system made up of physical, metaphysical, mental, and spiritual and other components. Modern medicine focuses on the physical side of disease, which is an important part of the equation. By using our magic, we can fill in the blanks and treat the other aspects of self that are affected by illness.

Coloring Magic

Color Correspondences

Color magic uses various hues to influence energy. It can attract or repel, strengthen or weaken. It expresses thoughts and feelings that don't fit easily into words. People choose colors of clothes, jewelry, walls, and carpet to create desired effects. In magic, we use altar cloths, candles, gemstones, bowls, and other altar tools to channel this energy. Coloring pages help people relax.

Different cultures may use different correspondences. Western cultures associate white with life and black with death; Eastern cultures tend to reverse those. It comes from interpretations. Red is the color of blood, which can suggest vitality or danger, depending on how you look at it. So there is no "right" or "wrong" meaning. Use the color associations that resonate with you.

Maroon: Crone, drama, respect, sensuality

Crimson: Determination, righteous anger, survival

Scarlet: Action, female sexuality, vitality

Red: Fire, strength, danger

Orange: Creativity, addiction, opportunity

Gold: God, Sun, justice

Topaz: Male sexuality, memory, fast effects

Yellow: Air, joy, charm

Lime Green: Growth, speed, end frustration

Green: Envy, money, health

Teal: Acceptance, abundance, happy home

Turquoise: Work-life balance, guilt, receiving

Blue: Water, truth, family

Indigo: Will, spirit, psychic

Purple: Wisdom, emotions, power

Lavender: Knowledge, intuition, divination

Violet: Calm, gratitude, tension

Coral: Mother, nurturing, emotional energy

Pink: Love, compassion, partnership

Fuchsia: Fight depression, self-direction, self-worth

Rose: Maiden, romance, friendship

Brown: Earth, stability, memory

Tan: Construction, food, past life

Black: Dark Moon, defense, grounding

Gray: Balance, loneliness, rest

Silver: Goddess, Moon, dreams

White: Crescent Moon, purity, peace

Ivory: Full Moon, luxury, animal magic

Safe Travels

JD Walker

The anticipation of an upcoming trip can be exciting. Even if it's a business trip, it's a chance to break out of the old routine and maybe see or learn something new. What is not so exciting are all the missteps, delays, and accidents that can occur to ruin your trip. Here is a spell to help send you on your way and bring you back safely.

You will need:
Dried plantain leaf and comfrey root
Flannel bag or small bottle
Malachite, amethyst, or aquamarine stone (optional)
Image from page 267
Assorted coloring pens or pencils in primary colors
White candle
Appropriate incense, such as sandalwood, frankincense, or
  dragon's blood

On the evening before your trip, assemble your supplies and set up your ritual area according to your tradition. Arrange the dried herbs and flannel bag or small bottle on the altar where you can easily reach them. You will be assembling either a mojo bag or witch bottle, depending on your preference. Have the coloring page and pens or pencils nearby too.

In addition, you might like to have one of the stones mentioned above. Malachite is a general-purpose protective stone for travel. Aquamarine is good if your trip is mainly by water. Amethyst is helpful for air travelers. Small stones are great for mojo bags. Chipped stones work well in a witch bottle.

First, light the candle and incense. If you like, call on your patron deity or ancestors or elementals to lend their energies to your work.

When you are ready to begin, take the drawing and color the talismans in the corners, "invoking" the energies of each as you color them. Visualize the protective energies you are calling forth as you do. The dragon leads fiery protection; the clover, luck; the Eye of Ra, shielding from evil; and the compass, direction to keep you from harm.

Once the coloring is done, using a finger or a colored pen, begin at the start of the labyrinth by imaging yourself packing for the trip, getting into the vehicle (car, plane, etc.) and starting out. As you trace the labyrinth, see yourself progressing on the journey with as much detail as you can image. What landmarks might you see? See yourself stopping for gas or food.

The center of the labyrinth is your destination. Take a few moments to savor your plans and imagine the joy of doing whatever activities that brought you to this spot.

After a few moments, reverse the journey through the labyrinth with full visualization until you see yourself back home safe, being greeted by pets or whoever is there at the home. You're home safe and secure and fully content from a restful, fun journey.

Put the herbs and stones (if you have selected stones) into the mojo bag or witch bottle. Pass them over the candle flame and through the incense smoke. Tuck this into your travel bag when you pack. Thank any entity that you may have asked to join your working. Let the candle and incense burn out in a safe manner.

That's it! You're ready to travel. Just one last word: once you're home safe and sound, be sure to thank the spirits who guarded you on your travels with a candle and incense. Everyone enjoys a little appreciation!

Crossing Thresholds with Blodeuwedd

Monica Crosson

Blodeuwedd's story can be found in the fourth branch of the Mabinogion, and it is there where Math and Gwydion take up the blooms of oak, broom, and meadowsweet to create the beautiful maiden as a wife to legitimize Lleu's kingship. She does not love the one she was created for but instead falls for the huntsman, Gronw. In an attempt to control her own fate, she and her lover try to kill Lleu but fail. Her punishment: to fly the night sky to escape the hostility of the birds who rule the day.

A goddess of thresholds, Blodeuwedd ("Flower Face") stands with the rising dawn. She is the light of day that spreads across fertile fields—she is passion and promise. But she is also a harbinger of the night, as her name also translates to "owl": she is the darkness that settles in twilight hues and offers us a different perspective on our surroundings. She is initiation and rebirth. Her story is one that can be associated with many principles—seasonal change, sovereignty of the land, sacred kingship, and death and rebirth, among others. Some may look at her as the ultimate unfaithful wife. I see her as a powerful representative of the wild feminine, one to go to when we could use a spark of assertiveness, one who lends courage and reminds us that even on the darkest nights, dawn will always follow.

Courage in the Dark

We all must accept changes as we journey through this life. And as much as we might not like it, we need change in order for growth to take place. Fear can make us complacent even in the worst situations. Draw upon the courage of Blodeuwedd as you face challenges in life. Take that first step through the threshold and initiate growth.

You will need:

2 candles (black and white)

Coloring medium of your choice (include yellow, white, green, and deep blues or purples of twilight)

Light the candles, black representing your challenge and white representing your goal. Place them on either side of your coloring page.

Use yellow, white, and green to color the face of Blodeuwedd. As you do this, imagine your own spirit opening into full bloom, awakening your confidence, ready to take on a challenge set before you. As you move on to color the owl, imagine yourself crossing thresholds into the darkness of challenge in your own life. The owl is your guide and the flowers your armor. How does it feel as you navigate the dark?

As you finish your page, imagine dawn approaching. Take a breath and snuff out the black candle. You've taken the first step. Let the white candle burn out on its own as a symbol of your commitment to continuing growth.

Home Protection

Mickie Mueller

This coloring spell is designed to summon up the energies of protection to shield your personal space from harmful energy. By coloring it, you add your own intention and breathe the art to life.

I have drawn a sigil in the center of the shield using a sigil wheel method and the words *protect this home.* If you wish to add your own sigil, simply trace a quarter on a blank piece of paper, draw your own sigil, cut it out, and apply it to the shield, covering my sigil with it using a glue stick. You can also add your own protective words to the back of the piece if you wish to further customize it.

While you work on this, you should think about a time and place where you felt the most safe. Pull up the feeling of safety, and do your best to hold that within your mind as you work. Lighting a candle or lighting your favorite incense might help get you into a peaceful and magical state of mind.

Choose the colors that resonate with you and remind you of safety, protection, strength, and shielding. There is no right or wrong way to do it, if it feels right to you. I suggest that you begin with the blackthorn frame around the edge. As you color that section, think about the way that blackthorn was used as a physical and magical thorny protective hedge and was used to craft shillelaghs, which were technically walking sticks but could be used as weapons if needed.

Next, as you color the yarrow and mugwort growing at the bottom, imagine the spirits of these protection plants bringing the illustration to life as you add the color.

Hanging from the top of the blackthorn frame, three eyes are keeping watch. Blue is often associated with protection magic associated with eyes, but you may color them any color that feels right.

On the other side there are three protective gemstones. I imagined purple amethyst, black tourmaline, and yellow citrine, but feel free to color them to look like your favorite protection stones.

Roses represent what you love and value. They are protected by sharp thorns, and their energy lets love enter but keeps enemies at bay. Color them next.

The dragon is a fierce protector. This one holds the line, ready to obliterate any baneful intentions that might try to enter your home. Close your eyes and ask the dragon to reveal the color that will best protect you. Listen with your heart and intuition—the color that comes into your mind is correct. Finally, the shield finishes off this coloring spell. As you color it, imagine it activating the rest of the art you've completed.

Once you're happy with your coloring spell, you can frame it and hang it near your front door. If you prefer to keep it under the radar, place a group photo of everyone who lives in your household over the top of it in the frame.

Contributors

H. BYRON BALLARD, MFA (Asheville, NC), is a teacher, folklorist, and writer. She has served as a featured speaker and teacher at several festivals and conferences, including the Sacred Space Conference, Pagan Spirit Gathering, Starwood, Hexfest, and many others. She serves as senior priestess and cofounder of Mother Grove Goddess Temple and the Coalition of Earth Religions/CERES, both in Asheville, NC. She podcasts about Appalachian folkways on *Wyrd Mountain Gals*. Her essays are featured in several anthologies, and she writes a regular column for *SageWoman Magazine*. Find her online at www.myvillagewitch.com.

ELIZABETH BARRETTE has been involved with the Pagan community for more than thirty-three years. She has served as managing editor of *PanGaia* and dean of studies at the Grey School of Wizardry. Her book *Composing Magic* explains how to combine writing and spirituality. She lives in central Illinois. Visit her blog *The Wordsmith's Forge* (ysabetwordsmith.livejournal.com) or website PenUltimate Productions (penultimateproductions.weebly.com). Her coven site with extensive Pagan materials is Greenhaven Tradition (http://greenhaventradition.weebly.com/).

MIREILLE BLACKE, MA, is a registered dietitian, licensed alcohol and drug counselor, and freelance writer. Mireille worked in

rock radio for two decades before shifting her career to psychology, nutrition, and addiction counseling. She spends considerable time renovating her Victorian home, pining for New Orleans, and entertaining her beloved Bengal cats.

DANIELLE BLACKWOOD (Salt Spring Island, BC) is a professional astrologer with more than thirty years of experience as well as a registered counseling therapist (RTC) in private practice. She is the author of the best-selling book *The Twelve Faces of the Goddess* (Llewellyn, 2018). Danielle is a passionate lifelong student of folklore, mythology, and depth psychology, and helping others reframe their stories through an archetypal lens is at the heart of her work.

BLAKE OCTAVIAN BLAIR is a shamanic and Druidic practitioner, ordained minister, writer, Usui Reiki Master-Teacher, and musical artist. Blake incorporates mystical traditions from both the East and West with a reverence for the natural world into his own brand of spirituality. He is an avid reader, knitter, nature lover, and member of the Order of Bards, Ovates, and Druids. He lives with his loving husband in New England. Visit him on the web at www.blakeoctavianblair.com.

CHIC AND S. TABATHA CICERO are Chief Adepts of the Hermetic Order of the Golden Dawn as re-established by Israel Regardie. They have written numerous books, including *Golden Dawn Magic, The Essential Golden Dawn, Self-Initiation into the Golden Dawn Tradition, The Golden Dawn Magical Tarot,* and *Tarot Talismans.* Both are Rosicrucians: Chic is Chief Adept of the Florida College of the SRICF and Tabatha is Imperatrix of the SRIA in America.

MONICA CROSSON is the author of *Wild Magical Soul, The Magickal Family,* and *Summer Sage.* She is a Master Gardener who lives in the beautiful Pacific Northwest, happily digging in the dirt and tending her raspberries with her family and their small menagerie of farm animals. She has been a practicing Witch for thirty years and is a member of Evergreen Coven.

KATE FREULER lives in Ontario, Canada, and is the author of *Of Blood and Bones*. She owns and operates White Moon Witchcraft, an online Witchcraft boutique. When she isn't crafting spells and amulets for clients or herself, she loves to write, paint, read, draw, and create. Visit her at www.katefreuler.com.

SASHA GRAHAM is the author of *Tarot Diva, 365 Tarot Spreads, 365 Tarot Spells*, and *Llewellyn's Complete Book of the Rider-Waite-Smith Tarot*. She is the editor of and a contributor to *Tarot Fundamentals, Tarot Experience*, and *Tarot Compendium*. Her tarot decks include the *Haunted House Tarot* and *Dark Wood Tarot*. Sasha hosts *The Enchanted Kitchen*, a short-form magical cooking series for YouTube and Heyou Media's *Mobile. Mini. Movies.*

OLIVIA GRAVES is an online creator who hopes to inspire others to build personal and powerful practices of their own with the help of her foundational content on Witchcraft, and she also vlogs about her life in an attempt to show how Witchcraft is woven into daily life and not separate. When Olivia is not filming, editing, and making content, she's usually found teaching pole dancing, collecting oddities, painting, and reading.

RAECHEL HENDERSON is the author of *Sew Witchy: Tools, Techniques and Projects for Sewing Magick* and *The Scent of Lemon & Rosemary*. She lives in Wyoming and writes about living a magickal life.

JD WALKER is an avid student of herbalism and gardening. She has written a regular garden column for thirty years. She is an award-winning author, journalist, magazine editor, and frequent contributor to the Llewellyn annuals. Her first book, *A Witch's Guide to Wildcrafting*, published by Llewellyn Publications, was released in spring 2021. Her new book, *Under the Sacred Canopy*, was released in spring 2023.

EMMA KATHRYN is a Witch and obeah woman who lives in Robin Hood County in the middle of England. Author of *Witch Life* (Llewellyn, 2022), she drinks copious amounts of coffee, reads tarot, and can often be found wandering in the woods.

LUPA is an author, artist, and nature lover in the Pacific Northwest. She has written several books on nature-based Paganism and is the creator of the Tarot of Bones. More about her work may be found at www.thegreenwolf.com.

TISHA MORRIS is an entertainment attorney and author of five books, including her most recent, *Missing Element, Hidden Strength* (Llewellyn, 2022). Tisha is a member of the Beverly Hills Bar Association, LA County Bar Association, Women in Film, and co-Ambassador of the Author's Guild. Tisha lives in Ojai, CA, with her wife, poodle, and two step-cats and works on becoming a legal thriller novelist one day. Visit Tisha at www.tishamorris.com.

MICKIE MUELLER is a Witch, author, illustrator, tarot creator, and YouTube content creator. She is the author/illustrator of multiple books, articles, and tarot decks for Llewellyn Publications and also has a jewelry line with Peter Stone and a statuary line with Sacred Source. Her magical art is distributed internationally and has been seen as set dressing on SyFy's *The Magicians* and Bravo's *Girlfriends' Guide to Divorce*. She runs several Etsy shops with her husband and fellow author, Daniel Mueller, in their studio workshop.

JOHN OPSOPAUS, PHD, has practiced magic since the 1960s, and his writing has been published in various magical and Neopagan magazines. He frequently presents workshops on Hellenic magic, Neopaganism, Pythagorean theurgy, and spiritual practices. John is a retired university professor with more than forty-five years of experience reading ancient Greek and Latin. He is also the author of *Oracles of Apollo*.

SUSAN PESZNECKER is a mother, grandmother, writer, nurse, and college English professor living in the beautiful green Pacific Northwest with her poodles. An initiated Druid and green magick devoteé, Sue loves reading, writing, cooking, travel, and anything having to do with the outdoors. Her previous works include *Crafting Magick with Pen and Ink*, *The Magickal Retreat*, and *Yule: Recipes &*

Lore for the Winter Solstice. She's a regular contributor to the Llewellyn annuals; follow her on Instagram at @SusanPesznecker.

DIANA RAJCHEL is the author of *Urban Magick: A Guide for the City Witch* and *Hex Twisting: Counter Magick Spells for the Irritated Witch.* She splits geographic time between San Francisco, where she co-owns Golden Apple Metaphysical with her business partner, Nikki, and Kalamazoo, MI, where she writes, teaches, reads tarot, and community builds with her romantic partner, Synty, and their children. She is about eight years behind in her sleep but hopes to catch up someday.

SUZANNE RESS runs a small farm in the Alpine foothills of Italy, where she lives with her husband. She has been a practicing Pagan for as long as she can remember and was featured in the exhibit "Worldwide Witches" at the Hexenmuseum of Switzerland. She is the author of *The Trial of Goody Gilbert.*

MELISSA TIPTON is a Jungian Witch, Structural Integrator, and founder of the Real Magic Mystery School, where she teaches online courses in Jungian Magic, a potent blend of ancient magical techniques and modern psychological insights. She's the author of *Living Reiki: Heal Yourself and Transform Your Life* and *Llewellyn's Complete Book of Reiki.* Learn more and take a free class at www.real magic.school.

TUDORBETH is the principal of the British College of Witchcraft and Wizardry and teaches courses on Witchcraft. She is the author of numerous books, including *The Hedgewitch's Little Book of Spells, Charms & Brews* and *A Spellbook for the Seasons* (Eddison Books, 2019). Tudorbeth is a hereditary practitioner: one great-grandmother was a well-known tea reader in Ireland, while her Welsh great-grandmother was a healer and wise woman.

BRANDON WESTON is a folklorist, spiritual healer, and writer living in the Arkansas Ozarks. He is the author of *Ozark Folk Magic: Plants, Prayers, and Healing* and *Ozark Mountain Spell Book.* He is the

owner of Ozark Healing Traditions, a collection of articles, lectures, and workshops focusing on traditions of medicine and magic from the Ozark Mountain region. He comes from a long line of Ozark hillfolk and works hard to keep these traditions alive for generations to come.

CHARLIE RAINBOW WOLF is an old hippie who's been studying the weird ways of the world for over fifty years. She's happiest when she's got her hands in mud, either making pottery in the Artbox or tending to things in the "yarden." Astrology, tarot, and herbs are her greatest interests, but she's dabbled in most metaphysical topics in the last five decades, because life always has something new to offer. Charlie lives in central Illinois with her very patient husband and her beloved Great Danes.

STEPHANIE WOODFIELD has been a practicing Pagan for over twenty years. A devotional polytheist, teacher, and priestess of the Morrigan, she is an organizer for several Pagan gatherings. A long time New Englander, she now resides in the Orlando area with her husband, two very pampered cats, and various reptiles. She is called to helping others forge meaningful experiences and relationships with the gods.

NATALIE ZAMAN is the author of *Color and Conjure* and *Magical Destinations of the Northeast*. A regular contributor to various Llewellyn annual publications, she also writes the recurring feature Wandering Witch for *Witches & Pagans* magazine. When not on the road, she's busy tending her magical back garden. Visit Natalie online at nataliezaman.blogspot.com.